I0458396

Animal Vignettes

True Stories
of Friendship

Other Works

Fiction

Carolina's Legacy Collection:

"Our Good Thing: A Short Story"
Any Good Thing: A Novel
This Good Thing: A Novella
Every Good Thing: A Short Story Compilation
One Good Thing: An Epistolary

The Crux Anthology, "Ealiverel Awakened"
Edited & Compiled by Rachael Ritchey

Nonfiction

Animal Vignettes: True Stories of Friendship

*Finders Keepers: A Practical Approach to
Find and Keep Your Writing Critique Partner*
Joy E. Rancatore and Meagan Smith

joyerancatore.com/my-writings/

Animal Vignettes

True Stories
of Friendship

JOY E. RANCATORE

LOGOS & MYTHOS PRESS
SLIDELL, LA, USA

ANIMAL VIGNETTES: TRUE STORIES OF FRIENDSHIP
Copyright © 2025 by Joy E. Rancatore
Cover Design and Layout by Rachael Ritchey, RR Publishing
Cover Photography copyright © 2025 by Tony Rancatore, Jr.

Logos & Mythos Press Editing
www.joyerancatore.com
www.logosandmythospress.com

All rights reserved. No part of this book may be reproduced or transmitted in any form or by any electronic or mechanical means, including photocopying, recording or information storage and retrieval systems, without written permission of the publisher, except for the use of brief quotations in a book review or where permitted by U.S. copyright law.
For permissions contact: editorial@logosandmythospress.com.

Animal Vignettes: True Stories of Friendship recounts the life experiences of the author to the best of her memory. All names included are used with kind permissions.

Scripture taken from the New King James Version. Copyright ©1982 by Thomas Nelson, Inc. Used by permission. All rights reserved.

A selection of "Badge of Honor" from *Grief Like a River* by Mea Smith is used with kind permission by the author and publisher.

A selection of "Life Lessons in Courage and Woodworking" from *Every Good Thing* by Joy E. Rancatore is used with kind permission by the author and publisher.

"His Eye is on the Sparrow" by Civilla Martin, *A Tale of Two Cities* by Charles Dickens, *Hamlet* by William Shakespeare and "We Give Thee But Thine Own" by William W. How are all works in the Public Domain.

All photos inside this book are the property of Joy E. Rancatore and her family. Written permission must be made to reproduce or redistribute any images.

Hardcover: 978-1-954465-03-9
Paperback: 978-1-954465-01-5
Ebook: 978-1-954465-02-2
Audiobook: 978-1-954465-04-6
Large Print: 978-1-954465-05-3

Library of Congress Control Number: 2025920536

Logos & Mythos Press LLC
Slidell, LA, USA

*In Appreciation of the
Two-legged and Four-legged
and Finned Companions
Who've Kept Me Sane or
Made Me Pleasantly Crazy
and with Hope for Those to Come*

For Casie

CONTENTS

Author's Note

Listen to the author read her note to you.

bit.ly/animal-vignettes-author-note

GROWING UP, I READ VORACIOUSLY. No book, magazine or pamphlet was safe from my insatiable thirst for knowledge and stories.

One of my favorite reads arrived in our mailbox each month. *Reader's Digest* fueled my imagination while igniting my passion for narrative nonfiction. After the humor submissions, I always flipped to sections with dramatic rescues or trauma situations and anything with animals.

True stories about animals have been a lifelong favorite I've revisited over the years. James Herriot's country vet books led to more books and movies than I can list where animals' stories have been recounted—the good, the sad and the sidesplitting; the heroic, the everyday and the always unexpected.

True-to-life stories—told in a storyteller fashion—have been my comfort literature. I didn't realize that until I submitted to my need to be an author and began pumping out ideas and stories of my own.

I first published fiction and leaned toward the narrative tone I grew up with. As I created, I recalled the lilt and mood of stories swapped on front porches to the rhythm of rocking chairs around shelling bowls or shucking buckets.

Saying goodbye too soon to one of my dearest friends revealed my need to embrace my natural style and tell the stories I've held in my heart. The time had come to add my animal stories to the great conversation of tales that made me the creature-loving, storytelling woman I am.

The animals I've had the privilege of loving inspired these true stories, but Casie motivated me to share them with readers. I only wish she were here to flip the pages as we laugh and cry over a cuppa and her own tales of Bassets and chinchillas.

My desire for *Animal Vignettes: True Stories of Friendship* is for you to be reminded of personal memories—joyful and heart-wrenching—that led to your present and shaped life and love in some pivotal way. I pray you are encouraged, uplifted and positively altered.

With that purpose in mind, I offer this collection of vignettes—moments in time, held in prose and shared with story-seekers. Slice-of-life stories and tales of animal antics speak to me and, I hope, to you as well. Let's Share The Read!

Joy

Places Timeline

Mobile, Ala.	April 1, 1983, to April 10, 1983
Artas, S.D.	April 1983 to Spring 1986
Cincinnati, Ohio	Spring 1986 to 1986/1987
Little Rock, Ark.	1986/1987 to March 1988
Pleasant Hill, S.C.	March 1988 to September 1992
Mooresville, N.C.	September 1992 to March 1994
Grenada, Miss.	April 1, 1994, to Summer 1998
Waynesboro, Miss.	Summer 1998 to May 2005
Hattiesburg, Miss. *William Carey College/University*	August 2001 to May 2005
Gautier, Miss.	May 2005 to June 2006
Wake Forest, N.C.	July 2006 to August 2010
Slidell, La.	August 2010 to Present

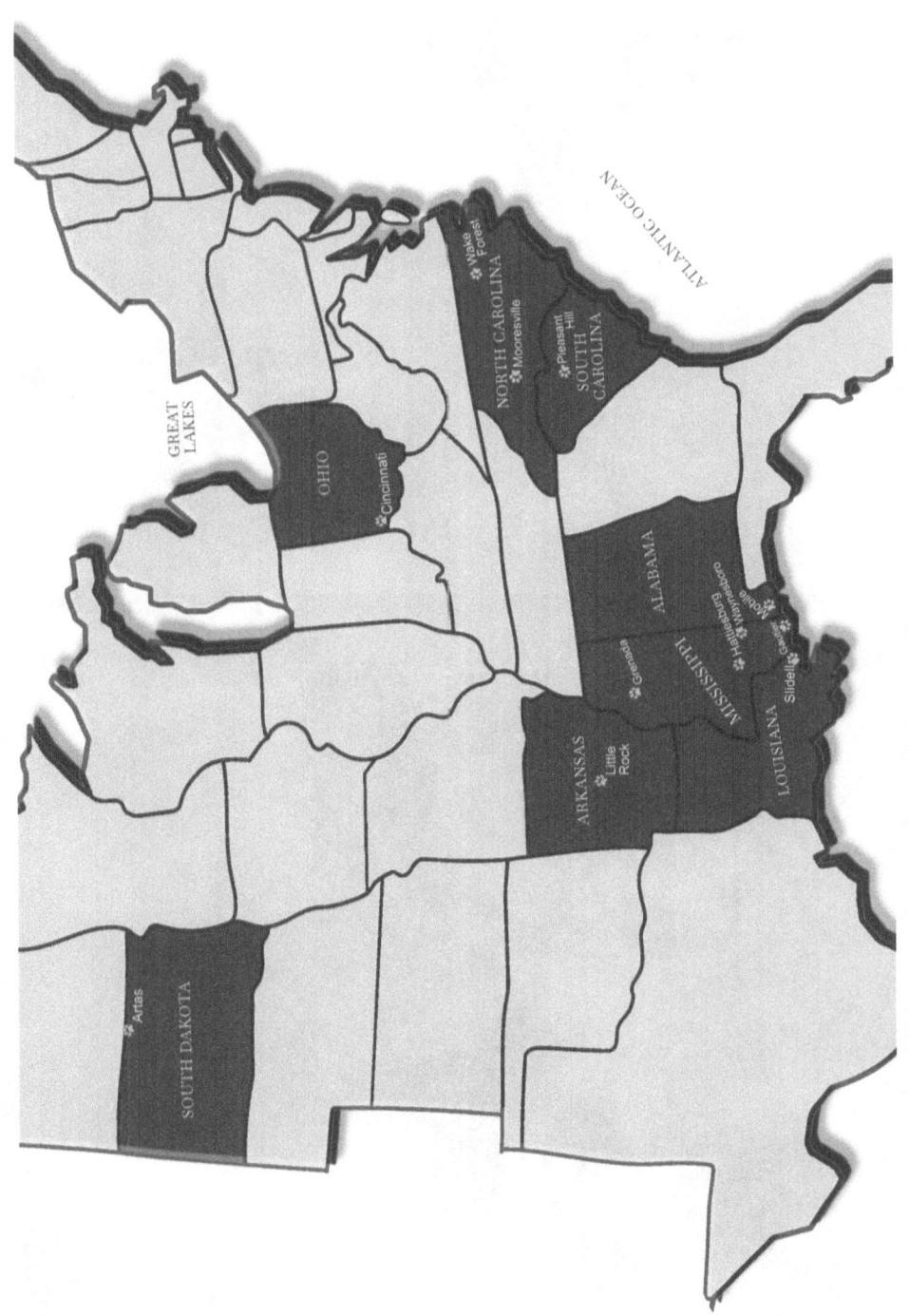

ATLANTIC OCEAN

GREAT
LAKES

OHIO
✿ Cincinnati

NORTH CAROLINA
✿ Wake Forest
✿ Mooresville

SOUTH CAROLINA
✿ Pleasant Hill

ALABAMA

MISSISSIPPI
✿ Hattiesburg
✿ Waynesboro
Mobile
✿ Grenada

LOUISIANA
Slidell ✿ Gautier

ARKANSAS
✿ Little Rock

SOUTH DAKOTA
✿ Artas

Pets Timeline

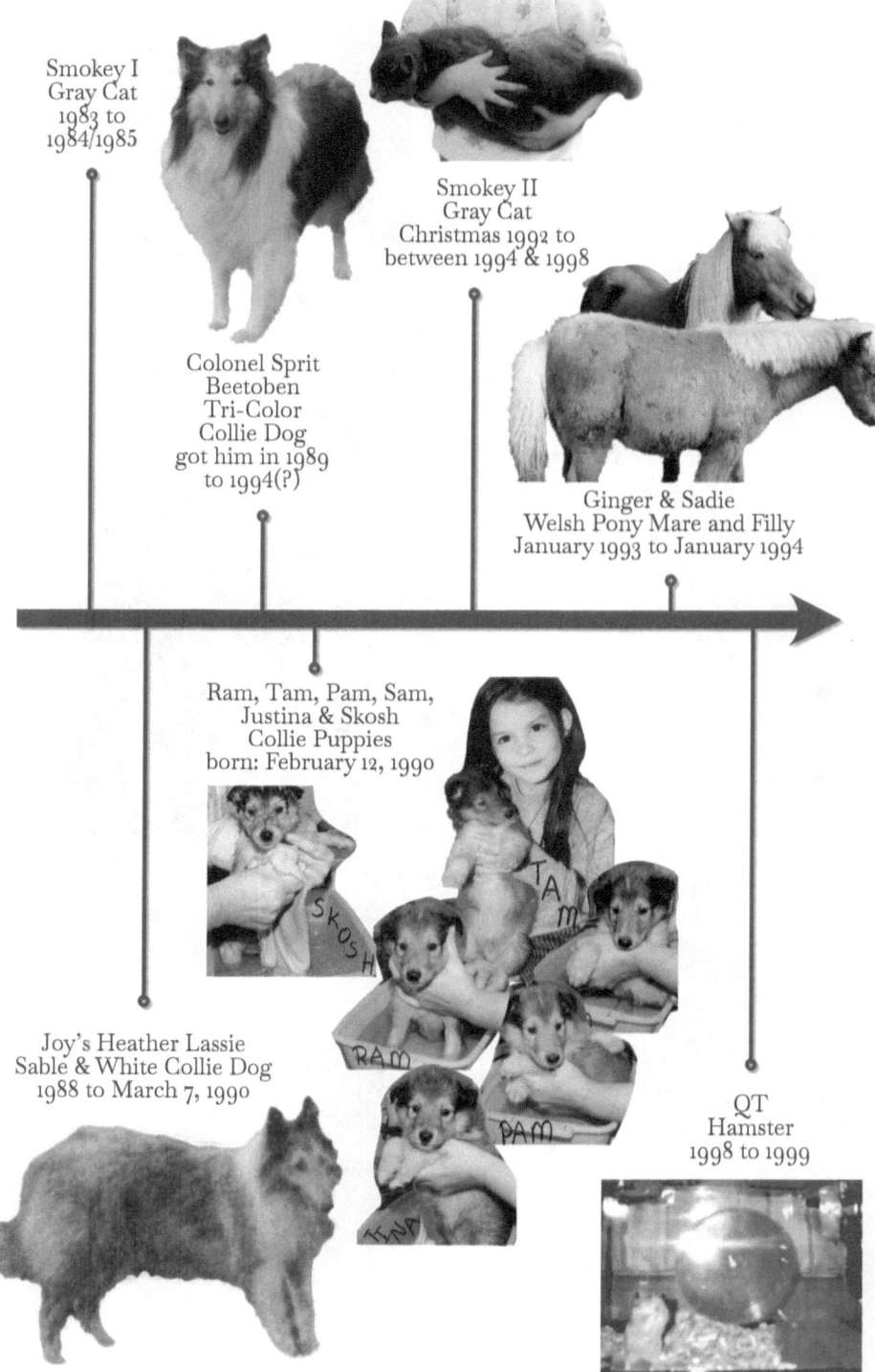

Smokey I
Gray Cat
1983 to
1984/1985

Smokey II
Gray Cat
Christmas 1992 to
between 1994 & 1998

Colonel Sprit
Beetoben
Tri-Color
Collie Dog
got him in 1989
to 1994(?)

Ginger & Sadie
Welsh Pony Mare and Filly
January 1993 to January 1994

Ram, Tam, Pam, Sam,
Justina & Skosh
Collie Puppies
born: February 12, 1990

Joy's Heather Lassie
Sable & White Collie Dog
1988 to March 7, 1990

QT
Hamster
1998 to 1999

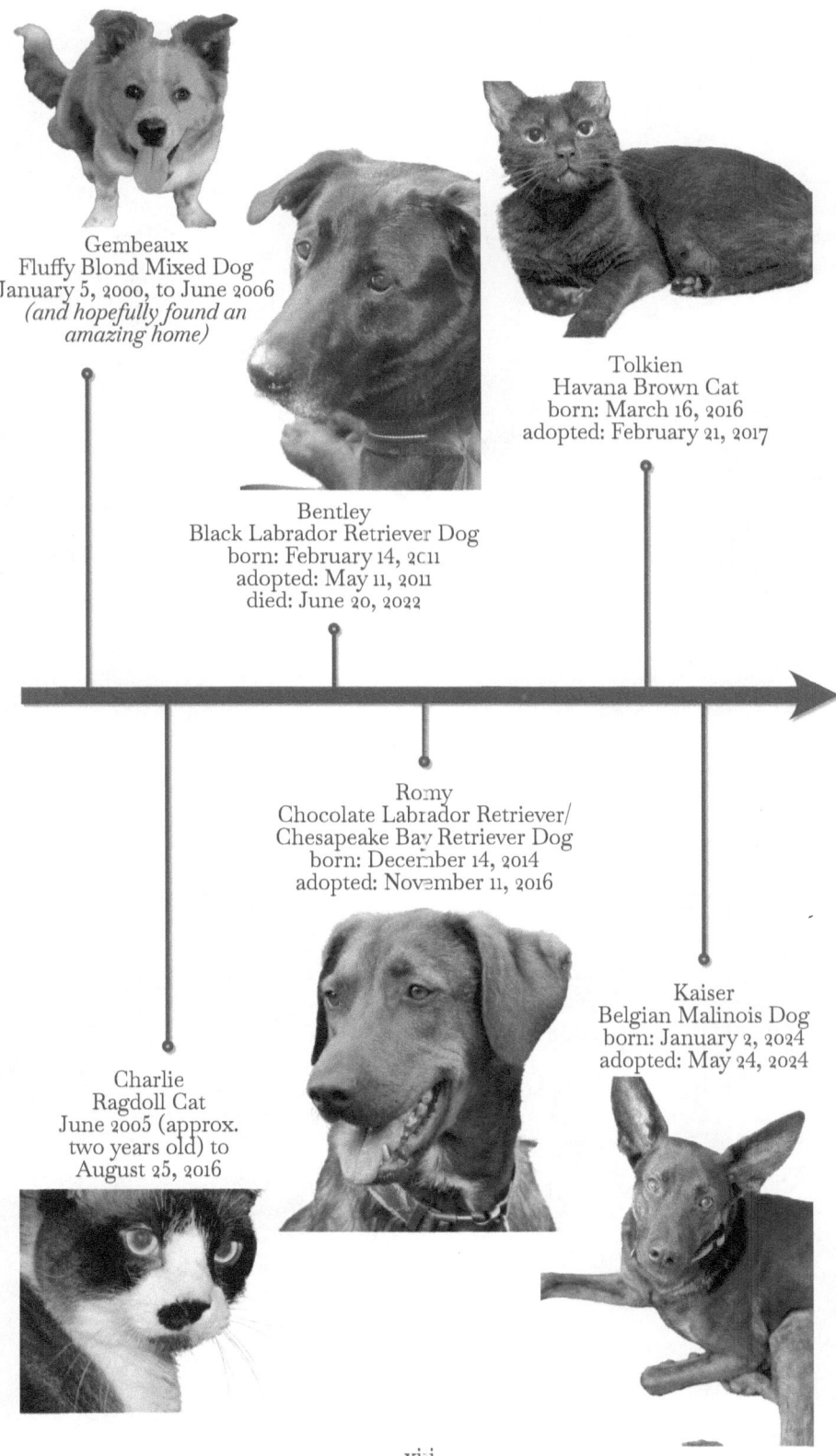

Gembeaux
Fluffy Blond Mixed Dog
January 5, 2000, to June 2006
*(and hopefully found an
amazing home)*

Tolkien
Havana Brown Cat
born: March 16, 2016
adopted: February 21, 2017

Bentley
Black Labrador Retriever Dog
born: February 14, 2011
adopted: May 11, 2011
died: June 20, 2022

Romy
Chocolate Labrador Retriever/
Chesapeake Bay Retriever Dog
born: December 14, 2014
adopted: November 11, 2016

Kaiser
Belgian Malinois Dog
born: January 2, 2024
adopted: May 24, 2024

Charlie
Ragdoll Cat
June 2005 (approx.
two years old) to
August 25, 2016

Animal Vignettes

True Stories
of Friendship

Vignette One

A Workshop: Two Authors & a Kitten in a Stroller

ON A SUN-HALOED DAY AT the fledgling age of two years old, I uncovered a profound truth: my best friends in life would often be fur-covered.

While drafting this book, I attended a writing workshop at one of my local libraries. Two author friends, David Armand and Colleen Hildebrand, challenged attendees to conjure up our earliest memories and write about them.

In true academic fashion, I set my intention to complete the assignment, despite a heavy load of skepticism. I doubted how adept I would be at the exercise or how far back my brain could remember. I also doubted any early memories would aid me with my work-in-progress: a book of stories about the animals in my life.

I set my brain's gears in motion and urged them backward along the windy rails of my memories until they screeched to a halt on my earliest one. At least, I think I unearthed the vision from the recesses of my brain.

My remembrance of a cat and a pink plastic doll stroller is more a slideshow click-through of hazy images than a full memory. I could be recalling a picture of myself, I suppose. Either way, I count this tale as my first memory.

Though I was born in Mobile, Ala., we moved to Artas, S.D., when I was 10 days old. Since my initial memory occurred outside, it must not have been winter—or I would have frozen to death—and it must not have been summer—or I would have keeled over, like thousands of cattle that die of dehydration during that sweltering season.

Perhaps it was early fall. That sounds safe.

I distinctly remember the sun's blinding glare against stark white concrete, my eyes squinted in self-defense and the downcast warmth kissing my milky skin. I also remember wearing an off-white terry cloth romper with strawberries on it—a style which accentuated my Buddha belly. Although I wasn't a chunky child, my belly always seemed to protrude as I toddled about. At least that's what the pictures that guide my recollections reveal.

Our family had a cat—one of three Smokeys we've had through the years. He would have been Smokey I. Since this feline was in South Dakota, he was also the one whose ears froze off—true story.

I had some sort of blanket or towel. I'm guessing it was one of the thin, soft blankets I used for my baby dolls. Whether I had a doll nearby or not, I'm unsure, but my guess would be my homemade one wasn't far.

At that time, I didn't have one of the most famous baby dolls of the 1980s. The named toys with lifelike hair and eye color combos, meant to match the children who adopted them, were in high demand with a waiting list. A dear church lady determined I should have one and gifted me a handsewn doll, complete with brown hair and brown eyes ... just like me.

In my memory, I stood on what I recall as a patio. Carefully, I burritoed Smokey into my blanket. Only his little head poked out— I can neither confirm nor deny the presence of ears. Once Smokey was sufficiently bundled, I laid him in my doll's bright pink plastic stroller and proceeded to push him around the maybe-patio.

That's the extent of my first memory. Our minds are remarkable, are they not? They have the ability to retain precious moments to be unwrapped by our senses of smell or touch: the earthy smell of outside with grass and dirt and the blanketing warmth of the sun. Our minds can also vault up trauma-filled memories that never should have been lived through. What I recall, I do so with surprising—though potentially inaccurate—clarity.

Whether Smokey enjoyed the stroller experience, my memory doesn't reveal. As an adult who's been closely involved with cats most of my life, my educated guess is he would not have been pleased. I envision a mighty and daring leap, a blanket flapping in the breeze behind the bounding feline and a shriek of dismay from the young cat-mama-in-training.

Regardless of the way that scene played out, I can make one statement with certainty. My early memory—nearly tucked away too deeply, if not for a workshop, two authors and a kitten in a stroller—reiterates that I always have been fond of animals ... perhaps more to their chagrin than my delight at times.

As I set out to compile my animal stories into the book before us, my memories continued to prove the hypothesis that animals have always been instrumental for me. I learned that not only have I been an animal lover my entire life, but also the creatures I've encountered have been companions and guides for life's journey. They've nudged me along the path of growth to who I am today, carried me through grief and turmoil and brought great joy to my days.

Many of my memories—good and bad—center around animal companions, and for both the memories and the beasties, I am grateful.

Vignette Two

Animal Surprises Beautiful & Tragic

I HAD WANTED A DOG my whole life. When you're five years old, that's quite a long time. By then, I had decided I would likely never get my wish.

Skepticism has been a lifelong characteristic of mine, it seems. Another early character ... quirk, shall we call it? ... was my imperviousness to surprises. I knew when something good was coming.

For instance, I had an inkling something was about to happen before my first surprise birthday party. Gifts were rarely safe from my intuition ... or sneakiness. I knew the large, wrapped box under the tree was the electronic art toy I'd begged for, and I couldn't wait to watch my pictures light up. If a feel and a shake didn't reveal gift-wrapped contents, I had a secret skill. I could unwrap and rewrap a present in a few moments—often without the need for more tape—without leaving any sign of disturbance.

Regardless of my methods, I predicted most good things before they happened. The time I was given a gift without wrapping paper, though, not even a glimmer that a surprise was brewing had entered my mind.

As I would learn, surprises tend to multiply in the most unlikely ways and come in a multitude of forms ... not all of which are positive.

One misty morning, I opened the screen door to our Pleasant Hill, S.C., backyard. Shock and joy collided in the expression I cast upon the scene before me. I don't recall my feet hitting the concrete steps as I bolted toward the fuzzball wriggling in the grass.

We tumbled end over end. She licked me all over, leaving traces of puppy breath tickling my nose. I covered her in my kisses and hugged her plump belly to my chest. I believe we tied for which of us was more thrilled to have a playmate.

I hopped up and hollered for her to chase me. She caught me and jumped against my legs. My poor balance sent us toppling down the hill. My giggles and her puppy yips followed us until we halted on our backs where the soft but prickly grass cooled my flushed neck. I looked over at my very own puppy, her tongue lolling and snout grinning.

Could she really be mine? Our partnership was sealed with her name—Joy's Heather Lassie—and a giant lick from a tiny pink tongue.

I called her Heather, but she grew into the spitting image of the Lassie I had watched every week—except she was in color and all mine. I believed she would rescue me from any danger. More than my potential hero-in-fur, she was my first friend.

As Heather matured from the rough-and-tumble pup into a sleeker version of the same imp, I accepted my second surprise. My father increased the four-legged population in our household when he bought another Collie.

Colonel Sprit Beetoben—who was named, with the nonsensical spelling intact, before we got him—was older, calmer, steadier. His tri-color coat stood out as more stately compared to Heather's simpler sable and white.

Though we didn't perform a ceremony, I imagined one in my mind. They were wed and joined in canine companionship. I would discover surprises multiply following such unions.

When I learned Heather was expecting, I did what any young pet owner would do: I worried and fretted and entertained question after question without reaching satisfactory answers.

Would she be okay? Unassisted deliveries of multiple puppies sounded terrifying.

What kind of mom would she be? After all, Heather remained a naughty, wild pup herself.

How would she be able to lay still long enough to nurse and bathe babies? Heather was never still—she even twitched in her sleep.

Most importantly, would we get to keep at least one? The thought of a new puppy to snuggle and call my own softened some of my fears.

As often happens while waiting and anticipating, time became taffy. It slowed and stretched and lengthened until it disappeared.

I woke, bleary-eyed to the news: puppies … six of them!

Never have I shed sleep as quickly as I did that morning. I bounded down two flights of stairs and out the door that opened near the two dogs' yards. Sprit had his domain; Heather had hers. A gate allowed them passage to each other's turf from time to time.

I flew past Sprit behind his chain-link fence and searched for Heather's perfectly triangular ears and slick coat. Around the second yard I flew until I glimpsed an oddly bumpy pile inside Heather's wooden doghouse.

She raised her snout and, I swear, grinned at me.

Heather proved to be an amazing mama. She kept all six pups in line, tightly tucked them in, patiently suckled them and protected them from anyone she thought meant them harm.

Six full-blooded Collie puppies: three boys, three girls.

For a girl who'd gone from a lifetime of wishing on stars for one puppy of her own to a furry family of eight, I decided I must have some pretty lucky stars. When I looked at the wriggling litter, I saw new playmates.

My mom—as all moms do in regard to pets—saw more work and mess in her future. My dad saw dollar signs. The price such well-bred puppies could bring would supply needed supplemental income for a preacher at a small village church.

We kept their value and our excitement a surprise. Only a few people in our church knew about the puppies—the elderly widows across the street, perhaps an elder or deacon. My father wasn't overly trusting of others—a trait I may not have inherited but have developed, thanks to surprises of a less pleasant sort than furry friends typically provide.

The day came for our meter to be read. That was back when a man pulled in the driveway and ambled from his little truck to the side of the house. He'd squat and squint at the meter, jot numbers on his clipboard and meander to the next house—after a chat with the preacher.

"Those sure are pretty dogs. And, she's had pups! Six, you say? Full-blood, I see. 'Bout how much can you get for those, you think? Wow! Well, you have a good day now!"

The interest that extended beyond typical nosy Southern conversation and the specificity in his questioning left an uneasy feeling. Whether I felt it then or later seems irrelevant as the heartburn-like feel of distrust, remorse and disgust rises in my chest alongside the end of the story.

"I have a surprise."

My mother's voice sounded ... different. She was trying to sound excited—maybe trying to set me up to focus on the positive. Tragedy's storm cloud never can be kept at bay, though.

Mama led me to a room off the kitchen, likely our schoolroom. Some parts of my memories remain hazy around the edges. Others appear as if they're unfolding before my eyes today—like the bundle of squirming, silky pups with the squeaky, searching sounds they made.

The story came out. I don't remember how it was presented that morning, but as I've heard and told it for nearly four decades, I'll relay it here.

Under the cloak of darkness, a shadow entered our canine kingdom. Sprit, ever the stalwart colonel, took to barking. He barked and barked and refused to stop, but by the time my father descended both levels of stairs and emerged from the house, evil had been unleashed.

My father recruited my mother, and they set to work. Puppy by puppy, my parents gathered the babies into the warmth of our home before they felt the cold of their mother.

Piecing together facts uncovered later, we suspect Sprit refused the poisoned meat that killed my dog and left her six puppies motherless in mere minutes. Sweet Heather—a puppy at heart with her simple, trusting nature—didn't heed Sprit's warnings.

Before my seventh birthday, I learned that an autopsy of an animal is called a necropsy. I added the macabre fact to my already extensive and random data repertoire. I had been developing the collection most of my brief life because I was an avid reader and careful listener who spent most of my time around adults.

The vet that performed the necropsy told us exactly what poison stole my first canine companion. For years, I remembered—clung to— the long word that represented the evil and deadly substance. With time, though, my brain replaced that information with a blank that I believe started with an "O."

It's funny how our minds cover things and yet allow us to sift through memories, like files, and retrieve specifics ... like the image of a black wrapped bundle in the back of our ... was it the station wagon?

I remember the words, "Don't look." Did my mother say them? Did I say them to myself? I mostly didn't look. I remember not wanting to, but I also remember a sideways glance because I needed to.

Heather was my dog. She was my responsibility, and she was dead. Was she really dead? Were they certain? I thought I should take one last glance. No movement and a gut-wrenching dog-shaped lump confirmed the truth.

We speculate the murdering thief hid in the nearby woods, watching his prizes disappear in my parents' hands and cursing the sentry who'd alerted the house and foiled his ultimate goal.

The police came. An officer sat at our dark wooden dining table with its heavy, fancy chairs that I always imagined belonged in a castle. He jotted notes in a spiral notebook engulfed by his large hand. Even at my young age, I understood they couldn't do anything and doubted how many resources would go toward the case. Catching a dog-killer wasn't simple, and a girl's tearful plea of "Find the bad man who killed my dog" was easier asked than accomplished.

We'd never know for sure who killed her. Distrust settled in my soul that day. I still eye anyone in my yard with great suspicion, even if they are in an officially marked vehicle with a clipboard.

What I came to accept as I grew into this hard world was that, even if whoever was responsible were never caught, even if no one else ever knew, God knew, and the killer knew. I prayed he'd one day feel guilt and remorse over what he had done.

The story doesn't end there, though.

I grieved and cried and raged until I thought it wasn't possible to feel any more. But then, I accepted a six-week commitment of caring for Heather's pups. They weren't even a month old yet and needed food around the clock ... special formula we mixed up. They had to be bathed every day.

The vet had told us, "You know, the mama licks them clean every day." We used tiny soft washcloths and water with my baby shampoo ... no tears in their eyes under my watch.

They also needed brushing and snuggling and playing and loving. I gave them all that in abundance.

Ram, Tam, Sam, Pam, Justina and Skosh.

Six puppies and one stately papa, still standing guard, ready to bark us all to attention should the need arise again.

We kept them safe from further nefarious acts within a makeshift pen inside our closed garage until, one by one, they met their people. I watched kids embrace their first puppies, and I prayed they'd get to hold theirs longer than I had mine.

I begged and pleaded to keep at least one. My father gave me a deadline. "If they're not all gone by such-and-such day …."

And so, I hoped and prayed and wished on the first star I saw each night. The day approached rapidly. Justina and Skosh remained.

Skosh—the runt—oh so tiny and oh so precious to me. When we bathed them, she was so small, she looked like a drowned rat. Her name came from a Japanese word meaning "a small amount." She had been my baby from day one, and I wanted her most of all. A family came and chose her. They seemed nice, but the green monster rose inside and kept me from sending them off with a genuine smile.

Such emotions are powerful. Even today, I recall that fuzzy scene with a verdant tint and feel jealousy's bitter bubbling in my chest.

Only Justina remained. She was named for one of my brothers. I remember her as the softest with the roundest belly. I can still smell her delightful puppy scent. On the day before she would be mine, I reminded my father of his promise. He informed me we had visitors scheduled to come the next day. One more wish; one more sleep.

Justina went to her new home on that deadline—no amount of crying or logically explaining how, technically, she should have been mine on that day, not after that day, could change the course of fate. In the wake of her departure were me and Sprit and a deeper relationship with disappointment.

The regal Collie became my constant companion for the next several years. Through two moves, more losses and the uncertainty that comes with the pains of growing up, Sprit lay beside me and gave me strength and friendship, unfaltering and unquestioning.

I told him stories, secrets, dreams and fears. He kept them all. What he gave me in return were my first dose of courage and my first chance to develop my voice.

On the cool concrete of our basement entrance in Mooresville, N.C., he caught my tears in his fur. In the damp serenity of our earthy, moss-covered tree ring between the manse and church, he and the nearby gravestones first heard my faerie tales.

Perhaps the greatest surprise for me in life has been the truth that animals show us who we are or who we can be. They do so through their empathy, love and companionship. Such epiphanies can also come through lessons hidden in the memories we cherish of the creatures we've called our own.

Animals are a great deal more than pets. Their stories mingle with ours until they become chapter titles in our lives' books. Animals are companions and friends. Animals are therapists whose hour is never up and whose door is always open. Animals are sounding boards, inspiration and encouragement.

Animals shape us into who we are.

My first experiences with pet ownership instilled in me a great responsibility to our furry friends. I recognized risk and reward to having animals. I committed to not promising anything I couldn't or wouldn't uphold. That incident made me the frank realist I am. I hope those traits have helped me prepare my children as they begin their individual journeys into the world.

Beautiful or tragic, animal surprises make us better in some great or small way ... if we let them.

Vignette Three

Chickens in my Bathtub & Mealworms in my Pantry

LIFE IS STRESSFUL—A FACT I decided to simply accept, after a revelation brought on by chickens and mealworms.

Stress-caused tension ebbs and flows to some extent. Certain seasons recede and allow respite in the shallows, while others batter unmercifully. One of the latter times hit me while I was polishing my first novel for publication.

I had no idea what I was doing. I'd revealed my plans to the world and divided my time among family, homeschooling, work and—of all things—chasing a dream that seemed ridiculous.

The ludicrousness of my pursuits felt especially pronounced in the middle of the day. I juggled teaching, grading, keeping kids fed, staying on top of my husband's ever-changing work schedule and making sure all our social obligations were met ... while approaching deadlines and imagining the mocking jeers of the thousands of people online who would know if I failed to produce a book when I said I would.

That's about the time my husband, Tony, decided we needed chickens.

We were new to the business of chicken rearing and accepted the task with careful attention and a basketful of anxiety.

While we live in the mostly sweat-inducing climate of southeast Louisiana, March and April can still get downright frigid in Slidell. After a night or so of fretting at the window, Tony borrowed a heat lamp, and we emptied a plastic bin. In went the chickens, on went the lamp; there went the bathtub.

Anyone who's never had the pleasure of being around chickens may not know an important detail we weren't familiar with either: they stink.

As the days passed and the chicks grew, our tiny bathroom took on the feel of a sauna with an added warm aroma that soon snaked into the hallway and neighboring rooms of our adequate—in other words, far from palatial—home.

Chickens poop—a lot. It's pretty much all they do; well, that and eat and drink and peck. That's a chicken's day in a nutshell. It didn't take long for their bin to fill up with excrement.

It also didn't take long for the biddies to outgrow their makeshift coop. Turns out, chickens can fly, and wherever they land, they do what chickens do. They poop.

As I juggled all the tasks and questioned my sanity for pursuing crazy dreams, I did so from a chicken poop sauna, attempting to keep chicks confined to a bathtub while disinfecting the rest of the space. As I type this account, I realize how those brain cells I've been missing leached out.

heat + feces + chemicals + sleep-deprivation = loss of brain cells

That equation makes sense and answers many questions.

Tony and his dad built a spacious coop and roost on the other side of our backyard, and the chicks kept growing in the tiny biddy coop on our patio. The bathroom slowly released its noxious fumes, while my patio collected a Jackson Pollock chicken crap exhibition.

Meanwhile, I set a date to launch my first book baby into the world. I ventured into my role as book publicist and planned to utilize any method possible to let the world know I was releasing a book.

When my chickens start to lay eggs,
my books will hatch at your favorite bookstore!

I haven't seen that exact marketing technique taught in any of the fancy promo courses, and I can't say with certainty it sold any books. Perhaps I should have included cute chick pics.

The day arrived when the weather leaned toward our typical balmy temperatures and the chicks were ready to fly the coop—actually, fly *to* their large permanent space. They seemed chickenly grateful for their new home. I continued typing, revising, editing, learning.

Book launch day came. It was everything I thought it would be and more. At least, I think it was. It's all a bit of a blur—as most long-awaited and highly anticipated events tend to be.

In between live videos on social media, I passed a hallway full of dirty laundry. The depths of the darkness of my loathing for those fabric mounds rise in my chest, even now. I'd never considered the plight of our dirty clothes post-publication, but the reality of the situation struck me as especially cruel and unusual punishment. I was a published author; surely I shouldn't have to do laundry anymore.

Alas! Authorship doesn't make laundry disappear.

In addition to adding publisher and marketer roles to my juggling act, I became an event coordinator with book signings to plan. I prepared presentations and gifts for the hordes of adoring fans I envisioned meeting and designed graphics to let them know where they could find me and my books.

Around this dream-come-true time, I made three discoveries:

1. I only thought I was juggling a ton before I published.

2. It was going to be a long, long time before I became famous.

3. Someone put a bag of mealworms in my pantry.

As it turns out, chickens enjoy treats as much as the next pet. The treats that set their tailfeathers to waggling happen to be mealworms.

I'm still not sure why they had to be in my pantry. It was a startling discovery to make as I reached for that night's supper ingredients.

I will admit, my initial reaction was a blend of shock, disgust and anger. In times of stress, I tend to react with rage at anything or anyone who makes the situation more difficult. I confess my anger at my husband for adding chickens to the insanity of my life and for tossing mealworms in my pantry for no logical reason I could deduce.

As I stepped back from the shock, I breathed deeply of the non-chicken-tainted air and discovered a revelation. Stress will always be here, there and everywhere.

Odd discoveries—like mealworms in a pantry—give us something to laugh about in the midst of anxiety. Those disclosures can only accomplish such a purpose, though, when we release our death grips on frustration and rage.

Years have passed since my early days of dreaming and chicks in my bathtub. I'm still dreaming and juggling. I'm still not famous. Stress continues with no sign of stopping. We still have chickens, though none of our original flock remain. They're not a long-living bird, it seems.

We gathered second and third flocks. Those chicks didn't get to live in a sauna-poop bathroom. Like kids, second and third flocks don't have as many pictures taken of them as first flocks either.

I often forget we have chickens ... until my husband brings me breakfast. As the poached eggs' yolks cascade bright yellow richness over my biscuits, I forgive Tony again for adding chickens to our life.

The birds and their edible contributions gift me clarity for stress and for living. Tony and I find ways amidst our far-too-busy schedules to share small moments—a quick but filling breakfast in bed or a half-hour watching our flock peck around the yard. We embrace such gifts with gratitude and strive to never take them for granted or overlook the opportunity to experience one.

Before chowing down, I raise my biscuit-and-egg-covered fork in salute toward the backyard and our feathered friends. I thank God for the gift of humor to file the sharp edges of life's stress.

I also thank Him I no longer have chickens in my bathtub and mealworms in my pantry.

Vignette Four

Gratitude Takes Wing

I BELIEVE ANIMALS SHOW GRATITUDE. They teach us to be grateful, even in life's most torrential times. I also believe I can dispel anyone's doubts on the matter through two stories.

In the late 1980s, in the aftermath of one of the worst hurricanes to hit near Pleasant Hill, S.C., one of God's tiniest creatures discovered a shelter from the storm in our garage.

For the sake of being factual, I might be mixing two separate events together. We did, indeed, live through Hurricane Hugo and its aftermath in September 1989. A hummingbird did, indeed, seek refuge in our garage during a storm.

Whether the two occurred simultaneously seems beside the point. Both instances affected me in my formative years and remain vivid recollections, dodging the typical haze surrounding childhood memories. Gratitude anchors both stories and links them in my recollections.

For anyone who doesn't live in hurricane-prone areas, the combination of gratitude and a destructive hurricane probably makes little sense. For anyone who does live in hurricane-prone areas, that pairing probably makes even less sense.

The hummingbird's example should convince anyone of the ability of all God's creatures—even the tiniest of winged beings—to express gratitude, so I'll share his tale before my experience with the hurricane.

At some point during the storm's fury, a hummingbird zipped into the refuge of our garage. While he remained safe from the storm, unbattered and dry, the time came for him to return to his proper place in nature.

Try as he might, that wee winged creature couldn't navigate the necessary dip to swoop beneath the garage's overhang and into freedom. Instead, his terror grew, which resulted in frantic and repeated flights into walls, ceiling and rows of hanging tools.

When my father discovered the bird and his plight, the creature had exhausted himself to the point of death. The hummingbird collapsed, enervated, onto the bristles of a broom. Slowly, carefully, my father lifted the broom from its hanger on the wall. He crept toward the door. One step at a time, the tiny bird gasped and clung to his makeshift perch, too spent to display fear at the nearness of the human or the vibrations of the broom.

My father carried the hummingbird to the cheerful red feeder on our front porch. He held the broom head steady, level with the yellow plastic flowers, until the rested creature shifted one foot at a time to the feeder's perch.

Time stilled. My father sat and observed. The hummingbird rested.

Finally, the bird took one small sip, then rested. He took a longer sip and another. A few sips in, his wings vibrated once, twice. One more sip ... they revved to life.

He rose up and back, hovered, then zipped forward and down for more sustenance. Up and back, hovered, then zipped forward. After a few more rounds, the little warrior buzzed inches before my father's face, hovered for a moment—beak to nose—then zipped away.

The next morning, my father emerged from our front door, coffee and Bible in hand. He prepared for his daily devotional reading on the porch where he'd carried the broom the previous day. As he reached for his coffee mug's handle, a sound alerted him to company.

With his distinct hum, the hummingbird buzzed inches before my father's face, hovered, then approached the feeder for his breakfast.

Every morning for many weeks, the hummingbird continued that pattern, zipping in for breakfast but always thanking his rescuer first. Season after season, the bird returned to the place that had been his shelter in the storm. Each time, he renewed his routine, remembering to first tip his crown and say his thanks.

Hummingbirds are my favorite birds, partially because of that one.

I also feel a kinship to the mini flyers. Like them, I'm small and fast—always zipping here, then there.

A third reason they've always been my favorite rests in the three powerful life lessons that bird taught me.

First, he gave me an outstanding example of gratitude. I may not always do so perfectly, but I have tried throughout my life to say thank you to the people God's placed on my path to help and guide me.

The hummingbird painted for me a real-life picture of Jesus' unsurpassed love for His children. God even cares for those tiny creatures and their well-being—in sunlight or storms. His love for us must be incalculable because He declares in Matthew 6:26, "Are you not of more value than they?"

Finally, that wee bird taught me resilience whenever I face one of life's storms—literal or figurative.

Hugo was the first major hurricane I experienced. I'd grown up with the stories, though: Frederick. Camille. I would grow into my own names with their devastation and destruction and lasting effects: Ivan. Katrina. Ida.

Those names haunt our Thanksgiving tables—names uttered in reverence, respect, sadness. We remember the loss, but we also remember the resilience, the rebirth, the lessons. We also remember the preparations and the charged calm before the storms.

The feeling of impending terror in my bones remains a phantom tingling as I recall asking my mother, "What will it be like? Will our house blow away? Why can't we bring the dogs inside?" At that point, we still had both Heather and Sprit.

I walked a step behind, following every detail of the mental hurricane prep checklist my mom ticked off with each bustling action.

- Fill all the gallon jugs with drinking water.
- Fill the bathtubs so we can flush the toilets.
- Get the candles ready, matches alongside.
- What kind of batteries does that flashlight need again? Put extra AA batteries where they're easy to find.
- Set out the card games.

"Really, why can't we bring the dogs in?"

I decided there was no way I'd be able to sleep that night and told my parents so as I was tucked in. The next scene I remember is my mom picking me up from my bed and the thick darkness around us. I fought through sleep's fog to ask what was happening.

My bed was against an outside wall where our chimney stood sentry. Apparently, visions of chimney bricks crashing through my ceiling and burying me prompted my mom to interrupt my slumber.

Down in the basement, I pressed my face to the window, straining to catch a glimpse of our dogs. Two chain-link yards with the shared fence between. My eyes inched from link to link—one doghouse. Inch by inch—second doghouse ...

No!

I remember the chill of the glass as I palmed the window and swallowed a scream. Heather's doghouse flew over the fence and flipped into the yard. The house smashed into the ground with a crash that reverberated deep in my heart. From there, the wind continued its tantrum, tumbling the house diagonally over and over around the yard.

Sprit stood in the downpour, a soggy sentinel in his yard. Maybe he was the smart one to not seek shelter in his house. But Heather ...

My beautiful dog.

As the storm continued to rage outside, a tempest whipped within me. I remember the red-hot flames of my anger toward my father for making our dogs stay outside in a hurricane. As the winds surged again and rattled the windows, I decided I'd never forgive him.

Whether I relinquished my resolve to stay awake until light rose and I could go to my dog, wherever she ended up, or I clung to consciousness, I'm not sure. Either way, the morning stillness—that eerie, other-worldly illusion of peace that follows monster storms—brought us news.

Somehow, someway, Heather breached the fence between her and Sprit and hunkered down in his house while he—ever the gentleman—kept watch. They had both survived.

My anger dimmed. Instead of bright red, the emotion dulled to a brownish-orange, like embers at the base of a dying fire that may have calmed but haven't extinguished.

After finding Heather and Sprit in good shape, I couldn't imagine what my parents meant by "bad news." My favorite tree between our house and the church had been lifted from its roots and laid on its side, never to stand guard over my daydreams again.

Trees have always been companions to me. I've looked to them as stalwart guardians and secret-keepers. When I conjure images of how that tree looked when it stood erect, I envision a willow that encased me from the world. I could hide, safe beneath its waterfall limbs.

Thinking back with a more practical memory to how the tree stretched across the yard post-storm, I'm fairly certain it was a pine. A child's imagination knows no bounds.

Regardless of its scientific classification, the tree was the first place I remember as a retreat of solace and solitude and a willing listener to my stories. In one night, with one giant storm, it was gone.

Hurricane Hugo destroyed so much more—people's homes, businesses—and took too many human lives. I know a tree isn't on the same level of loss, but for a six-year-old girl whose friends were books, stuffed animals, two Collie dogs and a tree, I grieved.

I wept for that tree. On a level I wouldn't have understand at the time, I believe my tears fell for the loss of a piece of me and of peace itself. I had witnessed the power of nature firsthand—a force that could pluck a massive tree, roots and all, with the ease of my hand around a dandelion. I faced the fact that nothing is certain or sure on this earth—not the pillow where I lay my head, not my pets, not even a tree.

Tears only get so much time after a disaster, though, and cleanup waits for no emotion to subside.

As we continued our circuit of the yards—ours, the church's, our neighbors'—we expressed gratitude for the lack of serious structural damage and commenced picking up the endless sea of shingles that littered as far as my eyes could see.

I remember the warm shimmer of pride that I could help. In my corner of the world that had been sent topsy-turvy, I felt tiny and powerless. I couldn't right my downed tree or erase the terror of the night before. Shingles, though—I could pick those up and set our yards right again. The smiles of our widowed neighbors rewarded me.

Life would be okay. The sun would return.

I may have lost my tree as it was, but the upturned roots and the attached earth provided a new fort. I could climb in and explore the tippy-tops of the branches I'd only glimpsed before.

Plus, I was helping uncover the bright green grass of our yards once more with my cleanup contributions.

I can still feel the next memory in the palms of my hands: the insatiable burning after a morning picking up shingles and the anguish accompanying the realization that we had no running water to rinse the lingering sting from my hands. Despair settled while my agony leaked out as tears.

My children have heard me recall that vivid memory during every hurricane aftermath we've been through as I distribute gloves to one and all.

The pain did subside, thankfully, after my mother poured some of our carefully reserved water on my hands.

Natural disasters cause victims' emotions to turn and twist like spin-off tornados. Mine were no exception. From terror to relief to mourning to thankfulness to loss and hopelessness to pride to despair, I was emotionally spent.

No electricity brought an unexpected joy, though. In the still darkness, our family gathered card games and board games and played together.

Each night the lights stayed off, we played by candlelight. When power was restored, the sense of loss of quiet family game times extinguished my excitement. We turned out the lamps, re-lit the candles and played one more night.

Gratitude in the rays of light following a storm manifests in various ways. I thanked God for covering my dog in His protection, for transforming my hideout, for giving me a way to help ... and relief from the unexpected pain of providing that help.

I can accept and respect any physical storm with a name that sends shudders down the spines of all who live through its wake. The ones in my past have become life markers. They have taught me lessons, made me strong and taught me to love my neighbors and community. I can also weather the metaphorical storms of grief, loss, pain and illness, even when they devastate my life's landscape.

To paraphrase one of my favorite songs, "God's eye is on the [hummingbird], and I know He watches me." I will trust Him to see me through the storms and ask Him to help me always, in every situation, show gratitude like that colorful, winged creature did.

Vignette Five

Origins of a Fluffball

THE SUMMER BEFORE MY SOPHOMORE year in high school, we moved to Waynesboro, Miss. It's a town travelers have to know about to get to, but the views and the serenity are worth the drive.

I had just driven home from school and emerged from my toasty car into the frosty January afternoon. My dad met me and said a surprise waited in his office, a small room off our garage.

While other details remain blurry, one memory remains clear—the sight of a tiny blond fluffball and the feel of his silky fur against my face. He had the roundest belly and the most delightful puppy breath.

How such a tiny nugget ended up on our property, far from the town's map-dot civilization, I'll never know. I suspect there's more to the story than what I was told.

According to my father, he heard crying while he was working in his office. He walked outside to search for the source. The noise emanated from beneath my sister-in-law's car, which was parked under a tree down from our driveway. My Marine brother Justin was stationed in Hawaii, and they had left his wife's car with us.

Sure enough, beneath the green sporty vehicle huddled a scared, hungry, lonely ball of fluff.

As far as the origin of the pup's name goes, I can only speculate this many years removed. My best guess is I came up with "Jimbo" because I had declared my brother Jim to be my favorite brother for many years. I had been begging my parents to let me learn French and was already a budding author, so I took a creative twist with the spelling. Hence, the little bundle of fur with his tiny pink tongue kisses was dubbed Gembeaux.

I fell in love immediately. I hadn't expected to find a new fur baby to love at that point in my life. Since that time, I've found—more than once—the best experiences often occur apart from my expectations.

For instance, when I stop fixating on visions of countless readers flocking to my events, I experience truly precious and meaningful moments with one special reader. When I pause my daydreaming and buckle down for focused work, powerful words emerge that may captivate or even soothe someone's heart one day. When I stop wishing on stars for a pup of my own, one appears in a somewhat magical way.

Perhaps Gembeaux's origin story uncovered the key to contentment. Life can be enchanting when we open our eyes and hearts to the unexpected and cease attempts to manufacture our own good things.

Vignette Six

A Kitten in an Overcoat & Other Feline Gifts

DOES EVERY FAMILY HAVE A sibling that stays in hot water with the parents? Justin, my brother closest to me in age, was a frequent recipient of eye rolls and steam billowing from ears.

As an adoring little sister, I never understood how our parents could be mad at him. Looking back, I can think of a few times where their displeasure made sense ... like the time he showed up at our house in Mooresville, N.C., with a tiny gray kitten in his overcoat pocket. Merry Christmas to me!

Smokey II was the first cat that was all mine, and I adored him. Plus, he had been a gift from my big brother who I thought was pretty amazing.

My new baby had a doomed name, though, I'm afraid. He was the second of three gray cats our family has had over the years. Smokey I, who lived with us in South Dakota, had his ears freeze off during the first winter there. I can't make this stuff up.

That Smokey didn't survive the second frozen season. I'm sure no one is surprised. Most people know a swiss-cheese, asymmetrical tree house can't provide enough warmth for any creature during a blizzard.

Smokey III was Justin's cat, so his story is not mine to tell. Perhaps my brother will include it in his feline tales.

I vaguely remember heated words between my father and brother regarding Smokey II's appearance, but the kitten got to stay—outside only. Thankfully, Mooresville has milder winters than Artas.

Cats have total confidence in their right to act however they please and no reason to mask their opinion of humans. Smokey II was no exception.

He followed me around our yard, playfully scampering behind me and batting at grass blades that I would wiggle along the ground beside him. Whenever I swung on the swing in our carport or sat in the openings on the brick wall and leaned against the support posts, he curled up and purred nearby.

Smokey had a morning ritual. He would crouch in wait behind bushes. At the start of my father's daily walk to our church to work on his sermon, the feline would leap out and attack the preoccupied minister's legs.

The feisty gray cat lived with us in North Carolina and then Mississippi. I can't remember the exact timeline, but at some point in the second location, he ran off. We lived on the busiest road in our town, and we frequently saw cats on the sides of the road who didn't survive a run-in with a fast car. I choose to imagine he found a new home or started an indie cat band and hitchhiked to Nashville where they became big stars.

Justin took the loss of Smokey II hard and was eager to give me another cat. He waited until I was on my own, though. He and I have similar opinions about allowing cats to live outside.

A few weeks after graduating from college, I moved into my first house in Gautier, Miss. Justin and his wife, Tonya, drove over from their home a few hours away to bring me a fat and fluffy house-warming present whose name was Charlie.

At the time, Justin and Tonya had a few other cats, including Charlie's "brother," Bennie. As large as Charlie was, Bennie was skinny. And as playful as Bennie was, Charlie was lazy.

They were polar opposites, but that didn't stop Bennie from trying to play with Charlie every chance he got. Charlie didn't mind his playful companion, but a cat can only have his nap interrupted for so long before he has to put his paw down and lay on his skinny buddy.

Charlie settled in quickly and happily to his new home. I think he was content to be an only cat. He had the royal run of the place, too, and delighted in rubbing his good fortune in to my dog Gembeaux who barked at Charlie through the French doors every chance he got.

A few weeks after Charlie became my roommate, I returned home from work to find him listless and bleeding in his litter box. As the night shift reporter, I worked late, so the only option for his care post-midnight was an emergency vet about thirty minutes away.

I bundled him up and sped off to find out what was wrong with the fuzzy cat who was rapidly becoming my best friend. Forty-eight hours and thousands of dollars later—an amount my amazing brother covered since his just-bought-a-house, just-graduated-from-college sister called him, freaking out—Charlie returned home with me. He had a new lease on life and a life sentence of a special cat food. Apparently, crystals in a male cat's urethra are common.

Charlie's emergency bonded us, and whenever I was home, he was never far from my lap. When I had friends over or was cooking in the kitchen or cleaning the house, I'd hold him on my hip like a furry toddler. He'd rest his paws on my shoulder and survey his kingdom from the comfort of my arm.

I loved to rub my face in his silky, warm fur and rest my cheek on his fluffy belly. He comforted me after long days of reporting and longer nights of deadlines and council meetings.

Unfortunately, I developed an allergy to my new companion. A weird crusty rash appeared around my eyes and on the tops of my cheeks. I've never been a fan of doctors, so I put off going to anyone for a few months. I simply ignored the rash and pretended it wasn't there. Denial serves me well enough in some situations.

I had almost reached the point of asking around for a doctor who dealt with mysterious allergic reactions when the mess magically cleared up. It never returned, and I guess my body adjusted to Charlie's fur.

For the record, I was willing to live out my days with a rash.

Charlie became my comfort, my companion and my confidante as I navigated the choppy waters between the peaceful shores of college life and the ocean depths of the adult world.

While college was challenging and had an adjustment period, my professors and friends and tiny campus served as safety nets. Once I moved out, bought a house and entered the work force, I both embraced my independence and questioned my ability to handle it.

I did not feel prepared to be on my own. I had so many unanswered questions and uncertainties. Those fears quadrupled after Hurricane Katrina hit on August 29, 2005.

While I had no desire to leave my home, my parents were insistent I evacuate. Animals should never be left in the path of a hurricane— that was one of the lessons I learned during Hurricane Hugo. When I declared I would, under no circumstances, leave without my furry companions, they recruited the aid of my sister Jane and brother Justin.

Gembeaux took shelter in my sister's backyard in Mobile, Ala., while I continued to my brother's in Pensacola, Fla., with Charlie. He and Bennie quickly settled into their routine of Bennie's insistent playfulness until Charlie grew weary and lay on him.

As the storm approached, I stood outside at my brother's house and watched massive pine trees bend nearly to the ground. My thoughts whipped as frantically as the leaves around me. The hurricane hadn't even hit yet and was hundreds of miles to our west. How bad was this going to get? Would I have a house to return to?

The days following Katrina's two landfalls—first in southeast Louisiana and second on the western corner of Mississippi—and the breaking of the levees in New Orleans swelled with tension and darkness, uncertainty and terror.

Communication was spotty at best. My then-boyfriend, now-husband had just started graduate school in Kentucky. We were able to talk a few times. I can't remember exactly how since both our cell phones with coastal numbers were as useful as paper weights.

My house was one of the lucky ones. I had only minor damage in Gautier, most to the fence in my backyard, which meant Gembeaux had to stay at my sister's house for a few months.

The bigger issue was my newspaper office in downtown Pascagoula. The headquarters of *The Mississippi Press* flooded and would be unusable for many months.

Our sister paper, the *Mobile Register*, opened its doors to our staff. For the next several months, we worked out of their offices. Our staff drove into Jackson County each morning to cover the disaster cleanup in our towns and then returned to Mobile to file articles and photos by deadline. I stayed with my sister, Jane, and her family in Mobile during much of that time.

Charlie remained in Florida, so my little family stretched across three states as I adjusted to a new normal for a time.

The weeks following major hurricanes are filled with stillness and an absence of sound. Even with the constant drone of generators and whirr of chain saws, post-hurricane silence drowns all other noise.

I can't call the quiet eerie. Well, I suppose I can in the areas where only foundations remained, negating any need for generators or chain saws. In neighborhoods where damage stands, leans or lies as reminders, however, the quiet envelops families as they grill whatever the freezers are no longer equipped to hold and neighbors have pooled together for that evening's communal dinner.

Community is defined in daily actions during disasters. In the stillness after nature's tantrums, humanity rises—resilient, resolute, reaching across the fences, streets and yards. Dividing lines vanish.

As I visited families who had lost everything and attempted to record their stories, we stood on unsettlingly clean concrete foundations—all that remained of their lives. I felt a shroud drape my heart as I witnessed greater devastation than I'd ever imagined in my 22 years.

I weaved through debris, lifting a picture frame with glass splintering across the faces of a family. I spoke with the couple who rode out the monster storm beside the water in the cab of their pickup truck. They still had their lives and the truck, but nothing remained of their home.

One of our photographers and I pushed off from a boat launch with some marine patrol officers from Mississippi and Florida. We were on a recovery mission … not rescue. I took a heavy pause to comprehend the distinction between those two words and felt reality's weight in my soul as I frantically attempted to prepare my mind and heart for the sight of a recovered body. Thankfully, I didn't have to test my mental and emotional steeling. I witnessed the beauty of nature's post-storm calm as we floated around the bayous, wondered at the might that tossed giant boats on land and homes in the water and worried about the dogs we found on an otherwise abandoned houseboat.

Area shelters held many more stories. I heard their whispers in the fear-filled eyes of children, clutching new teddy bears that weren't the same as the lovies they'd lost with their homes. I saw their influence in the shivering bundles of fur whose eyebrows danced nervously above snouts resting on twitching paws.

I interviewed a family who took shelter in the Superdome following the levee disaster. They may have found shelter but not safety.

The stories weighed on my shoulders, and I bowed beneath their heaviness. In my prostrate position, I entertained doubts about my abilities as a reporter and questioned my career choice.

I brought my concerns to my managing editor. His words were kind, reassuring. We were living through an *unprecedented* time. Unprecedented was that fall's buzzword.

He went on to say I was capable; reporting wouldn't always be like that. He supported whatever decision I made, but he urged me not to make any changes in the midst of the unsettling madness. Give it time; see it through. He was right.

Returning to my house, my Charlie in tow, improved my mindset and soothed my heart. It took us a while longer to repair the fence and get Gembeaux home. Having both babies back where they belonged restored my peace and comfort.

I stopped doubting my place behind the pen, but restoration post-Katrina didn't lead to an easier job. The tough assignments continued as I wrote three articles about two teen girls whose lives were stolen by a drunk driver.

My detective contact with the local police department called me one evening. He was on his way to pick me up. "Prepare yourself."

When we arrived on the scene, the bodies were gone, but the wreckage remained. Once a cute, practical car for a new driver to get to and from school and cheer practice, two pieces rested askew on the side of the road littered with other pieces and parts.

Witnessing the wrecked car, meeting the girls' grieving families and attending the funeral with crying cheerleaders and shocked relatives shifted the foundation of my heart.

I can't explain what that tragedy did within me, but I've carried its influence into my adult life. I had planned to name my daughter after them. Instead, I may one day have a character named Jasmine Gabrielle, and she will be a tribute to the two girls who never got to be adults.

Stories surrounded me, and not all were tragedies. I appreciated the assignments at the local Christian rehabilitation center where I covered graduations of people embarking on new lives, free from addiction's death grip. I watched families embrace, relationships restored, after years of alcohol- and drug-induced divisions.

Those were the good moments, though none of my assignments were easy. When the constant static of the stories swirling around me and the emotions they evoked within me became more than I could withstand, I could always escape to the furry sides of Gembeaux and Charlie. Eventually, with their comfort in my home, I regained confidence in the fact that I was born to relay stories—good, bad; hard, light.

No sound on earth is as comforting and reassuring as a cat's purr. Charlie's purr was louder than any cat's I've heard before or since. Over the years, he got into the habit of sleeping with me. In his later years, he would snuggle up against my chest and purr me to sleep. Once I was sleeping soundly, he would crawl to the bottom of the bed and spend the rest of the night.

I dearly miss his purr and presence. Charlie will always be one of my favorite life stories.

Cats are independent beings at their core, whether they are spunky and opinionated like Smokey II or content to be babied like Charlie.

They also relish community. Whether their pals prowl the neighborhoods with them or snuggle with them while laughing or crying, they embrace those connections. I can relate.

Most of me desires nothing more than to be on my own—free from responsibilities toward others, able to follow my whims, or from the challenging emotions people invoke—and yet a deeper part of me knows I was created for community ... community with my family, friends and animals; community with fellow citizens whose stories I can tell or listen to or learn from. My community makes me a better human.

I am thankful for my brother and his feline gifts. Most of my childhood, I thought I was a dog person. Don't get me wrong, I love and adore dogs, but I might be more of a cat person, in more ways than one.

Perhaps my brother knew that long before I did ... and so did the tiny gray kitten in his overcoat.

Vignette Seven

Love at First... Smell?

I REMEMBER EVERYTHING ABOUT THE day we got Bentley—the sights, the sounds, the smells. He battled anxiety with flatulence and excessive licking and farted the entire car ride home.

When Tony and I married, I had my cat Charlie, but we hadn't yet brought home a pet together. Our kids were old enough to help us care for a puppy—they were three-and-a-half and one-and-a-half—and we'd been looking for a Labrador Retriever.

Tony stumbled upon a social media post for Bentley, who at that point had the unfortunate moniker Kelso. His owner was a college student who discovered her studies wouldn't allow her to spend enough time with a rambunctious pup.

On a hot day in May 2011, we met at a dog park in Metairie and fell in love with the dog's goofy grin. He was the right fit for our growing pack. We loaded him up in our vehicle with his bed, food and giant stuffed teddy bear.

He started on my lap, the noxious fumes wafting incessantly. We did our best to calm him with lots of pets and soothing words. He wiggled his way into Tony's lap, where he spent the rest of the drive across the bridge to the northshore of Lake Pontchartrain.

At some point on the ride, a Dierks Bentley song came on the radio. Tony said, "We should name him Bentley." We agreed the name fit him.

Bentley was adorable and loving and completely devoted to the entire family, though he took a special shine to Tony. My husband

would come home late from work and sit on our concrete patio. Bentley would jump up, paws on his master's shoulders, and playfully gnaw on the top of Tony's head.

When I recall Bentley as a puppy, I tend to only remember the cute, cuddly, adorable details. In reality, he was a mess—like any puppy—but he was our mess.

He chewed up toys and shoes we left out. He chewed on furniture. He frequently dug out of the fence and always traveled through as many stinky ditches as possible before we got him back home.

Gradually, he outgrew the running away and chewing stages. He never quite outgrew the anxiety, though. Its accompanying odor lessened over time as his nerves flared only during neighborhood fireworks shows or other particularly stressful events.

I mentioned how he came with a stuffed bear. He loved to snuggle with that bear, but he chewed it to shreds within a few weeks. We got in the habit of buying big stuffed bears after holidays when they went on sale.

His first Christmas with us came and went, and I hit the sales rack. They had a variety of bears, but a stuffed puppy with a festive Christmas collar around his neck caught my eye. I brought it home.

Bentley immediately snuggled up with the stuffed dog on his bed. I noticed he wrapped his paw around it and tucked it in to himself as he napped. He was adorable. After his initial snuggly nap, he commenced chewing. That chewing was different than how he had chewed his bears.

Something I should mention about Bentley is he hated collars. He tolerated the bandanas or other silly things we'd fasten around his neck, but, in his opinion, dogs were meant to run wild and free and bare-necked.

Every day and every night, Bentley would gnaw on his puppy's collar. He didn't chew the legs or belly or snout—only the collar. Once the restrictive device was gone, Bentley never chewed another part of his puppy. He was inseparable from the stuffed dog. Whenever he napped, the puppy kept him company.

One of Bentley's favorite outings was to go to my in-laws' house. We never put his collar on to go there. We'd pull up and he'd bolt out the car door, straight to the pond. He'd leap in and swim, as graceful as any otter, with his webbed paws.

Bentley's anxiety disappeared in the water and with his family. Over the years, he grew less anxious, even on New Year's Eve or the Fourth of July. We were his family, and he found comfort and peace in our home. Only rarely would his nervous physical reactions pop up.

We accepted him—smelly gas and all—and made sure he knew how much he was loved and how much we intended to care for him.

Come to think of it, our approach with him was a lot like how he loved his puppy and made sure his buddy didn't have to remain collared. He exemplified a friend worthy of emulation, with devotion manifested in comfort, love and acceptance.

I strive to be a Bentley-like friend, looking for ways to gnaw a figurative collar off to free a burdened friend, and enjoy spending quality time with those closest to me. Everyone has quirks and challenges. Friends either tease one another about such things— lovingly, of course—or simply accept them with a grin ... regardless of their effects on noses.

Vignette Eight

When Love Is Unlikable

ROMY IS PROBABLY THE MOST expressive and emotional dog I've ever known. She wears her feelings on her snout.

Yes, animals have feelings, and no one can convince me otherwise. Romy may be the best example.

She came into our lives after we said goodbye to Charlie, my cat of eleven years. He had been with me through some of the most pivotal moments of my life and was truly one of a kind. I will never know another Charlie.

Or another Romy.

I decided I didn't have to have another cat—none could replace Charlie anyway—but I thought Bentley would like to have a puppy pal to play with. We desired a canine Neapolitan set (black, chocolate and yellow Labradors), so I searched for a chocolate Lab to join our black pup and get us two-thirds of the way there.

Low and behold, I discovered Romy—a chocolate Labrador Retriever/Chesapeake Bay Retriever mix. At nearly two years old, she needed a family who would be home with her more than her RN mom could be. Romy's online picture was what one would expect from dating profiles. She looked practically perfect in every way—smart and calm and obedient. Plus, she was gorgeous.

After more than eight years with her, I can confirm she is, indeed, smart—perhaps too smart. The other two attributes? We're still waiting for the second and have resigned ourselves to life without a perfect version of the third. I'll admit, she is pretty gorgeous, though.

As I said, we began the search that led to Romy after I said goodbye to Charlie in 2016. I was ready to open my heart to another animal and hoped a second dog would be my loyal companion, like Bentley was to my husband.

Less than a mile after we drove away with her in the front seat of my husband's truck, Romy declared her allegiance firmly to Tony when she leapt into his lap—not in the sweet, "Hey, Buddy!" way of Bentley. No, her approach was more like a "What's Up? Let me climb on your head!"—as he merged onto a busy highway.

Tony frequently indicates that as the moment he should have turned around, dropped her and her stuff off and driven away without a glance in the rearview. Honestly, he makes a valid point.

Despite Tony's regrets, Romy has been what I call a "Daddy's dog" ever since, in the most adorable and obnoxious way possible.

Don't get me wrong, she likes me, too, and I believe she would defend me from any intruder until her final breath. She loves the kids and can be found exploring the backyard with our son or snuggling in bed with our daughter.

When I work, more often than not, she's curled herself directly behind my chair. For such a large dog, she can form the tightest ball.

Most often, I write all over the house or backyard. Especially when I set up on our covered back porch, Romy trots out with me and sniffs and inspects the yard while I set up. Once she's completed her perimeter check, she saunters back and plops at my feet, her head alert to any potential threat, while I type.

Tony holds her heart, though. When he is away from home, I have caught Romy snuggling with his shoes. When he returns from work or Boy Scouts or training or the backyard, she greets him with the pure, unbridled joy most often showcased in young  children and loyal dogs. She waggles all over to greet him. When he talks, she sits at attention and gazes up at him, never breaking eye contact, completely enraptured with every word. I swear cartoon hearts appear in her eyes and float around her head.

Sometimes, we gather around Tony for family devotions, and Romy either sits or lies closest to him and gazes up at him the entire time he reads or prays. Truth be told, she probably pays better attention to him than the rest of us do.

Her loyalty and devotion and love are commendable and cute, except for when her attentions are overbearing. She is always there, just out of sight, which means she gets stepped on all the time. As smart as she is, I thought she'd learn one day.

When Tony walks through the house or around the yard, she trots directly behind him. Whenever he stops suddenly or takes a backward step to change direction, there she is—literally up his butt.

She sprawls at our feet when we sit on the couch. If we're watching a movie and forget she's there, guess where our feet land when we pause for a bathroom break—usually on her head or tail. She forgives us immediately and, in true loyal dog fashion, acts as though she's apologizing for us stepping on her.

When I sit on the couch, I kick my slippers off and prop my feet on the ottoman. Romy loves nothing more than to use my slippers as her pillow. More often than not, she ends up with one under her shoulder and the other under her head or with her snout tucked inside it.

Even though she'll follow us when we head to bed and will sleep in the kids' bathroom or outside our door, in the moment when I get up and want my slippers to walk through the house, she refuses to budge. She presses down with all her weight to keep me from taking them.

I suppose it could be worse; at least she doesn't eat them.

Romy adds a degree of difficulty to meal prep. I spend most of my cooking time straddling a dog because she always finds the least convenient spot to lie. Typically, I'll start cutting up veggies, and she trots in to "help" by squeezing between my legs and the cabinet ... directly on top of my feet, most often with her bony puppy elbows or knees—or whatever they are called on a dog—poking painfully into the tops of my feet.

I tug my feet from beneath her and either stand awkwardly away from the counter or straddle her or make her move. If she does move, I guarantee she won't go far. Usually she shifts to a spot right behind me, where I will almost trip on her multiple times and then will have to straddle her anyway to conduct the next phase of cooking. I've found it easier to deal with wherever she plops first.

Her annoying habits stem from genuine love, devotion and concern for her people, I believe. Her motivations are never so obvious as when one of us sneezes. Before the first sneeze has fully left us and definitely before any follow-ups erupt, she's in our face, sniffing and nosing, worry oozing from her gold-flecked hazel eyes. We have to convince her we're okay with plenty of verbal assurances and physical pats and scritches.

When we first got Romy, Tony and I had a double-sized bed frame with space beneath where she loved to sleep at night. We also have a hardwood floor. The problem with that combination was Romy isn't still when she sleeps. She dream-runs and shifts and skitters and generally makes a giant racket with her claws.

The positive result of that issue was Tony and his dad made us a king-sized platform bed. No more rabbit-chasing dream scampers under our bed at night. Also, moving from a double to a king may have saved our marriage. We love each other but appreciate our space.

I suppose life with Romy and her overly devoted actions is like any relationship. Every one of us can be annoying at times, especially for the people who have to live with us.

Consider the COVID-19 lockdown when, for many folks, they had no escape from loved ones. Granted, they are loved, but everyone needs a break from time to time. Work. School. A trip to the grocery store. An escape to the camper in the driveway.

Romy reminds me that I can be overbearing to my family members from time to time, as they can be to me. Despite our flawed manners and imperfect love—or perhaps because of them—we can embrace our times together and apart and accept one another's love and loyalty and the genuineness of both. We can love each other even in the moments when we're unlikeable.

We intentionally close the bathroom door before Romy can join us because she's as invasive and sniffy there as she is when we sneeze. I'll end with that visual and an admission that, despite her annoying manners, I truly love Romy and appreciate her care for us ... though I hope she finds less obnoxious ways to show her adoration.

Vignette Nine

Regarding Cats, Colophons & Community

SINCE 2017, I HAVE CHOSEN a word of the year each January. I find this practice more useful and beneficial than the traditional resolution list.

2019 was my year for *perseverance*. As my chosen words typically do, that selection fit its year perfectly.

Perseverance means adhering to a goal—despite all challenges or discouragements or detours—until an intended destination is reached. While the end may not always look exactly as the original vision, the mindset to reach the end and accept however it looks is the same—a dogged determination to carry a task to its completion.

I welcomed 2019 with an acceptance of the knowledge that my goal to publish my first novel may or may not happen that year. The costs involved with starting a small business and publishing books are too large to fund from loose change lurking beneath couch cushions. I decided to plow ahead with my September release date in mind, uncertain if I would achieve my goal.

Completed tasks earned check marks. Opportunities presented themselves. Financing fell into place.

I didn't think I'd ever finish revisions—but I did. I didn't think I'd ever finish edits—but I did. And I certainly didn't think I'd ever finish formatting—but I did.

The process of transforming a document into a proper, printable book manuscript is not for the faint of heart. I had stops and starts. I thought I'd finished, only to learn I'd used the wrong margin sizes. The issues were almost enough to make me throw in the towel. Almost.

Publishing—like most worthwhile endeavors in life—requires a great deal of perseverance and support.

I legally set up Logos & Mythos Press and publicly revealed my company and publishing plans to the world through a new website and continued regular blogging on my author website. My critique partner, Mea Smith, and I launched our weekly podcast for writers and other creatives—QWERTY Writing Life. We also wrote the first book in our author resource series.

As the months ticked past, I revealed the cover and set a September 2019 launch date for my debut novel, *Any Good Thing*. I watched my first book baby soar into the world. Three months later, I celebrated with my co-author as we released our first book, *Finders Keepers: A Practical Approach to Find and Keep Your Writing Critique Partner*. When I look back, I'm amazed at how much was accomplished during that year of perseverance.

When I look ahead to all my big plans for the future, I could easily decide they're all too lofty, hyperventilate and reach for a paper bag. That's not my style, though, and wouldn't honor my 2019 word.

While I choose a new word each year, I carry all of them with me as I press forward, continuing my pursuit of this author dream and putting in the hard work and long hours to realize it. As the years pass, I'm not going to do everything perfectly, but I will persevere.

The title of this vignette is "Regarding Cats, Colophons & Community." Since I haven't mentioned any of those yet, one may rightly wonder if I've finally lost my last marbles. All three of the *C* words directly relate to perseverance, so I will continue with my cat's backstory.

Tolkien is no ordinary feline. He came to me in 2017 before his first birthday. We were the fourth address in his short lifetime and, honestly, his first true home. When I adopted him from a house a few blocks away, I was given the following account.

His life began with a breeder. Likely (to me, anyway) the barely noticeable dab of white on his chest—unacceptable in the show world for Havana Browns—and a medical condition we would eventually uncover led to the breeder's eagerness to be rid of the kitten.

Enter his second owner: a young girl with a soft spot for cats. She saved him from whatever other fate the breeder may have found him. Unfortunately for her, she brought the cat home to an allergic roommate.

That led him to his third address, one street from mine. The family there loved him and loved animals. They had at least two dogs as well as two other cats. To quote Shakespeare in *Hamlet*, Act III, Scene I, "Ay, there's the rub ...."

Their female cat was not pleased with the kitten addition. They kept them separated which led to their original cat being cooped up most of the time. Such an arrangement wasn't sustainable.

They posted on our online neighborhood group, complete with a picture that made me yearn. I went to meet him and fell deeper in love. "KitKat" came home with me. Although his original name matched his color, I decided he needed a new name—one far more fitting for the regal fellow who would become my Little Editor.

When I brought him home, he was understandably skittish and hid in our bathtub for a while. The kids and I visited him and decided to try the list of potential names I'd come up with for him. Amenhotep. Lewis. Maher-shalal-hash-baz. Tolkien. When I spoke my favorite author's name, the shy cat looked up at me. Tolkien, he became.

While Tolkien had not been abused to my knowledge, he hadn't lived as high a quality of life as he could have. As time went on, disconcerting and increasingly frequent yowls accompanied mealtime. He ate less and grew skinnier. He would have days like that and then bounce back for a couple of weeks. After a while, those time frames swapped, so I took him to the vet.

Tolkien was diagnosed with feline stomatitis, a chronic inflammatory condition that typically affects the entire mouth.

His gums were severely inflamed, causing him extreme pain, especially when he ate. He wasn't able to yawn completely because stretching his jaw was too painful. When the sweet baby tried to yawn, he often ended in a howl instead. He didn't really like to be petted, especially around his head—which made perfect sense once I realized the level of pain he was in.

Unfortunately, stomatitis has no clear cause and no definitive cure. Thankfully, Tolkien had an outstanding veterinarian who wouldn't give up until he did all he could.

We started with medicine. We bought special pureed cat food, hoping he could eat it. Finally, after two surgeries that left only four teeth behind, we felt we might have turned a corner.

Every few weeks, Tolkien would have a painful day or two when he couldn't eat. For the most part, though, he was far more active. The week after his second surgery, Tolkien curled up in my lap for the first time. I had fallen in love with him at first sight, but finally I thought he might reciprocate some fondness.

Somewhere around six months post-surgery, Tolkien stopped having painful days. He doesn't yowl anymore when he eats. He leaps all over the house—on top of the refrigerator, up into our highest windowsills, from the piano to the mantle and back, across the living room from table to sofa—without crying. He plays with our dogs, batting at them, chasing them and giving them a run for their kibble.

He sleeps with me some nights. At first, he'd stay at the far bottom of the bed, not even touching me. Slowly he graduated to lying on my feet, then my legs and, finally, every now and then, he tucks in within finger's reach. When I lie on my stomach, he gets to cuddle into his favorite spot—curled at the top of my legs, snuggled against my butt.

Tolkien enjoys being petted now more than he used to and loves having his chin scratched since he's no longer in constant pain. He's also got the widest yawn of any cat I've ever seen.

What's this got to do with writing and the other C words? Perseverance, of course.

We weren't sure what to do when we got Tolkien's diagnosis, which didn't sound positive. The thought of the vet bills was scary, especially for a young family still struggling to emerge from debt in order to work toward launching our own businesses. My community came together, though.

Tony agreed to persevere in our decision to do all we could for the cat. Tolkien was still a kitten, and our vet had a plan.

The doctor persevered in his determination to seek advice from more experienced professionals and from journals and case studies. He stuck to his guns and kept four teeth in to give our sweet baby a better quality of life for the long run than he would with no teeth to support his gums and jaw.

And then there was Tolkien. Even when I could tell he was in excruciating pain, he tried to play. He wanted to chase the string and bat at the mousie. Once he no longer lived under a constant onslaught of pain, he pressed forward to become part of his forever family.

He realized he'd reached his final destination. Four addresses were enough. Ours was for keeps, and the four nutsy humans and the two crazy dogs might be a family for him after all. He even loves family camping trips.

When I've been at my most exhausted or frustrated, Tolkien lies on my papers as I run over them with red ink or curls up in my lap as I type or research or write newsletters for my subscribers and social media posts for my followers.

Tolkien motivates me to persevere.

He inspects my work, shoots me condescending looks when I'm not working up to his standards and sniffs my coffee to make sure it's strong enough to carry me through the next task on the list.

When I was almost ready to throw in the towel on formatting my book myself, he sat over me as I worked. He snuffed at the books

I pored over, ruler in hand, as I tried to discern the right margin settings. He oversaw my research into the font I wanted to use in my book—which became a driving force behind persevering in formatting my way.

He lay nearby when I wrote the colophon—the description of and history behind the fonts used in a book—that I had been so excited to include for me and the one other person who actually reads them.

Whatever comes in the future, we will persevere and charge headlong into each challenge. Part of my publishing perseverance comes in the form of a partnership with the most amazing formatter a resourceful indie publisher could have ever found. Rachael Ritchey helped me clean up the first mess I made and saves me from ever enduring such torture again, plus she's been one of the most encouraging friends on this journey and in my writing community.

My perseverance was deeply and personally challenged in 2021 when I made a decision that went against everything my gut was telling me. When a particular vaccine rolled out, everyone had an opinion. I had mine.

I took many details into consideration and decided to make a choice I thought I should, despite my gut's protests. I chose the two-shot approach.

During those three in-between weeks, I dealt with random, sharp joint pains all over my body. I also didn't feel right. When the time came to get the second jab, I debated—go or not?

Some of the reasons I made the initial decision had faded away. The state of the future was changing to less of a *1984*-come-true than it had appeared when I sealed my fate. At the same time, I decided whatever damage the vaccine was doing in my body was probably already done; may as well finish what I started.

I drove across town for my appointment. They were running behind. I stood in line for what felt like forever and changed my mind at least a dozen times. Even as I walked behind the partition, I almost turned around and left.

Honestly, I wish I would have.

On the way home, I had to keep moving my hands on the steering wheel. They kept falling asleep. They were painful. Something wasn't right.

Over the next three months, I faced flare after flare, each one worse than the previous.

The joint pain settled in my hands and wrists at first, which made holding a pen or typing on a keyboard impossible. I couldn't chop vegetables, stir a pot of beans or open a can of soup. At times, the inflammation got so bad, my entire forearms felt as hard as tree trunks.

Many times, I sat on our sofa, my hands resting beside me, in so much pain I wasn't sure how I was going to continue. I nearly despaired when I thought the rest of my life would be spent in such agony.

The pain spread to other joints as well, and I fell victim to a fatigue far more debilitating than any I'd experienced before—including right after having both of my children.

As I type this, I am on a better side of life with rheumatoid arthritis. I have added an incredible doctor to my community. She supports my choice to proceed with all natural ways to counter the disease triggered by a vaccine. Strict diet and exercise and a regimen of supplements have eased much of my pain.

While I am not healed, I am able to type again, within reason. I know what I can and cannot do. I recognize triggers and know, without a doubt, that an anti-inflammatory diet and regular exercise keep much of the inflammation at bay.

In the early days, I felt crushed beneath the reality of what I faced. I'll never forget the day I read the details of what my symptoms meant, learned I faced my future with an autoimmune disease and read two words that stopped me in my tracks, terrified me and echoed themselves with each beat of my heart.

No cure. No cure. No cure.

Those words became an unwelcome mantra as I worked through all an unexpected physical challenge could mean for me and considered all the activities I may never do again ... at age 38.

To get to a brighter side of the realities of my situation, I grieved and processed and accepted. I have praised God and thanked Him for inexplicable peace and comfort in the face of life-changing uncertainty and for how He will carry me through—whatever the outcomes and however they may change from year to year or even day to day.

Friends grieved and prayed with me. When I finally shared my challenges publicly with followers of my author journey, I felt arms from around the world virtually embracing me through words of encouragement, commitments to prayer and even gifts to aid me should dictation become my only option to continue writing.

On my good days, I give my all to my work. On my bad days, I listen and rest. Through all the days, I will persevere. Tolkien showed me how.

As I push ahead in the crazy pursuits of an indie author, I do so alongside my cat and colophons and the supportive community God has given me to share the unpredictable journey of life.

Portions of this vignette were previously shared on Joy's Logos & Mythos blog. To subscribe to her newsletter with weekly updates on her author adventures, links to posts like this one and words of wisdom from her Furry Friends, visit

bit.ly/JoyERancatoreNewsletter

Vignette Ten

When You Know, You Know

A FEW TIMES IN MY LIFE, I've had moments of prophetic clarity where I think something may happen and envision it occurring. As I play out the possibility in my imagination, the scene becomes more likely and real and then ... I know. It will happen.

Such a scenario led to us adding a furry friend to our family in 2024.

One of the events I look forward to every year is St. Tammany Parish Library's Summer Reading Kickoff. The evening is always a blast, and I love seeing all my library friends in their element. They throw quite the party!

For the 2024 Kickoff, they added a new attraction: our local animal shelter.

Books + Dogs + Library Fun = Perfection

After chatting with some friends and picking up our registration prizes, we headed outside to pet some pups.

Within a few minutes, my kids told me one of the dogs had taken to my son. That's when I met Georgie, a several-month-old German Shepherd mix with puppy breath, giant ears and a tongue so floppy, it hung over the side of his smiling snout.

He was excited to meet me and eagerly greeted me with hugs and many sloppy kisses.

I tried to get a picture of him to post on my social media and encourage local folks to register for summer reading and adopt a dog. In true puppy fashion, he was far too wiggly for me to get a clear shot, so I had my son take a picture of him with me. The pup instantly stilled to rest his head against my chest, gazed up at me with soulful brown eyes and then proceeded to kiss me on the mouth. I decided the furry charmer may be special.

We tore ourselves away from the tail-waggers and headed inside for more literary fun. With puppy breath fresh in my memory, my mind lingered on the lovable pup nearby. When we returned to their location, Georgie was back in the trailer. Each time my son approached his window, the dog would sit forward and paw at the glass.

Definitely special.

My husband, Tony, had recently joined the St. Tammany Parish Sheriff's Department Reserve Division and was at his Police Officer Standards and Training (P.O.S.T.) class that night. He knew about the animal adoption and had informed us that under no circumstances were we to come home with a pet. He knows us pretty well.

As we laughed and talked with friends and the volunteers and petted more dogs, phrases like "better to beg forgiveness than ask permission" and questions like "But, how mad would he be, *really?*" may have flown around.

Spending time with Georgie and observing his interactions with other people and dogs and my kids showed me he would be perfect for us. I also knew how much my husband would love him.

A couple months earlier, Tony had announced he wanted us to get a German Shepherd. Here, before me, was a perfect option who needed a home.

I had a moment where I strongly considered taking him home then and there, but, after nearly eighteen years of marriage, I knew my husband pretty thoroughly. He would have been mad if we brought the dog home after he specifically told us not to, but he would love the little guy. Had Tony been there, I was certain, we would be filling out paperwork.

With my wifely knowledge in mind, I said nothing of hope to the kids and decided we would be driving across the parish the next night for the second Kickoff event to bring Georgie home.

For the rest of the night, visions of the pup joining our family and meeting Tony and Romy and Tolkien danced in my head. He would be the perfect addition.

We got home. Tony got home. We told him about the dog. He said, "Absolutely not." I said, "He's a German Shepherd mix." I watched his face shift and, again, I knew.

Tony sat next to me on the couch and asked something about the dog. I answered and then added, "I know you, honey, which is why 1. He's not here with us and 2. If you had been with us, he would be."

My husband gave me an unconvinced look. I gave him a confirming nod and serious stare and said, "Really."

I left the topic alone for most of the night and then mentioned how I was thinking about the homeless pup. "Y'all really want that dog?" My look was my affirmation.

Our goodnight was "We'll talk about it over coffee in the morning."

The coffee was mostly gone before I finally mentioned the dog.

"You know, I need to make final plans for this evening."

"The dog?"

I could tell he had hoped I'd forgotten.

"Y'all really want that dog." This time, a statement. "Oh, what the heck!"

"I'm gonna let y'all get that stupid dog" was how our sixteen-year-old daughter was roused from bed that early summer day.

As the day progressed and the kids came to the realization that their father wasn't joking and we were, indeed, going to adopt a dog that night, the name discussion ensued. Only our daughter loved the name Georgie. I thought it was cute and fit his puppy personality, but he had a great deal of growing ahead of him. He needed a bigger name.

We focused on the German heritage, and fairly quickly, my husband said, "Kaiser." Our daughter said, "Yeah!" Our son said, "I like that!" I was less convinced.

That name continued to rise above other suggestions, and I softened toward the idea of him being an emperor.

The day went surprisingly fast, and the time came for my husband to go to work and for the kids and I to hop in the van for the ride to Madisonville. Traffic was light, and the miles flashed past.

A few concerns lingered in my mind:

1. Someone else may have already adopted him or someone could beat us to adopt him that evening.
2. We could get him, and he and Romy could be a total sibling fail.
3. He could eat my cat.

We pulled up to the library more than twenty minutes before the event would start. My daughter spotted the St. Tammany Parish Department of Animal Services trailer—all set up with dogs milling around.

My heart beat rapidly against my seat belt, and I attempted to suppress the worry that, despite our best efforts, we would be too late. We may be just in time to watch Georgie ride away in another vehicle—which, yes, would still have been wonderful because the point was for him to find a home. Of course, my active prophetic imagination had already decided ours was his home.

I'd visualized him snoozing in our house during the kids' school, zipping around the yard with Romy and chilling with the family in our camper. I was committed and attached and had begun to yearn. I admitted to myself—no one else—that I would be more crushed than the kids should we have arrived too late.

We found a parking spot and power walked toward the trailer. I saw my friend Jillian, the adult programming coordinator for our library. She stood by the trailer and smiled at us.

"Is he still here?" No response had my heart skipping beats until I was close enough to hear her.

"They've got him on that side tonight."

We turned the corner, and I couldn't look fast enough. As I spotted the pup, one of the amazing caretakers with the shelter rounded the other side of the trailer. His face lit up. "You lookin' for Georgie?"

I nodded, and I think he mentioned adoption. I nodded again, and he said, "No way! Are you serious?"

"I'm serious!"

He headed straight inside the trailer to kennel the dog he was leading and retrieve the one we'd come for.

What was probably only a few seconds later, Georgie bounded down the steps ahead of the kindhearted, burly man who was still grinning. He trotted over and may have excitement peed a time or two—the pup, not the man.

From then on, everything happened in a flurry of activity. Our sweet Bentley's camo collar was way too big for the little guy, but we snapped the Lab's old leash onto a tiny maroon one they clicked around the pup's neck. The kids held him while I completed paperwork.

"Will you want to rename him?"

"Probably."

"Do you have a name picked out?"

A little hesitantly, I said, "Well, we were leaning toward Kaiser, but we aren't certain."

The second half of my sentence was drowned out by two or three volunteers' enthusiastic reactions.

"I'm a history buff, so I appreciate it."

"Yeah? That was my husband's major; the name was his idea!"

"We'll put down Kaiser for now."

I finished the requested details. They checked to make sure everything was completed. We took our first family photo. I put his medical records in my bag.

"Don't forget his food!"

And then, we were off. The pup wasn't sure about getting in the van at first. He was probably sifting through advice like "Don't get into vans with strangers." His hesitation made me wonder if he'd been dumped from someone's car. We'd have to earn his trust.

Honestly, I couldn't quite believe we were heading home with a new dog, but my first concern was abated: we weren't too late. I drove like a first-time mama—likely to the chagrin of the vehicles behind me. For his part, the pup immediately lay down and remained still and quiet all the way to the closest pet store, less than ten minutes away.

"Make sure you grab his leash. Take him in the grass."

"Do you think he wants water?"

"Let's see."

Out came the collapsible bowl and the water bottle we'd packed for our new family member.

"Just a little bit."

"Here you go. Right here."

He lapped once, twice. We dumped the rest, stored the bottle and bowl and entered the store.

Earlier that day, we had decided we would let him pick a toy—like we had done with Romy when we got her. We'd get one for her, too, and maybe some treats. We would have gotten food, but they sent us home with a bag. Romy's leash had broken, so my daughter shopped for a replacement.

In the excitement of the new baby who was so adorable, I immediately forgot the limited list and wanted to buy him an entire collection of ourdoorsy gear and toys and the handsome olive green harness that made me think of hiking and camping.

Some internal intelligence resurfaced as I was calculating his size and realized such a nice harness would be quite pricey. Oh, and he was a tiny puppy who would be getting much, much bigger.

We chose two nylon bones ("chew-chews" to Romy) and a great big rope, big enough for two dogs to share. My daughter picked a neon pink leash for Romy.

A lady greeted us. "May I pet him?"

"Sure!"

"What's his name?"

"Kaiser. We just adopted him."

"Awww ... he's so sweet! You smell my dog, don't you?"

Animals bring humans together through the connection animal lovers share. When I go to the grocery, I avoid people at all costs. In a pet store, the presence of animals encourages me to talk with anyone who expresses interest in my dog or stands on the other side of a leash.

After a few minutes of pets and chats, away we went.

"Oh! Treats!"

I decided against the gourmet ones when I realized they might upset Kaiser's tummy. I tucked the cute shapes away for future days, though. We'd bring the dogs back together sometime and get them a bag full. Maybe on his "gotcha" day.

For then, we chose a box of simpler treats. We put everything on the counter. The total shocked me back to reality, and I thanked the good Lord for reminding me of the necessities and keeping me from the table full of adorable puppy gear—which I still wanted to clear into a cart.

Back to the van. That time, my daughter picked up the dog and put him in. I wondered again about his brief past and what car-related trauma he may have experienced.

I cautiously weaved our way out of the shopping center parking lot, toward the interstate, after texting my husband we were on our way with Kaiser.

Tony had to close at his work, and I didn't want him to wait until midnight to meet our little guy. I pulled alongside the restaurant where my husband is a manager and reached for my phone. *Just parked.*

My excitement was too much for me to sit in the van and wait. I got out and opened the sliding door. Kaiser's impish grin greeted me, and I snapped a picture before taking his leash from my son. The dog hopped right down and happily sniffed around while we waited.

Thankfully, the restaurant wasn't busy, and Tony soon rounded the corner. As soon as I saw his eyes when they fell on the puppy, I knew I had been 100% right. He was already in love. Kaiser immediately pulled me to Tony and did another excited tinkle.

Tony knelt and rubbed the pup's cheeks and giant ears. Kaiser didn't hold his licker and showed his instant fondness for the guy who must be part of his new life. Our new addition was acclimating as I had envisioned.

A few minutes later, we headed home for the next test in the process, discussing our strategy on the way. After a few disagreements, I insisted I stay with Kaiser. My daughter would unlock the door and wait with Romy while my son would pass through our house to open the gate for Kaiser and me. Once the pup had a chance to jog around the backyard and get some sniffs in, we would release Romy.

I may have had a few panic moments as I worried if I were handling their introduction properly. So much rode on the next few moments.

Once, when Bentley had been young, we came close to adopting a second dog, a gorgeous Siberian Husky. We took Bentley to the adoption place so they could meet. A few sniffs in, the Husky whirled on Bentley and issued a growl that communicated loud and clear he would not be joining our family.

Anxiety set aside, I decided we'd waited long enough. My son went to tell his sister we were ready. Romy bolted as soon as he cracked the door.

The pups raced together, tails and heads up, ears perked, noses twitching. Nose touches and sniffing commenced. Seconds later, they were off—running around like they'd known each other forever.

Honestly, my glass-half-empty nature had me expecting a switch to flip as the night went on, but it never did. The new pair had one intense moment where Kaiser had firmly claimed the dog bed, and Romy attempted to reclaim ownership.

Growling rumbled and barking escalated. Kaiser's voice rose in a whiny howl-bark that went on for some time. Romy stopped growling and barking and listened intently. I got the distinct impression he was telling her his story.

"I just got outta the slammer, sis. You know what they had there? Bars. And concrete floors and a chain-link fence. Several dogs in one kennel. I had to stand my ground against the bully roommate who killed the other dog with us. You know what we didn't have? A soft bed or ropes or chew-chews. I sure would love to sleep on a bed, sis."

Their discussion ceased. Romy gave him a final sniff. There was licking, and then she lay down nearby while Kaiser gnawed on one of the three chew-chews he'd pawed to himself on the comfort of Romy's bed.

They'd reached an understanding. Concern #2 had been dispelled. The remaining challenge was the dynamic between Kaiser and Tolkien.

Tolkien was instantly disgruntled at the chaotic entrance of a strange new dog—worse, a rambunctious puppy—into his domain. At the beginning, though, they took some tentative, peaceful sniffs and nose touches. I thought we may have another smooth transition. And then, Tolkien ran.

The kind guy from the shelter had warned me about that. He said the biggest issue when introducing cats and dogs is always the cat running and the dog instinctively chasing. Unfortunately we don't have a house we can cordon off into sections to keep them separated while they got used to the idea of one another.

Sure enough, the two imps launched an ongoing Tom-and-Jerry chase around our tiny, cluttered house at all hours of the day and night.

We learned fairly quickly that Kaiser did far better at night with all the lights off. We also learned to not leave items lying about the tables, desk or counters that we wouldn't want Kaiser to chew up. As the cat leapt from surface to surface, racing ahead of the dog, Tolkien inevitably knocked things to the floor. Anything on the floor became fair game for Kaiser's teeth.

The mischievous pup chewed up mail, a bath mat and even a math test booklet. The dog literally ate my kid's homework.

When I did laundry and the hall was lined with sorted piles, he would help himself to someone's sock or underwear and carry the item back to his bed with him—triumphant with his trophy. He'd add it to his hoard of two ropes and three chew-chews that he stashed away from Romy.

We discovered Kaiser has an interesting drinking habit. He will drain a bowl in a couple minutes of noisy and sloppy slurping ... and then ask for more. Apparently, that tendency is common for his breed. Our vet gave us the information when we introduced them. Dr. Firmin also told us Kaiser is a Belgian Malinois cross who was a couple months younger than we originally thought.

Tony may not have gotten the German Shepherd he wanted, but I think he's pleased with the sweet fellow who quickly took over our house and stole our hearts.

As Kaiser's somewhat grown into his ears and paws, he has learned to better control his bladder, though he still drinks like a fish, and we have learned to empty the bowl at bedtime.

Back to Kaiser and Tolkien: their game of chase grew more intense, with Kaiser pounding his front paws up on the table or my desk. Tolkien would hiss and scratch. Kaiser mimicked the pawing right back. Several times Kaiser caught up to Tolkien during the chase. The dog clearly wanted to play, not maul.

Finally, the chasing de-escalated, and the occasional nose touch returned. By the time we'd had Kaiser a month and I made a lengthy post and photo dump on the shelter's alumni page, the animals had reached a point where I felt confident in writing that they were adapting and in speculating in the comments that they may improve to a point where I could be posting Kaiser/Tolkien snuggle pictures one day.

Positive growth continued. Tolkien spent more and more time on the floor instead of leaping from tall surface to taller surface. Their chasing and playtime became a mutual sport. When Tolkien took the opportunity to swat Kaiser's butt as he passed by, I knew we were progressing to the friend zone.

Just over two weeks after my hopeful post on social media, I got to add a new photo in the comments. Around midnight the night before, Tony let the dogs outside. As they settled back in for the night, he realized Kaiser wasn't alone on his bed.

Butt-to-butt, there they were—Tolkien and Kaiser. Since then, they have been caught a few times awfully close to snuggling. They still fight over my lap and have only successfully shared it once or twice ... for a limited time.

With all three major concerns about adding a new fur baby eased, we have reacclimated to life with a canine duo and furry trio. At this point, I can't remember life without Kaiser. He fit seamlessly with our family, and our adoption of him reminded me that when you know, you know.

Vignette Eleven

Potty Training & Pets or How Much of My Life Have I Spent in the Bathroom?

DURING THE DRAFTING OF THIS book, I perused photos of the pets we've had through the years and found a surprising number taken in our wee bathroom. The discovery made me wonder, exactly how much of my life *have* I spent in the bathroom?

Before I meander down the rabbit hole of random research to answer such a question, I should admit our pets frequently join us in the bathroom.

Bentley and Charlie were kind companions throughout both kids' potty-training years. Romy is happy to accompany me; more accurately, she tolerates my entrance into her naptime sanctuary.

Even Kaiser and Tolkien have been known to join in on a potty party. Though, Kaiser—still in his puppy stage—usually makes his presence weird.

Tolkien, an unwilling participant, frequents the high, wide windowsill in our bathroom for bird-watching and doesn't like to have to get down until he's ready. Which, let's be honest, could be in the middle of *ahem*; and, when I forget to look for him prior to *ahem*, it can be quite startling to have a cat nearly jump on my head. Such a surprise can literally scare the *ahem* right out of me!

Back to my original question: How much of my life *have* I spent in the bathroom?

Anyone who's had kids—or knows someone who's had kids—knows potty training is not for the faint of heart and requires copious time spent cooped up in a bathroom or sitting alongside a kid's toilet in the middle of the family room while an oddly proportioned mouse on the TV screen creepily urges kids to enter his house.

Those reminiscences led me on a search of "How many hours does an average person spend in the bathroom in their lifetime?" My query provided the drastically wide-ranging answers of 92 days (thank you, portlandloo.com) to 813.3 days (thank you, posh.co.uk).

I believe moms spend more time when we factor in the bathroom assistance we must provide. Being the nerdy person I am, I decided to factor the added bathroom business into the mix.

Figure a woman has two kids, and she spends a solid two years in the potty-training stage with each. Using the higher lifetime guesstimate, since I have to think those early days require much more time, and an average lifespan of 79 years, times two, times two—and carry the one—we're looking at an additional 41.1797468354 days. Call it 42 days?

Note to mathematicians: When dealing with bathroom issues and children, always round up. Always.

Note to fact-checkers: I didn't think to search "average age of women in the U.S." until after I'd made all the calculations, and I wasn't about to head back to the beginning to add 0.1 or subtract 2.67 or add 1.2 (depending on which source we believe). I'll assume higher and let my rounding skills handle any discrepancies.

Now, when the grandparents and/or parents reach the ripe age of revenge where they require toileting assistance, who gets the less-than-pleasant task? *Las mujeres.*

"But Honey, it's my mom. That wouldn't be appropriate."

"Sweetie, it's my dad. That would be weird."

sigh

Let's factor in at least two additional helpless bathroom-goers for our average woman's numbers. From the experience of folks close to me, caregiving time ranges from three months to three years. Call it 2 years?

Using the same averages from our toddler word problem—because we know old folks also require the higher end of the spectrum for such activities—times two, times two—and carry the three—we're looking at an additional 41.1797468354 days. Call it 45 days ... adding a few for advanced age, of course?

Now, I'm ready to grab my handy-dandy calculator and add together the total damage.

By the way, I'm also rounding up because anyone who's ever had a period or given birth understands the added time-draining complications that come into play for a woman's bathroom needs. Heck! I'm throwing in an extra week to the final for those reasons.

We're up to 907.3 days spent in the john, the loo, the water closet.

Call it 1,000 days? This round-up is for the early days of diapers and for the occasional times the bathroom doubles as a hiding place, which—I've noticed—isn't as peaceful for women as for men.

"Where's Dad?" asks Johnny.

"In the bathroom," Mom replies.

"Okay." Johnny accepts the fact and wanders away, forgetting he ever needed his father.

Contrast that with the opposite scenario:

"Mom! Mom! Mom!" Johnny's calls grow louder as he approaches the closed bathroom door. "Mom! Billy hit me! I'm hungry! I can't find my left shoe! My zipper's stuck, and you're the only person who can help, but it has to be right now ... at this exact moment. Ready or not, I'm coming in!"

And no, I'm not anti-men. I actually think women should do a better job of teaching them how to successfully divert potential bathroom interrupters from disturbing our peace. After all, we apparently have the correct words, tone and inflection perfected when dad's whereabouts are requested. We have a duty to share our remarkable skills.

Back to my math: how do our total days spent in a bathroom translate to a percentage of our lives?

Well, given the average lifespan of 79 years ... factor in 19.75 leap years ... that's 28,854.75 days of life on this third rock from the sun, which means 3.14436964451% of our lives are spent in the bathroom.

That sounds awfully close to a famous number in math circles, which makes me think of pi and leads me to the conclusion that all women everywhere deserve a pie ... of their choice ... baked by someone who is not them (but who can actually bake, because we've all had the disappointing frozen numbers and bakery that-looked-better-than-it-was samples and bless-her-heart-she-thought-she-could-bakes).

I'll take my strawberry pie made with fresh Ponchatoula strawberries, topped with homemade whipped cream. Thank you very much.

Lest anyone think I'm cynical over the bathroom situation, I should add good things can happen during the "pi" percentage of our lives.

Potty training allowed me quality one-on-one time with each kid. Often, they would say the funniest things or hit me with the deepest questions while sitting there, waiting for something to happen.

I'll never forget the time the devil was likened to an octopus by one kid or the time another declared they were ready to drive—about thirty minutes into another unsuccessful hour-long spell of cramped quarters for me and dangling legs for them. Ah! Bathroom clarity!

Of course, I'd also be remiss if I didn't mention how the best ideas most often arise while on the porcelain throne. To be honest, I'm pretty sure the idea for this vignette originated there.

If anyone has ever texted or emailed or messaged me and received a coherent, sensible, well-thought-out answer, it likely stems from a piece of my pi time.

Before I'm judged for that fact, I must ask: who else has tried to write a reply while her husband's frantically searching for the wallet/keys/ring/phone he misplaced (again), while the kids are fighting over the TV and the dog has just found a recently hand-edited book and mistaken my hard work for his chew toy?

That scenario is far from far-fetched, so extend some grace when:

1. I don't respond;
2. I respond five days later; or
3. I respond with something indecipherable.

Oh, and math-minded sorts, mind your business if you find errors in my calculations and chalk them up to the 907.3 days of gaseous exposure I'm in the midst of enduring. Keep in mind I didn't factor in the time spent watching animals poop or cleaning up after them.

That's a whole other set of word problems, and nature calls.

Vignette Twelve

Animals Adored; People Permitted

IF WE MEET AND YOU have a dog or cat or horse or pig or any other kind of animal, your pet will get my undivided attention. You'll be there, too, though you shouldn't expect much of my enthrallment to shift your way.

It's not that I'm trying to be rude; you're a fine person. I'm sure you have many delightful things to say, and you have stories coming out of your stories; however, your companion is adorable and in need of scritches and I very much want to make a good impression so the next time we meet, I'll be greeted enthusiastically. My personal goal is to be the favorite aunt to each animal I encounter.

Also—please don't be offended—I'm far more likely to remember your pet's name than yours if we're meeting for the first time. I suppose it's easier for me to match names to pointy ears and whiskered faces.

I actively look for animals everywhere I go. When my love of books and writing crosses paths with animals—well, that may be a small taste of paradise for me.

In December 2020, my critique partner and I convened at a delightful rental above a barn in Picayune, Miss., for a writing retreat. The dwelling and encircling scenery provided the perfect spot for me to be inspired. We were surrounded by horses, dogs, cats, chickens and cows.

One evening, Mea alerted me to a thick fog creeping across the pasture toward the barn. We locked eyes and telepathically communicated our mutual creatives-are-eccentric need to run, unhindered, into the mist.

I'm not sure how long we spent, leaning against the fence, taking pictures and soaking in the mystical brume snaking tendrils around us as the sun sank slowly, slowly, suddenly. At some point, we broke from the atmosphere's spell for our return stroll across the pasture.

Out of the mist, a thunder rumbled. Behind the ethereal shroud emerged a herd of horses, galloping toward us—head-on.

I can't speak for Mea, but I felt no fear, only exhilaration. In that moment, we were simply companions—all creatures of the fog. The maned royals rushed at us, stopping only when they were within hands' reach. They bowed heads to our offered pets and welcomed us into their shadowy realm.

Never have I felt so in touch with nature—so in communion with God's creation. I can't forget the experience and know I'm unlikely to relive such an encounter.

That weekend, I molded *One Good Thing* into a recognizable form and got to know the characters more intimately. Rachael's voice crept toward becoming real, nearly audible, less foggy.

I also felt we may finally be breaking free from the smog of the pandemic's lockdowns and the weight of their shackles. Finally, we could breathe deeply and move forward with plans and hope and life.

Perhaps that was a pivotal weekend in more ways for me because my experience reminded me of an important truth. Nature, sunrises and sunsets: they were created for us. In our busyness and our failure to soak those gifts in, though, we lose something crucial, a key to life ... to truly *living*.

I may need more weekends like that one to slow down, observe, commune with nature. Of course, animals are part of nature, so the solution may exist closer to home, curled up with my dogs and cat on their nearby beds.

That writing weekend, a cat befriended me after greeting us on a return from the pastures. She rubbed her fluffy Russian Blue whiskered cheek against my leg, my hand, my lowered cheek. She lay beside my computer on the picnic table as I wrote.

I'm curious what about the act of writing—of creating tales—lures animals to the creative.

Nearly every time I write at my desk, Tolkien perches nearby—on the desk by my hands, on the top of my old desk chair behind and above my head or curled on a dining chair nearby. Both dogs—Bentley and Romy, now Romy and Kaiser—lay close to my feet. The preferred spot seems to be curled impossibly tightly in the cat's bed, directly behind my chair—where their splayed ears and tails rest, in constant danger of my seat's wheels rolling into my blind spot.

When I sit on the back porch to write on my laptop, the dogs flank me—sprawled on the cool concrete. When I work in bed, Tolkien lies on or against my legs, eager to oversee my progress—or chastise my lack thereof.

Perhaps the flutter of the muse or the rush of awakened creativity draws the animals. Maybe creatures simply know how to appreciate God's great and precious gifts of nature and creativity better than humans. Isn't that ironic since they were fashioned and crafted for our enjoyment—joys we often overlook in our endless pursuit of busyness?

Sorry ... I paused to soak in the animals around me and give thanks for their companionship and the lessons they teach me.

If I zone out when we meet, please remember I'm busy communing with your furry friend. Give me a minute and then gently remind me I can benefit from some human companionship as well.

Oh, and please repeat your name.

joyerancatore.com/one-good-thing/

Vignette Thirteen

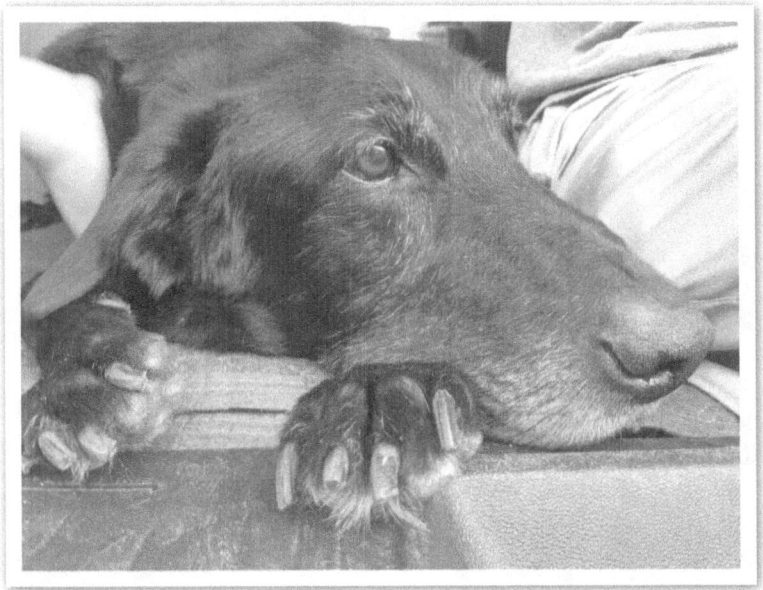

How to Say Goodbye

THE DOWNSIDE TO OWNING PETS is, unless we choose a tortoise or a parrot, we're going to be saying goodbye to a companion or ten during our lifetime. The upside is, I believe they teach us how to say it right.

I've had to say goodbye to more than a couple animals already. I've had tragic goodbyes, goodbyes without closure and goodbyes at the end of a lifetime. None of them were easy; all left a mark.

My first dog's end was the most tragic with a jarring life lesson. I learned firsthand that a human being could care so little for an animal's life—or the feelings of her young owner—that they would enter our backyard in the dead of night to poison the adult dogs and take six full-blooded Collie pups. All for money.

People's greed and disregard for life make me sick. Ask anyone who works in an animal shelter or rescue if they agree. They will, and they'll have far too many similar—and worse—stories to share.

I thought after such a hard first goodbye, future farewells would be easier ... not so much. Of course, I suppose goodbyes aren't meant to be easy. They are part of life, though. Our grief reveals to us how deeply we love.

My dear friend Mea Smith paints a lyrical image of this reality in "Badge of Honor," from her poetry book *Grief Like a River*.

> *Grief is not something to "get over."*
> *It's not something to shed,*
> *a season to weather,*
> *baby clothes to pack away.*
>
> ...
>
> *If you could leave grief behind you,*
> *if it didn't change the texture of your heart,*
> *I don't think you're doing it right*
> *or you didn't love those you lost with all you have.*

Saying goodbye to my dog Gembeaux was the worst in a different way. One year out of college, I was preparing to sell my first home, get married and move several states away, all while working my full-time job as a night reporter and my side job mucking stalls at a boarding stable early each morning.

That time of my life was simultaneously one of the most joyous and most stressful I had ever experienced.

I was still figuring out how to be an adult on my own and faced relearning how to do so as part of a team. I knew money would be tight, and I was stressing about not having a new job lined up yet. On top of that, I had to give up my Gembeaux.

He was a sweet, precious dog, and I loved him so much. Unfortunately, somewhere along

the way, he had developed a dangerous side. He even bit me, an episode in my life I had almost completely blocked from memory.

Our brains are fascinating creations—they preserve beautiful memories for us, but they also block traumatic events. To recount what happened, I consulted my sister, Jane. Her brain had buried the details as well, so what I will relay here is the best I could conjure up from my gray matter's recesses.

While my cat Charlie and I had evacuated together to my brother and sister-in-law's house in Pensacola, Gembeaux had to stay in Mobile with Jane and her family. They didn't have a dog at the time, but they had an enclosed yard for him to occupy during the hurricane and the subsequent weeks before I could repair his fence at my house in Gautier, Miss.

At some point between the evacuation, my initial stay with my brother and then my back-and-forth between Mobile and Gautier while the newspaper office and my backyard underwent repairs, I was visiting Gembeaux in his temporary home.

I couldn't say if I was feeding him, playing with him or giving him a treat, but I remember exactly three details from the incident:

1. I remember bending down toward him—perhaps over the fence.
2. The next scene in my mind's replay is my sister holding my hand in an emergency room while I waited for stitches to my face.
3. The last memory is my terror that Gembeaux was going to be put down.

Apparently, if a dog attacks anyone for any reason, doctors are required to report them to animal control. The doctor in the ER had explained the law to me, and I was horrified at the thought of having to say goodbye to my little ball of fluff dog.

How we escaped legalities, I'm not sure. My guess would be sympathy for my post-Katrina nomadic lifestyle and the waterworks of an emotional young woman combined to convince the doctor to overlook the cause for my visit.

I don't know exactly when Gembeaux became mean—and, to be honest, he wasn't all the time. He simply had moments when he would snap. I believe a human with a violent temper was to blame.

While I was in college, I rarely returned home. I had reasons for that and don't regret my decision ... except for Gembeaux. I lost those years with him and wasn't able to watch over him or keep him safe. Those were the years when his temperament changed, and he was never the same.

Fast-forward to the goodbye: Tony was in graduate school in North Carolina, and we would be living in campus housing. Dogs weren't allowed. I asked everyone I knew if they or someone they knew would adopt Gembeaux. Of course, I had to explain he had some aggressive tendencies.

One of my couple friends seemed interested, but when they met him, he did not show his softer side. That possibility closed.

I went to the shelter where the woman explained their policy if he showed aggression. I was young and stressed and couldn't see any other option.

When I think back to that time, I wonder if I could have done more. Today, we have online groups for people looking for pets and easier access to shelters better equipped to rehab and retrain an unpredictable pet. Did we have those resources then, but I didn't look hard enough?

As I tell my husband, nothing can be gained by looking backward and asking, "What if?" That vain pursuit only makes us miserable and causes us to miss the right now.

Giving up Gembeaux and knowing—barring a miracle—he would be put down nearly broke me. I'll never forget the overwhelming feeling of guilt that sank heavy in my gut as I walked into that shelter with him. I thought for sure I was going to be sick.

I walked him into the kennel area and felt a sharp pain in my chest that I thought was my heart breaking as I led him into his spot. I knelt on the concrete beside him and whispered my apologies. I wanted to hug him to me and bury my soaked face in his fur like I had when he was a puppy, but I didn't trust him.

When I reached my car, all the guilt, worry, overwhelm and uncertainty in my heart overflowed through my tears. I will always regret how I left Gembeaux.

In my memory, Gembeaux will always be the bouncy ball of fluff that showed up at our home one day out of the blue—the inspiration for a series of children's books I hope to complete one day. I can't wait to see an artist's rendition of him and his nemesis, Mr. Mole.

Gembeaux was a special dog. While I'm thankful for my brain shielding me from hard memories—including vague images of red-faced yelling and unnecessary kicks—I'm equally thankful my mind has allowed me to reclaim what I needed to no longer forget the big picture or understand part of the why.

Another loss without closure occurred years earlier with Sprit. We had moved from Mooresville, N.C., to Grenada, Miss.—our second move with him.

I'll always remember that change of address because we unloaded boxes at our new house on my eleventh birthday. A precious couple in our church—who remain a kind and encouraging force in my life to this day—brought me a cake, and my heart has always been warmed at the memory of that sweet gesture.

Sprit had a too-small pen, and I took him out as often as I could. Instead of a proper halter and leash, though, we had a choker collar. He and I both hated it. One afternoon, he slipped out of the choker and raced away.

We lived on top of a steep hill overlooking the busiest road in Grenada. I remember at least four lanes, plus the turn lane.

Sprit galloped from the backyard to the front yard, down the slope, toward that road. I screamed after him as I tried to reach him—my two legs no match for his four. He barreled into the road, and I watched a car slam into him. He got up, though, and continued to run across the rest of the lanes and beyond as I sank to my knees and cried.

We never found him.

Not long after, my father swore he heard Sprit's bark in a neighborhood near our church. One afternoon, we rode around the area with the windows rolled down, listening. I heard a bark I was certain was his, but we could never determine which of the cookie cutter houses hid him.

While Sprit and Gembeaux's goodbyes felt unfinished and heavy; goodbyes to Charlie and Bentley held closure but were equally heavy. My heart broke yet again.

Is there a limit to the number of breaks a heart can endure?

A few months before we had to say goodbye to Charlie, he slipped out the door. He may have done that a time or two over the years, but he never went far and I was always able to scoop him up and bring him back inside. That time, though, he was gone—vanished. I was heartbroken.

Why would he run off?

He was declawed (an uninformed pet owner mistake I made) and had never lived outside. I was terrified of what might happen to him. I envisioned all sorts of horrible fates: cars, feral cats, vicious cat-hating neighbors, bobcats or dogs. He was only gone two days, but it felt like forever. I bawled frequently while he was missing.

I went outside once more to search. In my mind, I figured that was the last time I'd look. I thought it was unlikely he was still alive. I took Bentley with me. He had been barking in the direction of one of our neighbors' houses, a raised house underneath which many feral neighborhood cats flocked.

Bentley dragged me straight there and stuck his front half under the house. There, sure enough, was Charlie. I scooped my baby up and bathed him with happy tears as I carried him home, clutched to my heart.

Not long after, Charlie presented some concerning symptoms, and the vet diagnosed him with diabetes. We began a regimen of insulin shots. By the end, he had lost almost all his substantial weight.

Watching him melt away in front of me clawed at my heart. And then, he developed a gaping sore on his chin that wouldn't heal.

Despite his illness, he purred his mighty purr to the end.

When we said goodbye to him, I knew we'd made the right decision. Right decisions don't always settle comfortably on our hearts, though.

I told my father-in-law I couldn't bear the thought of laying Charlie directly in the ground. Would he help me make a cat-sized casket? He would, and he did. It was beautiful—like everything my father-in-law builds. We lined the box with the little catnip mat I had sewn for Charlie years earlier.

We buried my cat by the pond at my in-law's house in one of the most serene and tranquil spots on their property, where the sun splashes in warming patterns through tree leaves onto the dirt- and grass-mottled bank.

Often, I've wondered if Charlie ran away because he knew something wasn't right inside. Did he try to protect me from the burden of his illness? More likely in feline terms: did he want to hide away as he slipped from this life into the next?

We'll never know. I am grateful for our final months with him, though.

Saying goodbye to him was multi-layered for me. I wasn't just losing my sweet Charlie; I was relinquishing the last part of me from when I lived independently. In a way, I was saying goodbye to part of myself. That may not make much sense, but epiphanies uncovered by grief aren't always easily explained.

Slidell Veterinary Hospital showed genuine empathy for our loss. They understood I was losing a friend, a companion, a comfort ... family. A few days after we laid Charlie to rest, I received a card signed by the staff. Their thoughtful gesture meant the world to me.

They saw my grief and acknowledged its validity and depth. Their sympathy wasn't a one-time gift. A few years later, when Bentley's time came, we saw their tears the day they met us at our van to ease his pain.

During the final months of Bentley's life, our vet staff fought hard to regulate his cortisol levels to get him back to quality life. As he declined, they fought to keep him comfortable. They supported us in caring for him and giving him the best quality of life for as long as we could until the pain ceased his ability to eat and he was ready to say goodbye.

Each evening for the last week we had him, we laid a large moving blanket on the living room floor beneath him because we weren't certain he would survive to the morning. I would lay beside him and hug and kiss him, whisper memories and thanks before bed each night. Tony did the same.

As we retreated to our bed for the night, Tolkien took up his vigil beside his canine compatriot. He knew—animals always do. I believe he didn't want his friend to be alone.

Anyone who says animals don't grieve has never had pets. After we said goodbye to Bentley, Romy visibly grieved. Even now, when we mention Bentley's name, her expression changes.

Losing a pet is not easily overcome. For months after losing them, I would catch a shadow out of the corner of my eye and think Charlie was near or hear the clicking of Labrador claws on our empty tile floor.

When grief or depression or sorrow washes over me, I miss my animals' comfort. They always knew what I was feeling and would take their places in my lap, ready to comfort, reassure ... simply be.

Animals understand emotions better than many humans do, and I believe they know how to say goodbye with more care, grace, empathy and confidence than we do. I believe I've learned from them how to better say goodbye when their turn at the rainbow bridge comes.

I will be there, stroking their fur, holding their paws and thanking God for the memories and lessons they selflessly gave. I will honor their memories and relay their stories. I will also open my heart to other creatures who need a home and have hearts overflowing with love. I have thought several times over the years that I could never make such a commitment again.

Part of the reason I wasn't begging for a puppy when Gembeaux appeared was I had decided to abandon pet ownership. Losing them hurt too bad. All my animals had met tragic ends, and I didn't want to experience such grief again.

I felt like that after Charlie because our bond had formed during a pivotal time of transition. Plus, he was unique as far as cats go. I felt no other cat could be as amazing, and I couldn't love another like I'd loved him.

Honestly, I don't think it was until after we brought Kaiser home and I was deep into edits on this book that it occurred to me to think of the need to say goodbye to many animals in a different way.

Instead of viewing adding an animal to our home as more reasons for my heart to break, I consider the additions opportunities to love and be loved for as long as God grants the animal to my care.

Yes, kissing them goodbye will hurt deeply, but I get to give and receive such deep love ... often to an animal who hasn't experienced such a gift. Every animal I share a piece of my life with will teach me things, and I will snuggle them and play with them and make up conversations with them in my head.

Such joy is worth the grief that accompanies the goodbye.

Vignette Fourteen

Covered by Fur

HAVE YOU EVER HAD THE naked dream? You know the one. You walk down the hall of your high school, stark naked, as the bell rings and all the doors swing open.

I've had it. Heck, I lived it!

Okay, I didn't actually walk naked down the halls of my high school—or any public place, for that matter. What really happened was I had a book launch event at an incredible indie bookstore and ... no one came.

In the months leading up to my debut novel's launch, I visited many bookshops, which is no chore for me. Bookstores are some of my favorite places, alongside libraries.

As a newbie author without one of the big publisher names to back me, I knew it was a long shot for any store to risk a full event for me. When Blue Cypress Books, an adorable shop in New Orleans, willingly signed me up, my horizon brightened.

Stars filled my eyes, and I immediately conjured images from my naïve baby author mind of limos, lines out the door, adoring groups of big city literary elites with cocktails in their hands and Drew Brees asking for my autograph.

My mother-in-law packed snacks and serving trays, and my husband and I loaded our minivan with those goodies and our two kids and headed into the city.

The shop owner and staff greeted me with hugs and smiles and positive vibes. They had ordered what must have been tons of my books. Seriously, they were everywhere I looked.

My name was even in chalk!

I couldn't stop grinning and feeling like I had arrived. This was it—my first big moment, perhaps my big break.

Family and friends had been invited. The event had been advertised and blasted. Doctors and other discerning acquaintances had been invited, and the entirety of the NOPD had been notified.

We set out the hors d'oeuvres, and I took deep readying breaths to greet the masses.

The start time came and passed. Everyone in New Orleans is always late. Right?

The door opened.

"Welcome! Are you here for our author event?"

Flushed cheeks, lowered chins, shuffling feet passed me to books by authors who weren't me. Lather, rinse, repeat a few times.

My smile remained plastered on, but I suspect my bookseller friends saw through the mask to my sweaty palms, pounding heart and downcast soul. With one of the kindest and most genuine smiles I've ever seen, the owner, Elizabeth, asked me to share my presentation anyway. They wanted to hear it.

Smile bolstered, I launched into a discussion about Southern fiction and food in front of two booksellers, my husband, my two children and the occasional customer with averted eyes.

I hadn't even gotten to the jokes about dumplin's when Kitty Meow entered. She strode with intentionality—as cats are wont to do—straight for my chair. She leapt into my lap and sat to listen to a portion of my presentation with what appeared to be interest and approval.

Of all the bookstores in all the towns, Blue Cypress will forever hold a special place in my heart. They opened their doors to me, hugged me close and introduced me to their reading community as a friend.

I may not have gotten to autograph my book for a celebrity, but I got to talk about it and read a selection in front of the greatest audience I could have ever hoped for with special attention from one of the most discerning of book lovers, Kitty Meow.

Cats don't fling attention about willy-nilly. When a feline chooses your lap as a perch, you can be certain you have, indeed, arrived.

Stroking Kitty Meow's silky fur relieved the beet-red embarrassment I felt at being ignored—the invisible, unpopular girl once more. The feline's confident, calming presence restored my hope that my dream of being an author wasn't as laughable as the naked nightmare.

Psychoanalyzing such dreams typically leads me to picking apart what I'm most ashamed of or what I'm most afraid of people discovering about me. The truth is, I think that dream contains deeper meanings.

When we chase a dream, we feel a certain level of exposure when we leap toward achieving it. In the moment when we've left the figurative ground, we have no way of knowing if what's waiting on the other side is terra firma … or an abyss. Perhaps what awaits us is simply falling on our face before a heckling crowd where we'll feel our bare skin tingle with the goose bumps of exposure and embarrassment.

Kitty Meow, my friends at the bookstore and my family eliminated my exposed feeling and left me feeling covered, cared for and hopeful that—with hard work and perseverance—open doors will one day usher in readers for books with my name on them.

That's a dream worth leaping toward.

Vignette Fifteen

The Cat, the Toothpaste & the Newlyweds

I SUPPOSE IT'S SAFE TO confess at this point, when my husband was in graduate school at a Southern Baptist seminary in North Carolina, I smuggled a cat into our duplex. I also had an occasional bottle of wine.

For anyone unfamiliar with the Baptist way of life, they're publicly opposed to alcohol. The cat ban I haven't found a Baptist reason for, but we had a tight budget and could only afford the cheapest housing available, the duplexes. Animals were not allowed. In the more expensive housing, they were only allowed at a higher rate.

Though I've always leaned toward a follow-the-law-down-to-the-letter lifestyle, I'd already had to let go of my dog and wasn't about to give up Charlie, too. On top of that, I wasn't convinced we could even afford the duplex, so I saw no other option.

Since I'm being honest, the time surrounding our wedding was stressful. In the months leading up to that sweltering first day of July 2006, I worked a second job, mucking out stalls at a horse barn at zero dark thirty, to pay for our special day.

Looking back, I recognize I wasn't taking great care of myself. I worked late into the night, got up super early for the second job and crammed many activities in between. My diet was pretty bad as well; I remember more about fast-food drive-throughs in Gautier, Miss., than anywhere else.

One day between jobs, I was talking to my neighbors in my front yard. I had just come home from the tanning bed, and the sun was beating down unmercifully. The world suddenly went black, and I hit the ground. My neighbors, a sweet older couple, fussed over me and helped me in my house. Some AC and cool water were all I needed, but they scolded me for not taking better care of myself. As a mom now, I understand and would have said the same thing. In my early twenties, I thought I was invincible. I promised to drink more water, though.

Back to Wake Forest: I had left my first full-time newspaper job and moved without a new job set in place, which scared the mess out of me. I had sold my three-bedroom house and moved into a one-bedroom duplex which was collectively about the size of my previous living room.

With straightened spine and shoulders, I put my foot down and spit in the face of the no-pet policy while I tossed a towel over Charlie's cage and smuggled him into our new home. If anyone ever thought I was cut out to be a Baptist preacher's wife, my admission should clear up their misunderstanding.

After our wedding and honeymoon, Tony and I settled into our life as newlyweds. I got a job on campus as the news and information specialist. I felt like a traitor, switching from journalism to the dark side of public relations, but the job had opened up first, paid well and allowed me to work on my master's degree for free. I will admit, when the newspaper I'd applied to offered me a job a few weeks later, I was tempted.

Tony worked two then three jobs and took on a full load of his own classes. I worked during the day. He worked both day and night. We both studied constantly and rarely saw each other. We've often joked how one day we'll write the book on what *not* to do when you get married: *101 Ways to Ruin Your Marriage.*

We made the best of our small space, turning the tiny duplex into our home. Charlie missed the floor-to-ceiling windows in my old house where he would lay for hours in the sunlight, conversing with roaming neighborhood cats. In the duplex, he was strictly forbidden from getting into any of the few small windows.

All I needed was a self-righteous neighbor or school official to catch sight of him and kick my husband out of seminary. Whenever I envisioned being caught, it always ended in dramatic fashion—a thought that frequently led to a generous sip of my contraband wine.

With our move, not only did Charlie find himself in cramped quarters where windows were off-limits and he was shoved into the tiny bathroom whenever someone came over, but he also had to share his bed with Tony.

The double-sized bed had been sufficient for me and my cat. I should mention, Charlie was a large cat. We think he was part Ragdoll, a breed known for their large size, relaxed manner and amiability. He loved being held and snuggled, didn't mind being picked up and carried around and had grown accustomed to being the man of my house.

Charlie put his paw down and stubbornly took up at least a quarter of Tony's side. The cat had the ability to make himself three times heavier than he actually was when he didn't want to be moved.

For his part, my sweet husband positioned himself in the last quarter of the bed every night for months, careful not to kick Charlie or take up too much of my side. I have to think, though, his resentment for my cat had to be rising, like bread dough atop a dryer.

One night, I was comfortably sprawled out on my side of the bed, propped up with pillows and a good book. Charlie was anchored comfortably on his quadrant of the bed. Tony emerged from the bathroom, toothbrush and toothpaste in hand. I don't remember anything about our conversation or why he got this bright idea, but suddenly he laughed, said "Watch this!" and proceeded to smear toothpaste under my cat's nose.

Poor Charlie leapt off the bed, viciously shook his head and issued a series of snorts and sneezes. The toothpaste bubbled up, and I thought my cat was having a seizure and foaming at the mouth. He dashed under the bed, his eyes wide and wild.

I yelled at my new husband, likely threatening divorce, and Tony realized he may have made an error in judgment.

He finally fished Charlie from under the bed, took him to the bathroom and washed the toothpaste off his mouth. Charlie shot out of the bathroom, water droplets flying, and Tony plodded after him a few seconds later. He knew I was mad at him, and I didn't disagree.

"Don't you ever do that again!"

If my husband had any question about the importance of Charlie in my life, he had his answer. Charlie continued to anchor into his spot on the bed every night, but the battle grew more heated. Tony became more insistent with his nudging of the cat off his side of the bed. Charlie simply looked at him with haughty derision. I stayed out of their battle.

At some point, Charlie switched to sleeping on my side of the bed, renewing his nightly habit of purring me to sleep. Tony finally got a full side of the bed to himself, and the tension dissipated.

We had been married almost six months when Tony took me to the airport and sent me off on a work trip to Nigeria. We were not happy about being separated for nearly two weeks or about missing our first New Year's together as a married couple, but we couldn't afford for him to go with the mission team, and I had work to do.

During our time apart, we both got sick.

Tony had some sort of mutant strep/flu hybrid that knocked him out and shot his fever through the roof. He was so delirious, he drove from Wake Forest to his job in downtown Raleigh on New Year's Day because he didn't realize what day it was.

While Tony resigned himself to his fate on our couch, Charlie tucked in next to him and purred him back to health. They bonded and remained close from then on.

On the other side of the planet, I was bouncing along on rough dirt roads, sleeping in the bush, meeting some of the kindest and most beautiful people and seeing up close the effects of war between Christians and Muslims.

My emotions had been all over the place while I was gone, but I chalked up my moodiness to being away from my husband on a holiday. I felt quite sick one evening and attributed my illness to the water or food or both. I did forget to use bottled water a couple of times when I brushed my teeth.

Finally, a realization hit me: I had missed something rather important. Tony and I were going to have a baby. I was thrilled, and then I panicked.

I had been taking malaria medicine, the type with the strong warning, "Do not take if you are pregnant or plan to become pregnant." I went to the nurse missionary, confided with her my suspicion and shared my fear about the medicine.

"Should I stop taking it?"

"Absolutely not! It would be far worse for the baby if you were to contract malaria."

She calmed me down, told me everything would be fine and congratulated me on my news. I smiled and kept the excitement and worry to myself until our plane landed in Raleigh.

I'm pretty sure I blurted the news to Tony in the airport. He hugged me and swung me around, and we stopped for a test on the way back to our little home. The test was positive, and we were elated.

That night, we talked about our future and our baby and snuggled together on our couch ... all three of us—Charlie in my lap with his paw on Tony's leg.

Our little family was growing, while Tony and I were embarking on a longer process of emotional, mental and spiritual growth as a couple. Marriage is not simply "happily ever after, the end." A shared life requires commitment, dedication, hard work and growth—individually and together.

For a marriage to last, a couple must also persevere as a team to overcome challenges and communicate concerns, differences of opinion and aversions to things like toothpaste.

Vignette Sixteen

Animals, By Marriage

ONE OF THE PRIMARY FAMILY members we get to choose is our spouse. Animals are also part of the family we choose.

I've been married long enough to offer some solid nuggets of advice. Tip #1 is to marry someone as fond of animals as you are.

Lucky for me, in addition to marrying an animal lover, I married into an animal-centric family. My husband grew up with animals. Unlike my vanilla pets—dogs, cats, one hamster and a short-lived stint with two ponies—Tony comes from a long line of more exotic tails ... and tales.

Before we got married, Tony and I were on a date when his younger brother called with news. He'd found the best Father's Day present for their dad—a goat.

The goat's procurement and homecoming would require a whole other story which involves a group of young men, the influence of certain substances, the Goat Man, a ride in the back of a pickup truck in the middle of the night, a police officer, explosive diarrhea and a shotgun.

Since I wasn't an eyewitness to those twelve hours of insanity, I'll fast-forward to life with Billy. After the initial shock and confusion of finding a bleating adult goat with a violently upset stomach tied to his back deck in the early hours of Father's Day, my father-in-law became good friends with Billy and welcomed his addition to their property.

Billy lived his best life and earned his keep as a fierce watch-goat. Whenever an unknown visitor turned into my in-law's property, they would wind along a wooded and garden-lined gravel driveway. Straight ahead, the angry eyes of a goat would bore into the intruder.

On the car's approach, the goat would put his head down and stand his ground, hooves firmly planted with no intention of moving. Once the intrusive vehicle reached him, the goat would jump up, planting his front hooves on the vehicle's hood. He would not budge until my father-in-law intervened and called him off.

Despite a commitment to his bouncer duties, Billy was the nicest goat. I never saw him get aggressive with people or butt anyone. He would, however, steal beer, wine or other strong beverages. I learned not to set my glass down unattended. Once, I turned around to discover Billy's snout in my glass and his tongue lapping away. When we pulled the glass from him, he showed no remorse as red wine droplets drip-dropped from his once-white beard.

Billy began showing some concerning symptoms, so my father-in-law took him to the vet. None of us knew that castrated goats cannot eat grain. The substance is deadly for them.

When they got the diagnosis, my father-in-law brought the goat back to the house, cracked open a couple of beers, had a last drink with his buddy and then said goodbye like every red-blooded American man in the South does.

Billy was a good goat.

The Rancatores have a history of animals with a fondness for liquor. At one point, they had a flock of hens they called the Dixie Chicks. My father-in-law would share some of his after-work beer with the Chicks. Afterward, they'd happily stagger around his feet, pecking more sideways than normal.

None of the animals I've encountered during my years as a Rancatore are quite as outlandish as the gator my father-in-law walked on a leash in New Orleans East or the pet spider monkey that stole schoolchildren's lunches and terrorized ladies with wigs. Those are stories best told by Tony Senior on his back deck over a few cold ones.

Around the time we moved to Slidell, La., from Wake Forest, N.C., my in-laws had quite the menagerie with two cows, a bunch of pigs and plenty of chickens, in addition to their more domestic animals.

The livestock always had appropriate names. Brisket and Meatloaf were the cows, and Hambone and Hogleg and Oscar were a few of the pigs.

They bred the pigs and sold piglets for a few years. I had no idea how hot the market is for pigs. They're perfect for family celebrations requiring a full pig roast. One of the most interesting pig purchasers picked up the squealing piglet and put him into an old Astro van—no cage, no box, nothing. We assume they arrived home okay.

My husband's family has had their share of dogs and cats as well. When Tony and I started dating, they had Bristol, the dog who lived to be eighteen years old, despite having parvo as a puppy.

They also had Gizmo. He was one of the softest cats I've ever petted. I adored Gizmo with his blond fur. Though he could be moody, he loved me. When I stayed at their house, he would snuggle on my pillow. He'd even let me pet him for a few minutes. Once he was ready to go outside and prowl, though, he'd stand up, stretch and hop down from the bed.

Like Gizmo, my family by marriage seems to have chosen me back, and I frequently say I have the best in-laws in the world, for multiple reasons.

We swap feeding duties when we go out of town. We all love each other's animals. We share the excitement of choosing new members of the Rancatore clan and spend time together as one big happy family—dogs included.

When we lived with my in-laws for seven months after grad school left us broke and floundering with a nearly three-year-old and one-year-old, Bull was their main pet. He was born on the Halloween after

Hurricane Katrina. He was a black Labrador Retriever/Catahoula Leopard mix who was massive, hence the appropriateness of his name.

With our young son, Bull proved himself a gentle giant. The two were inseparable, and Bull worried over the boy any time he'd stumble and fall. For his part, our son knew Bull would always let him lean against him to eat his snack or to rest.

When we welcomed Bentley into our family, we introduced him to Bull. They became big buddies, and Bull taught Bentley how to be a good dog. They wrestled and chased each other. Bentley kept Bull young and playful, while Bull helped Bentley mature into one of the best dogs I've ever known.

They swam together in the pond and shared the water bowl while we camped. I brainstormed a chapter book about them and planned to title it *Bayou Dogs*. Maybe I'll write it one day.

Bull lived a good, long life for such a big dog. In the end, his hips failed him, and he couldn't get around like he used to. We wept for him and often remind each other of stories about him—how he broke Bentley's tail when they were wrestling and left his tail forever crooked; how he was such a shy pooper, he'd back his butt into a bush before he'd go; how protective he was of our son.

He was one of the best dogs.

Beyond pets and livestock, my in-laws have rehabbed countless baby birds over the years. The first one I remember was Skittles, a little house wren whose mama chose the bumper of their camper trailer to build her nest. No one realized that until we had set up at the campground for a week.

When the kids discovered the tiny creature, we had to figure out how to feed and care for it. Skittles survived the camping trip and then made himself right at home in their house. He grew and, before long, he was flying all over their living room, roosting in the rafters and perching on my mother-in-law's shoulder while she watched TV from her recliner.

Skittles slowly adapted to life in the wild. The other birds seemed to make a good deal of fun of him in the beginning, but he proved himself to be a wild bird, too, and made his own way.

Arrow and Waddles, the ducks, came at different times. Each was the lone survivor of an orphaned rest. Both still fly into the pond and waddle up to the house for extra corn from time to time.

Animals remember; so do people. Our family grieves together over the losses of our pets.

When I had to say goodbye to my Charlie cat, my father-in-law built his casket. As the end drew close for sweet Bentley, we were afraid we'd have to say goodbye while my husband and son were away at Boy Scout camp. Without us even asking, my father-in-law dug a hole and had all the necessary tools on hand ... just in case.

To the left of my in-laws' pond is a little cemetery where we can go and sit a spell with our old buddies, Charlie, Bull and Bentley.

Gone but not forgotten—eternally part of our eccentric, unique and endearing found family.

Vignette Seventeen

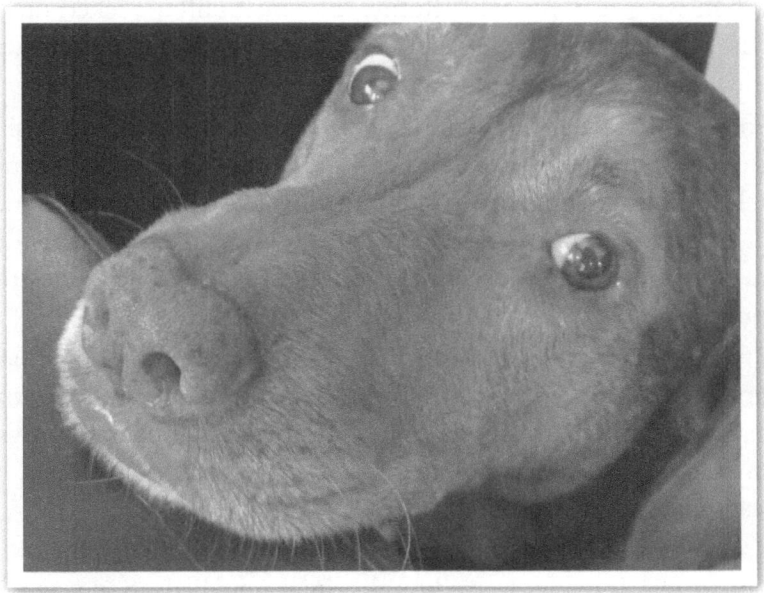

Personalities & Deep-Dish Pizza

PET PARENTING ISN'T ALL SNUGGLES and paw-shakes. Our fur babies can get into mischief, wreak havoc, destroy things and generally make us crazy. At the end of the day, though, we wouldn't enjoy life as much without them.

Romy, Chesapeake Bay Retriever/chocolate Labrador Retriever mix, was almost two years old when we got her, and we had no idea what we were getting ourselves into.

We had signs, though, like her leaping into Tony's lap as he merged onto a busy highway on our way home with her. We've often asked ourselves why we didn't turn around right then and take her back. We didn't, of course, and so our life has been an extra adventure since Romy joined our family.

Before we brought her home, we took Bentley to meet her. The dogs hit it off. We let them off their leashes to run and play. They looked like a couple of puppies. Jumping, bowing, hopping, nipping; tongues flopping and tails wagging.

When we got home with Romy, she and Bentley picked up their playtime. The transition seemed to be going smooth as butter ... until Bentley realized she wasn't leaving.

Poor pup! He was happy to have a friend, but he had no desire to have a new sister at age five. For her part, Romy did not exactly endear herself to him. Within the first couple of weeks, she stole his bed. We got a second one, but she hogged them both. I think what really set Bentley against his new roommate, though, was when she destroyed his puppy.

That puppy had been Bentley's faithful companion since before his first birthday. In no time flat, Romy had commandeered the stuffed animal and ripped it to shreds. White, fluffy stuffing coated our living room floor. We decided not to get any more stuffed animals. One massacre was hard enough to watch.

Romy moved on to the beds ... another stuffing explosion. We waited a long time before we bought them new beds. She was a little older and, well, she wasn't any calmer, but we felt bad for them sleeping on the hard floor. They each lay on their own beds, for the most part. Romy tended to sprawl out and end up with her head on Bentley's bed or butt.

For a while, everything was fine. Then one day, Romy got sick. Knowing her, she likely ate something she shouldn't have. Whatever the cause, the effect was vomit ... a massive amount of vomit. The mess coated one of the beds. It was beyond salvaging.

They were back to one bed. Bentley usually won its use, but they would sometimes share. We went on that way for a while until Romy peed all over the remaining bed. Cold, hard floor it was from then on.

Bentley eventually got used to having Romy around. He was never as fond of her as she became of him, though. She adored him. Wherever he was, she followed. Poor fellow couldn't get away.

After we got Romy, Bentley's attitude toward other dogs changed. He became a barking, growling mess any time we'd take him on the leash around other dogs. I'm convinced he wanted to make sure we didn't bring another rogue pup home.

Walks became a Romy-only venture because of Bentley's increasing grumpiness. At first, Bentley would bark the entire time they were gone. As time went on, though, the old fellow recognized the benefits. He had a blissful Romy-free twenty minutes whenever her leash came out. Sometimes we would snuggle; other times he'd lay at my feet and snore while I wrote.

Romy would return, grinning and panting. She'd noisily lap up half a bowl of water and then plop down beside Bentley and drop her head on his rump. He usually greeted her with a resigned and pronounced sigh.

While Romy loves hugs and snuggles and is loyal and affectionate—often to an annoying extreme—she has a dark side that emerges when food comes into play.

We cannot leave food anywhere. Most covers are not Romy-proof. Food must go in the fridge or the oven or the microwave. One especially impressive food-snatching occasion deserves a few lines.

I have an affection for deep-dish pizzas. When one boasts toppings of mushrooms and pepperoni, I'm ready to drop everything and commence yummy noises.

One Tuesday evening, my daughter and I were at her American Heritage Girls meeting, where I served as a leader for 13 years. I love how much the organization and troop has meant to my daughter and some of her closest friends, but those nights exhausted me for many reasons.

My sweet husband said he'd get us pizza, including a special surprise one for me, from my favorite place. The thought gave me something to eagerly anticipate.

When we got home, Tony greeted me with a stunned look on his face. He proceeded to describe the special pizza to me. My mouth watered. And then, he explained that he had checked the contents, shut the lid and pushed the box to the back of the stove before he went to hang out with our son.

When he returned to the kitchen from our son's room, the box was slightly askew, which Tony thought was odd. The lid was tightly closed, though, so he wasn't suspicious when he opened it. Imagine his shock when he peered into an empty box.

Romy somehow opened the pizza box, ate an entire deep-dish pizza and closed the lid to avoid detection. To this day, she owes me a medium deep-dish pizza with mushrooms and pepperoni—a fact I frequently remind her of.

Nothing is safe from being eaten by Romy, and she hasn't found many things she can't eat. We went camping once with my in-laws, and she stretched her tie-down rope far enough to pull half our chicken to herself. She scarfed it down, bones and all.

Whether chicken bones are really bad for dogs or not, I'm not sure. They don't bother Romy. Of course, she may be part goat. Sometimes, she will get an upset stomach and can't eat for a day or two. She might vomit or have diarrhea; she'll nibble on grass. And then, whatever the issue was will pass, and she'll be back to her normal eat-everything-in-her-path self.

She has eaten paper, rope, candy—wrappers included, which, incidentally, don't digest but pass through intact ... ask us how we know—plastic bags, paper clips and building bricks.

Romy also ate a corn cob. I had no idea until then that corn cobs are incredibly dangerous for dogs. They do not break down in a dog's system, which means they can't be passed. Once they get past the point of no return in one direction, the only option to keep a dog from dying is surgery.

Again, our dog proved herself to be on a whole other level. We had her in our vet's office within 30 minutes of the corn cob incident. They immediately initiated Operation Vomit—which is started by special eye drops, a fascinating fact I learned that day. She responded to the drops and proceeded to throw up ... a lot. Noses were squinched; candles were lit. We found a fully intact salami sandwich we didn't know she'd also snatched from the trash but no corn cob.

The next step was X-rays. They found no sign of the offensive corn cob, but they did find a large mass. Our vet called it an "incidental find," a medical issue without symptoms that's typically only found during other procedures. The splenic tumor was massive; the odds were low that surgery would reveal anything other than a more serious issue that could take her from us while she lay open on the table.

Since Romy was ten-and-a-half, more active than she had been in years (thanks mostly to her superstar new brother, Kaiser) and not in any pain, we opted against a surgery. While we weighed several factors in making our decision, an influential one for me was not

wanting her final moments to be the fear of surgery, away from us. We knew the tumor would most likely rupture, but we'd know what to expect so we could ease any pain and would be able to surround and comfort her in her final moments as we said goodbye with pets and kisses.

The corn cob remained a concern, however. We scheduled two follow-up X-rays to keep an eye on the situation and confirm the mass was really a mass and not an unusual fluke of the initial scans. The mass didn't magically disappear, but that corn cob sure did. Romy hasn't slowed down since her diagnosis, and the way she races around the dog park would never make anyone think she has a tumor.

She's proven again that she has an iron gut and continues to eat anything left within snout-reach. Romy and Bentley—and now Kaiser—appreciate our chickens and the snack contributions they drop as they peck around the yard. They also like when Tony drops some of the chicken feed on the ground outside the hens' coop.

We have to watch Kaiser around the chicken feed, though. One day, soon after we got him, he consumed a large quantity straight from the chickens' feeder before we realized it. I loaded the pups up for a trip in the van later that afternoon. Midway through our trek across town, every bit of that feed—sickeningly sweet yet rancid—came back up onto the backseat of our van.

Mealy, dark liquid dripped from the leather onto the floor in the trunk, between the seats and into cracks and crevices I had no idea existed. For weeks, we scrubbed and cleaned and sprayed. We left windows and doors open—an unwise decision, as I discovered when I went to crank the van and got nothing when I turned the key.

Of course, the vomit incident occurred right before my nearly 800-mile book tour to North Mississippi. The smell *had* to go, so in desperation, I soaked everything I could in vinegar. While the method helped, I fear my books and I smelled like salt and vinegar chips on the trip. My daughter still turns up her nose when her brother enjoys his favorite snack.

When we got home, Tony spent an entire morning peeling back carpets and unscrewing pieces I didn't know could come apart in the back of the van. He got the remaining bits and completed the extensive cleaning job.

Unfortunately, poop and feed aren't the only snacks our dogs can get from the hens. Romy discovered the oval items in the hens' box are quite delicious. Now we have to beat our dog to the eggs if we hope to have breakfast.

I've declared many times that Romy is the worst. While I stand by my statement most of the time, I have to admit she may not be the absolute worst.

My in-laws got a puppy for Christmas 2020—a black Labrador Retriever/hound dog mix. Clyde was the cutest pup—and still is—with his floppity ears, sad eyes and lanky legs. He is also in the running for the literal, hands-down worst.

And, Romy cannot stand him.

Our dogs have always loved going to Papa and Nonna's. They swim in the pond, run around the ten acres and enjoy an occasional rib bone or stray crawfish tossed their way.

Not long after Clyde's arrival, we took Romy over there. She was practically dancing as she jumped out of the van. When she turned the corner and spotted Clyde, she dropped her grin, made a U-turn and tried to leap back into the van.

It's safe to say, she loathes him.

Clyde is awkward in a manner that usually ends up annoying. For instance, he'll be so head-butting insistent he be petted, that he will send a beverage flying from someone's hand or overturn a nearby table. His spastic actions resulted in my mother-in-law having extensive knee surgery.

Thankfully, he has mellowed over time and remains adorable, and his deep and genuine appreciation for ear scritches is quite endearing. However, he's still a stinker. Next to Clyde, Romy—the dog who will literally eat the food out of your mouth—sometimes looks like an angel. Though, I say they're a close tie.

Speaking of looks, Romy has some expressive faces. She's the master of the side-eye and the mad mean girl face. She'll be woofing at something—most likely a leaf on the wind—and we'll tell her to stop. She'll huff another woof or two, her face still aimed toward the window, while side-eye glaring in our direction.

Other times—usually when I'm comfy on the sofa with Tolkien in my lap and won't let her join us—Romy gives me the if-looks-could-kill stare. She juts out her bottom lip, like she's pouting, and narrows her eyes at the situation.

When Romy wants to play, she hops like a bunny, bows, cocks her head, hangs her tongue over one side of her mouth and gives a different kind of side-eye—the I-have-mischief-to-manage one.

Bentley was never much for playing with her, although he and Romy could tear up the turf in our backyard when they sprinted after one another. Kaiser's the one eager to play now, while Romy gives him her I'm-too-mature-for-such-nonsense glare. She gives in on

occasion, and they'll snarl and snap, playfight or nip, until they bolt around the yard in a frenzied game of chase.

Romy and Tolkien have some interesting play times. Tolkien has a distinct yowl when he wants to play. The sound is loud and demanding. Other times, he twitches his tail or runs around and scratches things, with a crazed look in his eye.

Some evenings while Tony and I are watching TV, Tolkien will race around crazily and then crouch where Romy is about to pass. His tail will twitch; his backend will waggle once, twice. Romy will appear, and ... *Pounce! Swat! Swat! Swat!* He leaps up and boxes her snout with his paws.

She stands there, confused, every time—like she's trying to figure out what's wrong with his paws and why they're so sharp. You'd think by now she'd expect his antics.

Two endearing qualities of Romy are her empathy and loyalty. When I cry, she rests her snout on my lap and peers up at me with compassion.

When Tolkien has a hair ball or so much as a hiccup, she's on top of him, sniffing, sniffing, sniffing. She's the most obnoxious mother that ever lived, but she does care. She acts the same when we sneeze. It was sweet the first time or two, but her sniffing is seriously *invasive*.

All our animals endear themselves to us one way or another—some with their good manners, others with their impish ones. Even in their naughty moments, pets enrich our lives and add to our enjoyment of life. Their very presence and personalities brighten our existence.

As for Romy, we know she'll always be by our side when we need her ... or when we drop our guard over a medium deep-dish mushroom and pepperoni pizza.

Vignette Eighteen

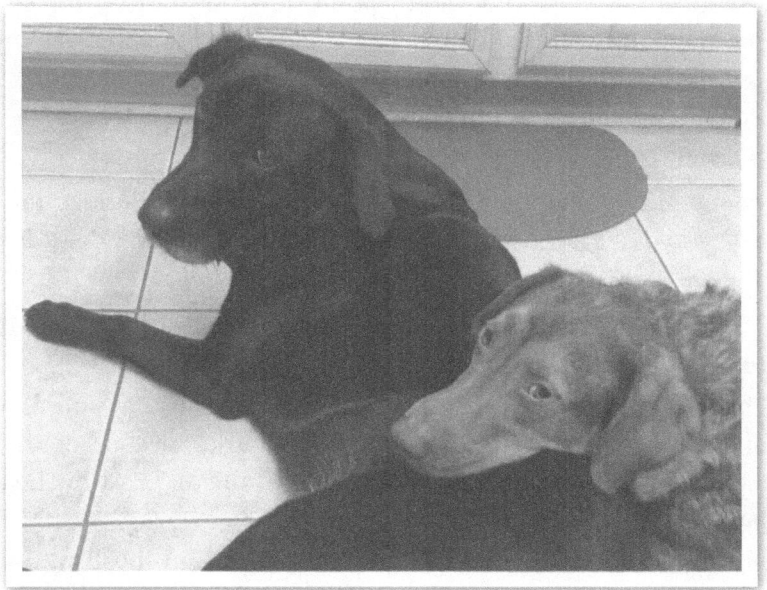

How to Speak Animal

BE HONEST. DO YOU TALK for your pet in the voice you imagine them to have? I boldly admit I do because I believe most pet owners do … whether or not they publicly claim the quirk.

Why we speak for our pets, I'm not sure. Perhaps to connect with them. Maybe—as much as we're around them and think we know them—our pets remain a mystery. Without a common language, we don't know what our furry friends are thinking or feeling, so we observe and imagine and give voice to their inner dialogues.

Bentley and Romy have quintessential Southern dog drawls. Romy's voice becomes Gollum-esque—if Gollum were from New Orleans—when food is involved. "I wants dat chicken. It's mine, my own … my preciouses!"

As Bentley got older, he became increasingly salty. We decided he was the stereotypical get-off-my-lawn old guy.

"Maybe I'd be nicer to other dogs if y'all hadn't tricked me. Last time I used my manners 'round another dog, she ended up comin' home with us. Where—I'd like to point out—she tore up my stuffed puppy, peed and vomited all over my bed, ate my birthday ice cream and generally proceeded to be a continual boil on my butt. Can you understand why I'm a might testy?"

Yes, Bentley; yes, we do.

Meanwhile, oblivious Romy curled up wherever Bentley lay and usually rested her head on his backside. She adored him.

"I loves Bentley. He's my buddy and the wisest dog that ever was."

When we had to say goodbye to Bentley, Romy was visibly depressed for months. Animals grieve.

They also know when someone is ill or nearing the end of their life. I remember many times when I was either sick or depressed, Bentley would climb onto the couch next to me and rest his head in my lap. He always knew.

During Bentley's last days, Tolkien lay with him most nights. He kept vigil beside his canine friend as Bentley slept.

One of the many times I took Bentley to the vet in his final days, an older dog walked over to him. They stood nose-to-nose for a solid minute. I imagine their conversation went something like this:

"It's the end of the road for me, kiddo," the elder canine confided.

Bentley replied, "Mine's coming soon, too. You scared?"

"Nah. Just hate to leave my humans, you know?"

"Yeah, I'm trying to get as much wisdom into the younger dog as I can before my time's up. Romy might make a decent pup one day … maybe."

"This younger generation …. You'll be fine, and so will she. All dogs wise up for their people when they have to."

"And your humans will be okay. They'll grieve, but they've got the memories you're leaving."

"Wise words. I gotta go now. The rainbow bridge is callin'. You take care of that family and enjoy your silver days."

I teared up, watching the interaction between the two dogs. The vet tech asked the dog's owner if he was ready. The man's voice was damp with soon-to-be shed tears as he answered, "Nope."

We weren't ready either. I held Bentley a little tighter for the next week and a half or so until we had to say goodbye to him. He was, as we often say, the goodest boy.

Our animal voiceovers aren't limited to the dogs.

My interpretation of cats' voices always comes out British. I'm not entirely sure why that is; perhaps it's the only accent from another country I can somewhat pull off. Also, I'm not sure why we continued with the British accent for Charlie when we always imagined him introducing himself with, "I hail from Spain."

Charlie was my storyteller. Tony and I would make up all sorts of outlandish tales that required him to be in an advisory role to famous people throughout history.

"I say! When Constantine came back from the Battle of Milvian Bridge, I did my best to advise him theologically. Far too superstitious, that one! Though, he was a fine leader and fierce fighter. I remember the time we ...."

"Luther and I had some great chats over pints. He wasn't there to start a rebellion, you know; we wanted to restore the church to the Bible's teachings—sola scriptura. I'll have to tell you one day what he said about the Pope. Luther did have a way with words, you know!"

One day I'm going to finish Charlie's book that I started writing years ago. Tall Tales *of Charlie the Cat* is sure to be a hit—at least for nerdy cat and history lovers like me.

Tolkien speaks in much more condescending tones. He mostly insults us and demands food in his British accent. He does often reflect kindly on Charlie as he was, indeed, "a good chap."

Since Bentley's passing, I have occasionally caught Romy and Tolkien looking close to snuggling. They'd both deny it if you asked them, I'm sure, but I think they like each other more than they'll admit.

"Preposterous! I care not at all for that wretched, smelly mongrel of a dog."

We're also convinced Romy hasn't figured out Tolkien is actually a cat.

"I hates cats. They's the worst. I bites 'em."

Sometimes she eyes Tolkien with total confusion. "That weird little brown furry puppy's gots sharp paws. That not right. Somethin' wrong with the little guy."

Romy has done her best to step into Bentley's role as top dog. When Tony and I sit on our back porch at night with a fire roaring in the chiminea and a tasty beverage to sip on, Romy attempts to stand guard and do perimeter checks like Bentley. The problem is, she's a scaredy-pup.

She sits on the edge of the patio, ears pricked, knotted eyebrows twitching in concern, head on a swivel.

"What's up, Romy? You look worried."

"Stuff's goin' down out there, guys. It's gettin' real."

And then she trots over and shimmies beneath my legs.

She's trying, Bentley. You taught her well; she's just not you. But, she's Romy, and she loves her family and will watch over us and keep us company and make sure we're safe for the rest of her days. She'll also eat any food left uncovered and unattended—or too casually lifted to our mouths. I doubt that will ever change either.

Since Kaiser's been with us, Romy has been braver. Perhaps it's the instinctual mothering coming out in her. Perhaps it's the commitment to passing down all she learned from Bentley.

Kaiser took a few months of maturing before showing interest in the art of the perimeter check. He was too busy chasing and eating bugs, chasing chickens and Tolkien and zipping his zoomies around the yard. He's slowly accepting the vigilant side of being a dog, though.

Romy observes Kaiser's lack of duty and puppy antics with a side-eye, which reminds us of Bentley's frequent and straightforward looks of disdain in her direction when she acted the same way.

We imagine Kaiser to have a certain teenager-from-the-streets sound to his voice.

"What's up, guys? Can we go to the dog park today? I've got the zoomies, and this backyard ain't touchin' 'em. While we're out, can we get another ball? How about some new treats? A rope? When are we gettin' new antlers from Uncle Clyde's house? Can we hang out with Uncle Clyde?"

As rapid-fire and long-winded as his words seem to us all day long, Kaiser has a switch that flips around 10:00 each night.

"Hmmph ... I don't wanna pee. It's sleepy-time."

Once we finally coax him up and out the door, he stagger-trots, barely hikes a leg, does his business and immediately stagger-trots back where he insistently paws the door. When we don't immediately respond, he glares back at us.

"Bed. Now!"

That's usually when Romy is slowly and methodically sniffing every inch of the yard. Clearly, Kaiser expects burgling to be done during business hours.

As a Belgian Malinois, Kaiser has the inbred ability to communicate quite clearly in his native language, which we're slowly learning.

The insistent and high-pitched *Yap! Yap!*, accompanied by a pulling paw—yes, he hooks his paw around our arms or legs and pulls whenever the situation calls for it—means he needs something urgently.

Because we're less intelligent beings who only fluently speak Human English, we have to use context clues to determine what he's telling us. He may need to go outside and pee or we might have overlooked the time and he's about to starve to death or his ball has, yet again, taken a wild bounce beneath a piece of furniture. Typically, though, the *whine-bark-yip* is the phrase relating to ball issues.

While Romy will bark her ferocious bark at the front door frequently—leaves on the wind, remember?—Kaiser rarely issues his K-9 bark. When he does, though, I know two truths:

1. Something real is out there.
2. No one will attempt a door breach when faced with that tone ... if they even made it past the Sheriff's vehicle in the driveway, that is.

Kaiser's six-foot-in-the-air leap should also send them packing. News flash to bad guys: when motivated, Malinois jump more than 10 feet straight up, and I'm not sure there are tape measures long enough to record how far forward they can catapult their freakishly athletic bodies. They are the choice dog of special forces and law enforcement for a reason.

Regardless of species or breed, pets communicate with one another and convey many of their thoughts with us. They see and understand more than we realize and feel the emotions we do.

However they sound in our heads, we know in our hearts our animals' loyalty and love for us are unconditional.

Vignette Nineteen

Attack of the Spiteful Chicken & Other Misfortunes

FOR A SEASON IN MY LIFE, disaster rose every time my husband went out of town. Happenstance, bad timing, the mirrors I've shattered coming back to haunt me—whatever the reason, I hope the curse has been broken.

The Season of Misfortune, as I've titled it, coincided with the introduction of a flock of chickens to the Rancatore family. Coincidence? I'll let you come to your own conclusions.

The first unfortunate incident I remember taught me that chickens may not be able to fly high, but they can fly high enough.

Parents know few more gut-punching sentences than, "Um, mom? You need to come see this."

I've learned to hustle when I hear that declaration.

On that occasion, I exited the back door in time to witness one of our Rhode Island Reds fluttering from the top of our fence into the neighbor's yard.

We live outside the Slidell city limits, which means we can have chickens. Our yard is big enough to accommodate a coop and to allow the chickens to free range from time to time. Our property butts up on all sides to four other houses and their backyards—all of which contain dogs who are in and out at various times of the day.

At the time of the Great Chicken Escape, the neighbors directly behind us had several dogs who barked constantly and did not seem like they would host a tea party in honor of our rogue chicken. My first thought was, "Well, she's about to be a snack." Thankfully, their dogs weren't out.

The next challenge came with how on earth to get our chicken back. We weren't exactly on speaking terms with those renters. Let's just say, the dogs probably learned their manners from their owners.

To assess the situation, I stood on a stump in our yard and gauged whether I could leap the fence or not. I determined my backend still had too much COVID-fluff to allow me to leap gracefully over anything much higher than the stump I stood on. As I was contemplating whether the chicken would remain contained in the yard long enough for me to drive around the block, my son came to the rescue.

"I can jump over there, Mama!"

Have at it! I thought.

As my son effortlessly leapt into the other yard, I longed to sink into the ground. My goal as an introvert is to be completely invisible, especially to strangers. I had seen enough of those neighbors to justify my worries that they would either complain about our trespassing or emerge and launch a lengthy string of expletives in the direction of me and my two young children.

I contemplated how nice it would be if the ground opened and deposited me in Mordor or somewhere else less scary than my current situation. While my imagination over-reacted, my son scooped up the hen without a peep from her, and chicken and boy returned to our yard before I fretted myself into a complete frenzy.

We ushered all the hens into their coop, and I informed Tony that the chickens had to stay enclosed unless he was home. Next time, those dogs might be out ... or I might be by myself and would have no choice but to climb a fence, which would surely end in a broken hip.

A second phase during this Season of Misfortune meant that, every time Tony went out of town, a chicken died. I decided I wasn't cut out for the chicken mom life.

One of the deaths was a red hen. I had no warning anything was wrong until I walked into the cage and found her, stiff and unmoving in a corner. Chicken-whisperer, I am not, but I did know enough to act quickly and remove the carcass.

Chickens like to eat. They aren't picky at all—they're a bit like billy goats in that regard. Though, I've never heard of a goat eating its sibling.

Yes, chickens are cannibals. Don't believe me? Drop an egg or a chicken nugget in their coop. Step back first.

The saddest time I had to scoop up a lifeless chicken was when we lost one of our little Silkies.

Silkies are the puppies of the fowl world. They're cute and cuddly and can make good pets. They truly are adorable with pompoms on their heads, fluffy bodies and fuzzy Hobbit-esque feet. Our daughter had been begging for a Silkie, so we gave in when we got our second flock.

What we didn't know about Silkies is they are high maintenance and dumb as a brick.

I am not being mean. I'm being candid. They are the least intelligent of all God's creatures. Honestly, I have no idea how they aren't extinct. They cannot get wet; they will die. You would think they would stay out of the rain then. Nope. When it rains, they will go *into* the downpour *out* of it. I have observed that exact scenario: a Silkie was under our shed; the rain started; the Silkie darted into the middle of the yard, where she proceeded to casually peck the ground, oblivious to the deluge.

My husband and son went on a campout with their Boy Scout troop, and that's the weekend we had torrential rains with tropical storm-like gusts of wind. I also remember feeling chilly. Not a good combo for wimpy chickens with pea-sized brains.

Their coop usually stayed dry, especially with a fence on one side and a tarp on another, but the wind gusts made dryness impossible. When I realized how soaked the little creatures were, my daughter and I dashed into the monsoon and brought all four of the Silkies to the covered porch. We wrapped them in towels, dried them with a hair dryer and tried to stay clear of their tail areas and the presents they frequently dropped during the process.

We got them as dry as possible. My daughter corralled them with towels while I stomped through the lake that was previously our yard in my husband's rubber boots—the boots that, incidentally, had a gash in one of the ankles. I discovered that bit of need-to-know information as I sank into a three-inch-deep puddle.

I found another tarp and some zip ties in our shed. Back in the weather, I crossed to the coop where I stood on planters, random bits of wood or whatever I could find while I covered a third side from the rain's blasts.

In case you ever find yourself in a similar situation, I advise you to add the few seconds it will take to search for goggles. When you're looking up and rain is falling down ... well, you probably know the results.

My favorite moment occurred while I precariously teetered on a flimsy planter to hook one of the zip ties. In an effort to successfully complete the mission before my makeshift ladder collapsed, I forced my eyes open as wide as possible. A branch full of rain-laden leaves directly above me chose that moment to dump its pooled contents.

After all my efforts, the ridiculous Silkies managed to get themselves drenched again the next night because they insisted on standing in the only wet corner of the coop. Again, off we went—rain slickers on, towels and hair dryer waiting under the covered patio.

My daughter and I ruffled feathers with the towels and blow-dried until we were afraid we might set their tails on fire. We wrapped them completely and dashed back across the pond to put them carefully in the dry part of the coop, after rigging up a barrier to the one boggy corner.

I'm not embarrassed to admit I cried the next morning when I found one of the Silkies unresponsive. If only they were a little brighter, maybe we would still have all four fluffballs.

Not all the issues that saved themselves for my husband to be out of town had to do with chickens. The washing machine tends to be a household tool that chooses the most inopportune times to poop out on me.

It was one of those days where I hadn't gotten around to washing clothes in a while, so I had a hallway full of laundry piles. My house was a mess. I had deadlines zipping up on me, and the kids were giving me a run for my money in school.

Basically, a typical Tuesday.

I got the first load and another subject with the kids started. Three subjects, a few metaphorical fistfights and a migraine later, I returned to switch the first load.

When I lifted the lid on the washing machine, my mind was focused on berating myself for not switching loads earlier. All that laundry to do … it would be late at night before I finally finished. Each load of clothes had to run through our dryer at least two or three times before they'd get completely dry.

In my preoccupation, I thrust my hand into the machine without looking … deep into cold, soapy water. The sight that waited was equally shocking. Our clothes drifted around, waterlogged and forlorn. That was one of those moments where I could have laughed to keep from crying. I'm pretty sure I just cried, as I sat down in the pajama pants I'd been wearing for a few days because they were cleaner than anything else I had.

The day ended okay. Thankfully I have incredible in-laws who live about ten minutes away and say, "Come on over!" when I call hysterically crying about clothes floating in soapy water.

That scenario occurred more than once before we discovered the issue on our thirty-year-old washing machine was a latch on the lid. When I opened the lid to toss in a wayward sock or some other piece of clothing I had overlooked, I learned to confirm if the latch got triggered again. If not, the cycle would stop before the water could drain.

Remembering those days makes me even more grateful for the new washer and dryer we have now. The washer isn't ornery, and the dryer produces dry and fluffy clothes with one cycle instead of maybe after three—as long as the kids remove the lint first.

I still can't understand why breakdowns of that sort always happen when Tony's gone, but they do. Some of the misfortunes sound so ludicrous when I relay them, I'm not sure he always believes me. The best example would be the time one of the chickens attacked me.

Once Tony clipped the chickens' wings, I didn't have to worry about them attempting more great escapes. The kids and I would let them out during the day and put them up in the evening or before we left the house to run errands.

Corralling them into the coop can be tricky, though, especially if they're not ready to roost and don't understand why they can't keep pecking at all the plump and juicy yard bugs.

I should probably back up and explain that a couple of our Rhode Island Red hens from the first flock could be downright mean. They'd give me and the kids the stink eye and charge us when we entered the backyard. They didn't act that way all the time, just often enough to make me wary of them.

You should also know they never acted like that toward Tony. He received only their undying affection and devoted attention as they flutter-hopped loyally behind him.

It took me a while, but I finally got almost all of the chickens in their coop. I tossed some extra food in for them, herded them gently and was about to breathe a sigh of relief. One more hen to go.

The moody red hen was right outside their coop. I gently picked her up and set her inside, in front of the fresh food I'd sprinkled for them.

"There you go, little red hen. Enjoy your night!" I said in my softest, kindest chicken-ish voice.

Instead of pecking contentedly at my careful provisions, that wretched hen whipped around and proceeded to flutter up toward me, talons outstretched.

Let me set the stage: Two or three feet from the door to the chickens' coop is a tree. Roots of that tree undulate around its base, including a few inches from the coop. The ground there is extremely uneven and slopes steeply to the tree itself.

As the chicken fluttered higher and higher, her beak and talons closed in on me. I attempted a backward leap. The uneven roots slowed my progress, and I took a talon-scratch to one leg.

I was squawking; the chicken was squawking. My neighbors were probably laughing. I fell on my butt. I shrieked as I grabbed a nearby stick. It was on then.

Stick in hand, I poked at that vile, fluttering chicken until I finally managed some sort of polo move that landed her inside the coop. Once I slammed the door behind her, I plopped down on the tree roots and swore I would never again deal with that demon chicken.

When I relayed my story to him, Tony chuckled. He clearly didn't appreciate the life-threatening situation I survived. He loved to taunt me with, "Watch out for this evil chicken!" as they all—Demon Red included—followed him and his bucket of feed like docile puppies. He would frequently hold the evil creature against his face and make puppy eyes at me. Trust me, the chicken's eyes cast only malice in my direction.

The next time Tony and I were in the yard with the chickens, I was near the coop. Tony was on our patio, his back toward us. Suddenly, that hen fluttered at me again for no reason at all. As I ran across my backyard, chicken flapping at my heels, I yelled, "I told you!"

He finally believed me.

When we discovered that hen's stiff body, I did not weep. And no, I did not kill her. In our battle royale, I was prepared to do whatever was necessary to see another sunset, but I want the written record to show I am no chicken killer—not even of killer chickens.

Reminiscing on such anecdotal trials made me wonder why we face such random and aggravating mishaps during our lives.

Perhaps seemingly unnecessary challenges and hardships serve greater purposes than we can see in the moment. They can build character, resolve and resourcefulness within us. Further, they can prepare us for more complex life challenges.

Maybe they simply serve as humorous tales to recount and to elicit a healing chuckle. Laughter is, after all, the best medicine ... even for talon scratches from spiteful chickens.

Vignette Twenty

Romy & Best Laid Plans on the Run

LIBRARIES HAVE ALWAYS BEEN AMONG my favorite places. With each move I've made, the library has been the second place I've found, right after a new church home.

I grew up in awe of the endless shelves of books. Their perfectly organized stacks speak to my CDO soul. (That's OCD for fans of alphabetizing.) As a child, I considered the library a place of wonder and magic. As an adult, I still do.

For years, I dreamed of seeing my name along a spine on one of the shelves or neatly typed on one of the cards in the card catalog— yes, I'm old enough for typewriters and physical card catalogs.

When I was still only a reader, I savored the delicious feeling of snuggling up with a borrowed book and getting lost in its world. Now, my local library is a place to write new stories and books, spend hours in research for them and discover inspiring authors or escape into unexplored realms. It's also become a place for me to share my fondness of reading and writing with kindred spirits.

One of the greatest joys I've had since becoming an author has been speaking for groups of readers and writers in libraries. Being face-to-face with literature lovers and finding ways to inspire or help them fuels my creator-teacher heart.

As our library cautiously shook off the restrictions of COVID and our community greeted in-person events with open arms, I couldn't wait to sit down with the literary community again. Screens are nice, but meaningful, unfiltered interactions happen best in person.

I felt quite giddy as I dressed for a special presentation meant to get our adult readers psyched about summer reading. I spent extra time choosing an outfit—folks would see more than the waist up, after all.

(Admit it: you kept your pajama pants on with your dress shirts for Zoom events, too.)

The night before, I had decided I would give myself extra time to enjoy the process of getting ready. I took the time to straighten my hair and put on makeup. I even pulled out the red lipstick.

Finally, I was ready to go. I put last-minute items in the little yellow-and-black cart I pull to events and prepared to walk out the door.

Even with all the primping, we would have arrived a good forty-five minutes early—plenty of time to leisurely set up and then sit and wait for readers to join me.

As my kids opened the door, oblivious to my struggles with gathering my almost-forgotten sunglasses before I pulled the cart behind me, leisure bolted out the door with our rascal of a dog, Romy.

We live in a neighborhood that could be the setting for a *Warriors* book with all the rogue clans of cats that run the streets and backyards. One of the feral felines passed through our yard as the kids opened the door, and Romy seized her moment.

She raced the wind across two neighbors' yards into a third and didn't slow down as she army crawled under that house, the base of operations for the largest feline clan.

Under and out, around and back under, Romy raced and barked and smiled her infuriating grin. She had those cats in quite the tizzy while she was living her best life.

It was spring. In case you're unfamiliar with springtime in southeast Louisiana, the season produces rain and lots of it. When it pours, all our yards become mudholes at best—usually more like bogs. You can bet the area beneath the house where Romy had been burrowing after rogue cats was one of the muddiest of mudholes around.

Meanwhile, I sprinted after her in dress clothes and heels, my once-straightened hair becoming increasingly frizzy in the oppressive humidity. I charged into the neighbor's cat yard, around and around the house, trying to catch Romy whenever she popped out for a moment before diving back beneath the dwelling.

I had the kids bring the leash and treats to lure her out. My voice felt scratchy from yelling the dog's name. Sweat cascaded inside my shirt, and I wondered why I'd bothered to shower that morning.

The cats evaded Romy's capture, and the rattle of the treat jar caught her attention. Success!

I snapped the leash around her neck and proceeded to parade out of the yard of the people I'd never spoken to.

If they were home, they didn't emerge, but I'm guessing they were either irritated at the ruckus or laughing at the sight we made. Clicking down the street in the heels that felt ridiculous given the circumstances, I led our processional, two kids in tow and a dog trotting alongside me.

For her part, Romy was content with the world and pleased as punch to be coated snout to tail-tip in mud.

As we marched up our driveway, I barked orders.

"Get one of the dog towels. You help your sister and hold the leash while she towels off as much of the mud as possible. Flip up the couch cushions so she doesn't get mud all over them while we're gone. You'll have to bathe her when we get back. Do the best you can for now. I'm going to try to fix this hair and get my cart in the car. Hurry! We have to go!"

Thank goodness for extra primp time. We squeaked into the library parking lot just in time.

Next time you attend an event with an author at your library, remember Romy. You'll probably laugh out loud.

If the author asks what's so funny, tell them you heard authors often battle muddy dogs and distracted kids to attend events. Then, let them know you're thrilled they made it and eager to hear about their books. They'll probably smile as wide as a Romy on the run.

Vignette Twenty-one

When a Silkie Takes a Stand

SILKIES MAY BE AS SURPRISING as they are adorable. They're also one of the dumbest chicken breeds. They run from anything they don't need to fear and toward everything they should fear.

If you put them in a corner of their coop and open the door, they'll pace back and forth in that one corner and never discover the exit—even when the door is three feet to their left.

They will teeter precariously on the edge of their laying box until they fall to the ground—even when there is a ramp one small chicken talon to the right ... oh, or wings.

For all those reasons and more, I would never imagine one of our special Silkies could become a model for standing one's ground.

Allow me to set the stage with a little backstory. Kaiser loves to chase. As a young pup, cats and chickens were his favorite chase subjects. We have both, so imagine his thrill at the good fortune awaiting him in his furever home. We were more than a month into Kaiser's life with us, and he showed no signs of halting his chase of the increasingly flustered and barely egg-laying hens.

On one of his many frantic chases, Kaiser had a particular chicken on a full-out sprint around the yard and back toward her coop. As they approached the enclosure, that chicken stuck out one wing as she drifted into the coop, strongly resembling a hood-sliding Bo Duke or a drifting race car.

[Despite the advice of early readers, I've chosen to retain those two similes for fellow fans of *The Dukes of Hazzard* TV show (not the unfortunate movie remake) and *The Fast & the Furious: Tokyo Drift*. If you've never seen either, I highly recommend both. Also, you should know: Daisy Duke is my idol.]

Back to my story: Shouts of "Leave it!" and "Index!" and carrying Kaiser back inside by the handle of his halter did very little to calm the repeated frenzied situation.

Our vet told us to leave them alone outside together. Often, humans' presence makes dogs more apt to chase and be imp-like. Whether that tactic would work or not, we weren't sure.

It was hard to want to push the limits too far when he would run them all around the yard and back again or corner them in one of the coops. Though he clearly had no intent to kill, his actions could cause such an unintended effect. Visions of exploding chicken hearts burst in my mind.

One day, Tony and I were outside. He was doing yardwork, and I was writing. The chickens were grazing, and Kaiser was stalking. One of our two Silkies was doing what she loved best—lying in the nesting box on whatever eggs the hens had laid that morning.

That hen had been known to forgo yard time to lay on eggs. She'd also been known to peck at Tony when he tried to retrieve said eggs. The downy yellow hen had shown some spice, but we were unprepared for the spunk she'd been withholding.

Bold and fearless, Kaiser strode into the coop which was empty of chickens save the lone egg-layer. With the confidence of a homecoming king about to invite the nerdy girl with giant glasses to prom, he walked directly to her, stuck his head in her box, grinned his grin and unwittingly unleashed the power of a Silkie pushed over the edge.

The miniscule hen fluffed herself up and somehow managed to kick out both legs and spur the dumbstruck pup in his bewildered face. She bowed up her chest at him and flailed her wings. Kaiser bolted away, tail tucked. He reached the patio and cowered beside me.

That Silkie may have been small and mostly dim-witted, but she  stood up when the eggs were on the line. She stared down the maw of a ravenous (actually, mischievous) Belgian Malinois and prevailed.

Kaiser has not dared to poke his head in her laying box again. As the months have gone by and he's matured, he has also ceased his incessant chasing, and our backyard has seen a time of mostly peace and coexistence. He still calmly herds them from time to time but only when he decides they're outside their appropriate or safe bounds.

The Silkie's fortitude reminded me what great things can happen when we take a stand in real life, no matter how small or quiet our voice may seem. When we call out the big dogs—the bullies—and demand accountability or correction, we may be surprised at the reactions and actions that follow.

I'm reminded of a particular news editor who was … unpleasant. He wanted to run scandal and intrigue and clickbait headlines before *clickbait* was a coined term. I had ethical, moral and *ick* issues with him and let my feelings wave.

Though I cannot remember the exact article or ethical issue his request presented, I do remember the day I stood up to him and explained why I couldn't, in good conscience, write whatever the topic was or do so in the way he wanted. He wasn't happy, but he didn't push the issue. At least I was heard. It helped that I also worked for two of the best, most ethical editors I've ever known, and they outranked him.

That was my first full-time job in my chosen career, and though my bosses and most of our newsroom staff were truly a dream team, I met several folks who considered journalism a man's world. Our introductions felt like hitting brick walls.

I experienced comments like, "So, you're the little lady's gonna be writin' about our fair town?" and looks that revealed I was too young, too naïve, too female to last long, let alone do anything resembling a good job.

You know what I did? I'll tell you what I *didn't* do.

I didn't get offended. I didn't cry. I didn't give up, pack up my recently bought house and go home. I didn't leap on social media (and wouldn't have even if it had been a bigger deal then) to complain about my mistreatment.

What I did was ... my job.

I did my work well. I did it to the best of my ability and looked for ways to improve. I wrote fairly and accurately with my readers in mind. I didn't steer clear of the tough issues, but I didn't set out to *get* anyone either—unless, of course, they deserved it.

And when I announced my forthcoming wedding and end date with the paper, the same fellows who looked down their noses at my arrival wept that I was leaving. One even snarlingly addressed Tony as "the fellow who's stealin' our little reporter from us."

Who knows what changes could occur thanks to a simple Silkie-sized squawk or stern but respectful refusal and a brave, though small, action like an intentional and forceful wing flutter or a fair and balanced news article.

Vignette Twenty-two

Of Birds & Basil

I'VE COME TO A POINT where I willingly admit a cold, hard fact about myself: I'm not the mothering, nurturing sort. I'm not fond of being needed or of forced caregiving.

Cases in point: every plant I've ever owned and my son's parakeets.

I should probably share about our family's expansion into the realm of indoor birds. Our son had been asking for pet birds for at least a year, probably more. He'd researched and saved his money and finally cleaned his disaster zone room.

We took him to a local pet shop where he talked to a fellow who walked around with a bird on his shoulder. Who better to answer questions about bird care, right?

Our son jotted down notes on what he'd need and how much it would all cost. A few days later, we returned with his wallet. He chose two parakeets—one green and one blue. Derrick and DJ.

DJ later became Coco when four eggs appeared—that was an eye-opening discovery. As squawky as the birds are, I'm not convinced they're not both females.

Back to the birds' homecoming: Our son set up the cage in his room, lined the bottom, carefully installed their water and food dishes and hung a perch, a swing and a cuttlebone. Out of the happy meal-looking boxes came the birds, and into their new home they went.

Since they reside in his room with the door closed (we didn't want to tempt fate or the canine and feline claws on the other side of the door), I almost completely forget about their existence. Their incessant chirping makes total amnesia impossible.

Months went by, and the need rose for me to step in and care for my grand-keets. Our son was about to embark on his annual week-long Boy Scout summer camp.

He meticulously walked me through each step of their care—the water changes and food process, the need to wake them each morning and put them to bed each night, which is simply uncovering and covering their domain with a blanket. He also asked me to be sure to water the basil he had just planted.

"You've got it! Don't worry about a thing!"

He didn't look convinced.

Camp day came. He was dressed in his Class As, and we were out the door with his giant camp trunk and backpack stowed in the van soon after 6:00 a.m. Hugs, reminders to tuck his shirt back in and goodbyes. I waved as I drove away.

That night, I put the birds to bed. The next morning, I woke them, gave them fresh water, replenished their food. I followed their daily routine until Thursday.

Thursday was a quiet day that began at 4:45 a.m. when Tony left for his 5:00 a.m. Jiu-jitsu class and I got up to write in the early-morning hours. The rest of my day was packed with prep and communication for my Logos and Mythos (LAM) Summer Reading Challenge, which I'd kicked off the Sunday before, and with final preparations for my writing workshop at the library the next day.

Late that night, as I lay in bed, thankful to finally be back there, I remembered: "The birds!"

It was too late to rectify my error, so while I lost sleep, they got extra—a full day extra. When I woke them early Friday morning, they gave me rather judgmental looks.

In my defense, I could have done much worse. I never once thought about that basil plant.

May it rest in peace.

joyerancatore.com/summer-reading/

Vignette Twenty-three

A Tale of Two Roosters

I KNEW VERY LITTLE WHEN we took on the role of chicken tenders—the caregivers, not the food. One fact I didn't know was not all the cute little chicks are guaranteed to produce eggs. Some have a different destiny.

Roosters are tricky creatures. Some have ferocious tempers; they will attack more than the hens they keep in line. Others can be more docile than the hens, but neighbors don't always view the little fellows as kindly as their owners do.

We ended up with one rooster in each of our first two flocks. I suppose that's pretty decent odds.

In the first flock, one of the Rhode Island Reds matured into Big Papi. He was a gigantic rooster. As he grew ... and grew and grew some more ... Tony decided keeping him would not be the wisest decision. Big Papi was showing aggression, and Tony worried he might hurt me or one of the kids.

Besides, a rooster as grand as Big Papi deserved wide open spaces and a larger flock to command. He went to live with some friends who have far more land and several larger flocks of chickens.

Last we heard, Big Papi had killed three other roosters and was the unrivaled king of the coop. Talk about living his best life.

Our second rooster was the polar opposite. King George was small, wimpy and adorable. He was a Silkie rooster.

Although the larger hens clearly didn't respect him and wouldn't allow certain rooster-specific antics, George kept order in his flock. If any of the hens fought, he'd put a stop to their bickering quick, fast and in a hurry.

The Silkie hens, Gabby and Kelsea, thought he was the best. In case you wondered, we named the Silkies after country music stars.

King George strutted as proud as a rooster four times his size. If Tony would approach, George would draw himself up to his full height and bow up at him ... until Tony scooped him up and had a face-to-face stare-down.

Unlike Big Papi, King George was a lover, not a fighter.

We would still have the little fellow, but we have neighbors. Most of our neighbors are delightful people, but everyone has *those* neighbors. The man declared that our tiny barely-rooster woke him every morning.

I have to interject that King George had a crow that wasn't nearly as loud as the hens' egg-laying announcements.

My husband is a far kinder person than I am. He strives to be a considerate, respectful neighbor. And so, King George went to live with another friend with more land and chickens and no petty neighbor.

While Big Papi took over and ruled his new roost, King George found himself in danger of worse bullying than Gabby and Kelsea received from the Wyandottes when they were left without their protector rooster. Thankfully, George's new owner fell in love with the little guy and gave him his own special area, free from harm from more alpha roosters (and hens, most likely) and close to extra attention and pets and snuggles from her.

We would have preferred to keep all our chicks, including the crowing ones, but we know the two roosters ended up in better places.

As I think back on my life and all the moves and changes, closed doors and unexpected opportunities, I feel a little like our roosters.

Given my way, I likely would have been content to stay in one small space, comfortable with the familiar. I would have been satisfied with not challenging myself and would certainly not have chosen to push myself beyond my comfort zone.

In a million imaginings, I would never have envisioned myself in bayou country, accepting frequent hurricane threats and embracing the culture and community of southeast Louisiana.

I never would have chosen many of the twists and turns that led me here. I certainly wouldn't have penned myself through the losses, the heartaches, the terrible mistakes that nearly cost me everything or the painful experiences where people's words and actions stabbed sharper than a tanto blade.

And yet, here I am, content as I ponder a great dichotomy of life. Life's worst hardships often bring us to life's greatest beauties. We can't have one without the other on this earth. In some ways, the bad enables us to better appreciate the good, and the tough times teach us lessons that lead to better days.

I'm reminded of the entire first paragraph of *A Tale of Two Cities* by Charles Dickens—a literary classic whose pleasure in its reading may be debated but its value in the canon of the Great Conversation is not.

> It was the best of times, it was the worst of times, it was the age of wisdom, it was the age of foolishness, it was the epoch of belief, it was the epoch of incredulity, it was the season of Light, it was the season of Darkness, it was the spring of hope, it was the winter of despair, we had everything before us, we had nothing before us, we were all going direct to Heaven, we were all going direct the other way—in short, the period was so far like the present period, that some of its noisiest authorities insisted on its being received, for good or for evil, in the superlative degree of comparison only.

Seasons of our lives can be considered in the superlative when we review them in their entirety—when we take in the good alongside the bad and acknowledge their close relationships. Such an exercise allows us to settle into the best of our times and express gratitude for all the worst moments that have led us there.

Thankfully, both roosters are living out their best of times, and I hope their worst of times is behind them. I can only hope the same for those I know and love, although I also know this life of contradictions isn't all there is. What awaits in the life to come is no dichotomy. It's simply the best of all.

Vignette Twenty-four

Humor Dances on Paws

I HAVE FOND MEMORIES OF watching *America's Funniest Home Videos* during my childhood. I recall the stitch in my sides and the ache in my cheeks from laughing so hard.

As an adult, I often catch a live version of that show since I'm surrounded by animals and kids whose humorous antics are typically unintentional—like the time Tolkien Cat got stuck behind Tolkien Author.

Allow me to explain.

My office has always been a corner of our living room/dining room/school room/kitchen/Grand Central Station. Over the years, I've shifted furniture and shelves and drawers around. I've switched old desks for new ones, repurposed shelves from other parts of the house and generally gone on redesign sprees from time to time to make the most of my tiny corner of the world.

The incident occurred when my two-tier brown desk faced the kitchen. Behind me was a white cubby shelf salvaged from my daughter's room. The shelf held all my books on writing and my most precious tomes—books by the Inklings. J.R.R. Tolkien's works have two cubbies to themselves. Of course, those are only my most prized. I have a Tolkien section on my shelving unit in my bedroom, and his core books also sit prominently on our fireplace mantle.

I digress.

Atop the white cubby, I set the red and black buffalo plaid cat bed I had bought for my sweet Tolkien Cat. I insisted he use it in my office area because I wanted him nearby. Unfortunately, my desk was too small for him to lay (if I were to accomplish any work), and he turned up his nose when I placed his bed on the floor. Also, Romy decided the cushion must be for her when it was on the floor and meticulously curled herself into the tiniest ball to fit mostly in it, resembling a canine version of fat-man-in-a-little-coat.

On top of the cubby shelf, the bed rested. Never mind it was too wide for the spot. I angled it just so in order for him to lay with all his main bits on a solid surface, which worked fine … until Tolkien needed to shift his snoozing position. After all, cats are level expert at avoiding bed sores and know to frequently alter their positions.

As I worked at my desk, a commotion scared the heart from my chest. I whipped around in time to witness a pitiful whiskered face with flattened ears and a tiny, grasping paw emerge above my Tolkien books. The cat bed crash-landed behind the shelf, and the cat hung on for dear life to his namesake's works.

After the initial worry that my baby might be hurt, I couldn't stop the laughter and didn't try. Thankfully, I had the presence of mind to pull up the camera on my phone and capture Tolkien's expression which had shifted from terror to confusion to pitifulness to resigned-then-resentful annoyance with my continued snapping.

I eventually moved the books so he could hop down. He ran and perched across the room, clearly peeved at me and the situation in general. He licked his rumpled coat and sought to regain his feline dignity but showed no leaning toward mirth.

Like Tolkien Cat, I struggle to laugh at myself. As much as I enjoy chuckling at another person's embarrassing moments, being laughed at ranks up there as one of my biggest fears.

I also loathe practical jokes. My birthday is April 1, no fooling. That joke stopped being funny around age four, so I don't find rogueries amusing—much to my son's chagrin. Every year, he looks forward to April Fool's Day and plans elaborate pranks, very few of which I allow him to pull off.

Good luck to his wife one day. He'll have a lifetime of pent-up pranking to unleash on someone more forgiving than his buzzkill mother.

I experienced what the color red feels like back in high school when I tipped over in my desk in the middle of Honors Algebra II class at the exact moment a group of cute older guys walked past. They paused and laughed—the slap-your-buddy-on-the-back kind of laughing. I closed my eyes and pled for the ability to open a portal to darkness and isolation in the slick floor beneath me.

Honestly, if not for my sweet teacher, Mr. Sanders, who swooped in and helped me up with the most genuine look of concern on his face, I'm not sure I would have willingly risen from my awkward position.

Thank God for kind teachers.

And ... I now realize I may have based aspects of some of the older men in my stories after him. I've got a soft spot for quiet old men. If they're grumpy, even better—though Mr. Sanders wasn't grumpy; precise, exacting and old school, but not grumpy. He was much like Senior in *Any Good Thing*.

As I recall instances of embarrassment in my life, I may have discovered the core of my concern: I fear looking or feeling stupid.

Now, I'm not the smartest person in the world, and I often get things wrong. I don't claim to know all things, but I fear being called out for saying or doing something downright stupid.

Tipping over in my desk wasn't stupid. Doing it and then being laughed at while in an unflattering position made me feel stupid, though.

Although … putting a desk with slick metal tips on its bottom atop a slippery floor is where the stupidity really rests.

Again, I digress.

I think my fears lie in a wonky version of imposter syndrome. I am a perfectionist, and I study and read and visualize and plan every aspect of everything I do to an obsessive degree.

The thought of being found unprepared or inaccurate or "stupid" in parenting, homeschooling, teaching, speaking, writing or anything else I care deeply about makes me shudder. I imagine being an unwilling participant in an *America's Funniest Home Videos* clip where I'm not laughing with the chortling masses.

I fear looking stupid so much that my imagination frequently runs away with me. As I visualize pulling into the tight parking lot of my kids' Jiu-jitsu school and backing into a spot, I envision the inevitable disaster—crashing into one of the deputies' cruisers. Lights and sirens blaring. Everyone inside staring through the full glass front. Laughter. Pointing.

As I write this, I emotionally prepare for the day someone who reads this—not a friend, more likely a peripheral acquaintance—asks, "Have trouble backing into any parking spots lately?" and follows their pithy question with a snicker.

Insert fake smile and laugh here.

I suppose that's the difference—acquaintances vs. friends. With friends, I don't worry about looking foolish.

Maybe I still anticipate the horror before something unfortunate happens, but true friends laugh with me and accept me—snorts and all. At the end of the day, the opinions of peripheral folks—the ones with the backhanded questions or compliments—do not matter.

In the company of friends, when I have fallen backward or up stairs or snorted—or admitted I thought a texted *OMW* meant "Oh, my word!"—I have had no tomato-red face or desire for a sinkhole to open beneath me. My smile and laughter are also genuine as my friends and I share the humor.

Visualizing scenarios in detail and feeling all the emotions that go with them, whether or not they ever happen, is one of my superpowers. The ability certainly comes in handy in my role as an author. In real life, such an exercise can raise my blood pressure or spike my cortisol levels to dangerous heights.

Instead of letting my imagination run amok, perhaps I can channel those powers solely to my writing. Maybe I'll more fully embrace laughing at my failings and unflattering moments one day. I doubt Tolkien ever will. I also doubt I'll ever coax him back atop that cubby shelf, which is why the dogs have taken over the little bed during my writing sessions.

Oh, and for others of my generation, when someone texts *OMW*, just know they're on their way. You don't need to text back *Oh no! What happened?* with proper capitalization and punctuation intact.

joyerancatore.com/any-good-thing/

Vignette Twenty-five

Part of the Flock

OVER THE YEARS WE'VE HAD chickens, Romy has come a long way.

With our original flock of chicks, Romy eyed them intently while drool dangled over her snout-lips. We always took great care when opening the birds' cage if Romy or Bentley were around. I never worried about Bentley eating them, but I thought he might bite at them if they bothered him. Romy, on the other hand ….

Our fears were not unfounded.

We had moved the first flock of chicks from our bathroom to the high baby cage on the back patio. While Tony was refilling their water, one of the two Cinnamon Queens made a daring break for it and leapt out of the cage and directly into Romy's waiting mouth.

Tony reacted immediately and stuck his hand in the dog's mouth to retrieve the tiny chick.

His hand emerged around the chick, but all I saw was blood. I doubted there was any way the tiny creature would survive.

Most of the blood turned out to be Tony's since he had thrust his hand in Romy's mouth as she chomped down.

We put Cinnamon and her sister, Sasha, back into the bathroom together overnight. We didn't expect her to be alive the next morning. When we checked on her, though, she was hopping around, happy as could be. We returned them to the cage with the other chickens.

As the flock grew, Cinnamon ruled the roost. She was always the most independent with the most spunk and yet she was also the most pet-like.

Once we moved the chicks into their larger permanent coop, Cinnamon waddled to the fence whenever Romy neared them. The hen would stare the drooling dog down. I swear she was telling her four-legged nemesis, "Bring it on!"

A few months before we had to say goodbye to Bentley, the dogs and chickens decided to coexist. I honestly don't remember how we discovered their amiability, but our backyard became an odd mix of canines and fowls grazing side by side—the chickens pecking at bugs and grass and the dogs nibbling on chicken excrement.

For months after we said our goodbyes to Bentley, Romy's face held a sadness I didn't think dogs could show. The chickens, though, kept her company after her buddy died, and she grew fonder of their presence.

Comfort after the loss of a loved one often comes from unexpected places. After losing my dear friend Casie, writing this book became a solace and comfort. I had never planned on writing a collection like this, but somewhere in the wrenching of my heart at that goodbye, a whisper through a windchime-laden tree told me I should.

Companionship can be found as well as comfort if we open ourselves to the opportunity. In times of darkness, we easily lose sight of people waiting in the wings to comfort us. They are there, though.

Casie and I met because of homeschooling. Several other homeschool moms we'd known for years came together more than once to cry and laugh and pour one out in memory of the woman who, we all agreed, was the best of us.

Sometimes we have to do a little seeking for our tribe, companions, compadres; other times, they've been beside us all along. My closest friend today has become that person, in part, because we linked arms along the gravel drive to say farewell to Casie together; though, we've walked parallel along life's twisty paths for many years.

Friendship has never been easy for me. In part, I was always the new girl, the ya-ain't-from-round-here-are-ya girl. We moved every three to four years, so I got used to saying goodbye and being the new girl again.

I don't remember witnessing a solid example of a deep, lasting friendship outside of the books I read as a child. Anne and Diana exemplified the best of those in *Anne of Green Gables*, and I longed to find a "bosom buddy" of my own.

Over the years, I had friends—lovely, Anne-and-Diana-like friends—in each place we lived, but the move would always come. Until my college years, I didn't have social media or email, and snail mail eventually lost its appeal. I'd move on; they'd move on.

It wasn't until my senior year of college when some friends opened my eyes to my defense mechanisms. They told me I was erecting emotional walls and shutting them out that year. I finally realized that's how I'd prepared myself for every move. Mentally and emotionally, I became accustomed to short-term bosom buddies.

I tried to stop the wall-building, to put off the armor and shields, to remain emotionally open, to understand that the next move didn't have to be the end of strong friendships. I continue to struggle with that tendency, though.

Somewhere along the way, I got into the habit of bringing battle gear to the start of companionships as well. Other friends have brought that fact to my attention in their truth-in-love manners. I keep struggles and dreams and curiosities and generally more close-to-the-heart thoughts veiled behind a steely armor. I am quick to help, to welcome, to check in, but rarely will I go deep in my conversations with anyone.

Talking about deeper matters makes me vulnerable, reveals my insecurities and weaknesses and means I may have to acknowledge issues I should change. I may even have to admit a need for help from time to time.

During the COVID lockdowns and following, I felt extremely inadequate as a mother. My kids had some struggles with friendships, and I was at a total loss about how to guide them. That's when I admitted to myself that I wasn't sure I knew how to be a friend.

Had I ever been the Diana to an Anne? I'd always tried to be the giver, never the taker; but had my seemingly selfless mindset actually been selfish? Was my determination to never ask for help the reason friends felt I kept them at arm's length and the reason I often felt completely alone, even while surrounded by people? Did I have any real, true, call-on-them-in-the-middle-of-the-night kind of friends? Was I that kind of friend for anyone?

I evaluated those questions as I entered my season of loss in 2022, and I came away with clarity and a better understanding of myself—the good and the bad—and of friendship.

Since the passing of my parents and Casie, I believe I've grown emotionally and as a friend. I hope I have anyway.

Part of that growth has meant guarding myself from leaping into new relationships like I used to do. While that sounds counterproductive, I'm learning not to barge into someone's life, shield held high, pretending to be invested in their lives while having no intention of showing them who I am behind a closed helmet.

Another aspect of that maturation is challenging myself to be more vulnerable in the few relationships I've found to be the most precious. I've worked hard to shed the armor and set down my shields in those situations.

I've also acknowledged a few truths. When I don't need to bare my soul to another person, I also don't have to steel up. I can be who I am without apology because I don't owe others an "I'm sorry" for being who I am. I also don't have to give everyone a reason for my opinions or decisions. We weren't meant to be everyone's cup of tea or bosom buddy, and that's a truth we shouldn't feel obligated to beg forgiveness over or explain.

We also don't have to remain entirely standoffish with people who aren't meant to be our tribe, but we don't have to braid daisy chains with them either. As an all-or-nothing person, I struggle with this concept the most.

Another aspect of growth for me has been the ability to cherish friendships from the past or with people I know can't be some of my closest friends. Just because distance or seasons of life keep us separated doesn't mean I can't find ways to reconnect or stay in contact from time to time. That all-in or all-out attitude I mentioned a moment ago doesn't have to dictate how I approach all my relationships.

Social media has one benefit—reconnecting with friends from long ago and far away and staying current on what they're doing and where they are. It's fun to watch their kids grow and remember how we were at their age. Locally, community or organizational activities allow me the opportunity to see others from time to time in person.

We can still be friendly acquaintances who, given a different season of life or place of residence, would likely spend much more time together. I don't have to feel guilty that I'm not more deeply invested in their day-to-day. I care for them and know they care for me. We don't have to check in daily or like every new post or have weekly heart-to-heart chats to prove we care.

While it is a joy to be part of their lives, even in small ways, I know we live in very separate places. We all struggle to keep up with the many responsibilities and relationships in our lives. For a long time, I labored under the guilt of not touching base more often with friends from all over. I finally cast off that burden because sometimes one of the truest forms of friendship is touching base on a whim with no feeling of guilt that it's been a year or more.

When we do have opportunities to reunite and reminisce, I cherish those moments and hope they do, too. When disasters strike or a need arises, we can be there for one another—and I hope we will. On the daily, though, I recognize our interactions will be less frequent, though no less important.

I am grateful to have a few actual "bosom buddies" now. They are the ones who I can be honest with, who will see my weaknesses and not run away or judge or condemn. I continue to be mindful of my tendency to reach for a shield or cover a flaw or avoid a hard topic, but I've seen the beauty of an armor-less friendship. I'm learning I can ask for help when I need it and share my burdens, even when they reveal my shortcomings.

While I am no relationship expert and have not magically become some mighty friend, I hope I've become a better member of my close-knit flock.

As for my backyard, whenever all the animals are roaming freely, dogs and hens make an interesting flock.

Cinnamon continued to rule the roost until her sudden passing in 2022. I doubt I could be as fond of any other chicken as I was of her. She would let us hold her and pet her, and she had a certain charisma that chickens rarely possess.

I had nursed her back to health during the aftermath of Hurricane Ida in the late summer of 2021. With a backdrop of fluttering clothes drying on the lines across our yard and a soundtrack of the ceaseless drone of generators, I coaxed water into the ailing hen and urged her to fight the sudden illness.

When my research led to the proper treatment of mites in chickens and kept the rest of our birds healthy, I thanked God for granting me wisdom to keep our flock intact. I'm not sure if her recovery or the restoration of our power relieved me more.

Cinnamon was a great chicken. Plus, she faced the fangs of the wild Romy and lived to cluck about it.

Life with the flock isn't all sunshine and mealworms. The silver-laced Wyandottes do not care for the Silkies. Since the Silkies are less than half the size of the Wyandottes (and far less intelligent), they didn't stand much of a chance in the pecking war that waged after we had to get rid of King George, the Silkie rooster.

The bullying in the cage got so bad, the little Silkies' backs were constantly scabbed or bleeding from their coop-mates' incessant pecking. Tony built a second smaller coop for the Silkies. Separately, their wounds healed; their feathers filled in; and they became much fluffier than they were before.

When the two flocks converged to free range in our backyard, bullying still occurred on a smaller scale. The little fluffballs had a champion, though. Romy would chase the Wyandottes whenever they bullied the Silkies.

Unfortunately, the Silkies haven't figured out Romy is their guard dog. She'll mosey up and stand between them, her nose to the ground, sniffing for whatever her feathered friends are finding to munch on.

As soon as the Silkies notice her, though, they streak across the yard with their ludicrous T. Rex runs.

Romy's sad puppy eyes remind me of melting chocolate drops as she watches them run from her. I swear, I can hear her say, "I just wanna be friends, guys!"

Sometimes the chickens are too busy pecking at bugs or dusting themselves in the garden to worry about the big brown dog in their midst. Those are the times I look out the window and see Romy standing with her head high and grin flashing, simply part of the flock.

Vignette Twenty-six

Where Wild Girls Gallop Over Dashed Dreams

I DON'T REMEMBER A TIME I wasn't horse crazy. I genuinely believe I was born with a whispered whinny in my soul and hoofbeats on my heart.

When we inherited two ponies from my oldest brother, John, I was young—nine or ten. Ginger, the mama, was a nutmeg brown Welsh pony with a blond mane and tail. Sadie was her fluffy, mischievous filly.

To say I was thrilled was an understatement. I finally had a horse—well, pony—of my own, and not just one but two.

I daydreamed about training Sadie as she got older, bonding with her and winning her trust so she'd have no fear of a saddle or bridle or anything else I'd introduce to her.

We boarded them at a barn owned by some family friends. Their ranch wasn't far from our home in Mooresville, N.C.—at least I don't think it was. My point of mentioning the distance is, I don't remember visiting often. I couldn't tell you if we had some sort of arrangement for them to be fed by our friends. I may not remember going often simply because we only had the ponies one year. My brother took them back once his family moved to a place where they could keep them.

I do remember asking to spend time with them. I also remember hearing "no" a lot, which could be a kid's selective memory. I also know I didn't have the kind of parents who would adjust their schedules for added activities like petting ponies. I can't imagine either of them sitting in the back of a van with the air running while tapping out a story on their laptops and waiting for a Jiu-jitsu class to end. (Guess where I'm writing this.)

While my memories of that time are scattered and potentially unreliable, they're filled with my favorite smells: leather, hay, sweet oats and horse. If they've captured that scent medley in a candle, I'll take two.

During that season, I also remember snip-its of hazy half-scenes: actions I witnessed, stories I overheard. As a PK—preacher's kid—I heard many things adults likely thought I didn't hear or understand. They may have been right about me not understanding, but I always heard.

Lovely, clearer scenes dance in my memories of that time as well: Learning to properly groom my ponies. Saying "my ponies." Sadie's fluffy fur and the feeling of oneness, of wildness and of belonging I experienced whenever I dug my fingers into her coat or rubbed my face in her pony down. Standing in awe at the advanced age of one of the other inhabitants of the barn and imagining what it would be like to have my own horse for more than thirty years—the bond we would share.

The ranch itself: It was the dream. Multiple pastures. Many horses. An obnoxious, lovable donkey named Number 7 who could be heard for miles whenever he hee-hawed. A dark, cozy, sweet-smelling barn. Two awesome dogs—Red and Blue. They were Australian Cattle Dogs—one red, one blue. Blue was the good one—the rule follower, the stately sentinel always at his post, despite being nearly deaf. Red was a mess, full of energy and mischief. Her three legs propelled her faster toward trouble than four could have. She was my favorite.

One of my most vivid memories was the day I rode Ginger around one of the big pastures. The grass was sweet, and the sunshine made it a deeper green than usual. Everything was tinged with yellow rays.

As we turned toward the barn, I noticed a flash of brown and whip of manes and tails out of the corner of my eye. Horses in the neighboring pasture—my memory shows a herd, reality was likely two or three—galloped toward our fence.

Ginger, spooked by the larger equines and their speedy approach and oblivious to the fact that a fence protected us from their stampede, bolted. My black and turquoise saddle—or was it brown, and my memory displays the saddle of my dreams instead?—slid to the left as rapidly as Ginger's hooves pounded.

I remember the world turning sideways, nearly upside down, as I slow-motion slid to the left with the saddle that must not have been properly tightened. My face drew nearer to the pistoning legs and hooves. And then, I let go.

The earth packed a punch as it absorbed my breath. I saw stars and considered what treatment would be for broken ribs. I cried—not in pain—out of fear for the well-being of my tiny pony whose fright morphed into terror at the saddle banging between her legs. Her panic fueled by the dangling contraption led her careering directly into a metal gate.

She was okay—though I think she was a bit banged up. I was okay physically, though I replayed that afternoon a million times. My imagination has always been vivid. I suppose I can call that training for my future as an author. In my redo, I hung on and used my legs to right the rogue saddle mid-gallop. I calmed Ginger, steered her away from the gate and saved the day.

Time galloped away, and Ginger and Sadie went back to my brother. I remember the searing heat of my anger when my dream was taken away. I was mad at everyone around me and carried that anger for a long time.

As with every emotion, my rage eventually subsided. Life went on. We moved to Grenada, Miss. I grew. My horse craziness did, too.

Fast-forward a few years: at night, when I was supposed to be sleeping, and during the afternoon when most kids would be watching TV, I was on my bed pretending my pillow was a black stallion.

We won races and jumped our way to perfection and a grand cup. I became an expert in posting, though I still have never sat in an English saddle. Every trip to the library, I came home with book after book on how to train horses, how to groom horses, how to jump horses, how to ride horses, how to heal horses. I read horse encyclopedias cover to cover and could recite factoids about every breed and identify each one from the other side of a pasture. I memorized every part of a horse's anatomy and every piece of their tack.

I envisioned saddling a horse so many times, I guarantee I could have done it blindfolded, if I'd had the chance.

As I got older, I designed my dream horse barns. I planned my future as a jockey or trainer or groom or barrel racer or show jumper or star of the magical schools of dressage in other countries. I filled notebooks with my research and plans for how to earn money to buy a horse, tack, food, boarding—even a truck and a trailer. I made five-year plans and ten-year plans.

My father encouraged the planning, which led me to believe that if I strategized with enough researched detail and a promised commitment to hard work, my dreams would become true.

They never did.

Around the time I recognized the encouragement for what it really was—an adult's amusement at a child's enthusiasm—I began to view dreams differently. I kept my dreams and wishes to myself and the first star to the left. I hid my drawings of ranches and rough renderings of Arabians. I learned that rarely in life do dreams come true, no matter how much I wished them or how willing I was to work for them.

Dreams belonged to the whispers of the night and mists of the heart. They were smoke and mirrors. I didn't stop dreaming—that would be like roping wind for an imaginative being like me. I simply denied knowing my dreams when around others.

Over the years, I improved at denying dreams and learned to bury them from myself as well. It's easier to smooth the dirt and toss the shovel than to stand beside a gaping hole and feel the ache of a desire laid to rest.

More recently, I've uncovered some dreams and claimed them publicly. I declared them mine and expressed my plans to achieve them, then I shared them with others.

Now, I'm an award-winning published author. I may not be a household name and may not make any money from my words yet, but I'm speaking my dreams into the wind. As I declare and plan and take hold, I see dreams becoming reality.

If it happens once, twice, could it happen again? How far can the wind carry my words? What other dream pieces—like a hopeful girl atop a black stallion—could be blown back together and mended with renewed hope and faith in the power of dreams?

Vignette Twenty-seven

The Little Editor

WRITERS WITH CATS NEVER WORK alone. We have a built-in support system, critique partner and demanding editor. Of course, we also have a comforting companion-in-fur.

Cats gravitate toward the written word: a bed of books, smooth papers on which to rest their paws during nap time, a computer keyboard to sit on as they ponder the next great American novel.

Tolkien has committed himself to keeping me on my proper task, whether that is writing, revising, editing or any of the other million hats I wear as an indie publisher.

I often catch him sitting at attention on the rug by the front door, staring. He's not mindlessly staring; he's staring with purpose—intent on conveying the message that I've been dilly-dallying long enough. It's time to work.

When I pour my coffee or brew my tea, he follows me to my workstation. If I head to the office chair at my desk, he bounds ahead, leaping atop the desktop and around the L-shape to sit and observe my setup before claiming his supervisor's chair. He either lies beside me to look out the window at the chickens pecking around the yard, behind me from his perch on the top of my old chair or in front of me atop one of my printers.

Tolkien has also been known to lay in my lap or nestle beside me in the chair. In fact, the first time he sat in my lap was in my black leather office chair soon after the surgeries to remove his teeth. My eyes may have teared as I took his attention as a feline thank you for ridding him of his excruciating pain and for giving him a home.

I don't always work at my desk. If I use my lap desk and laptop, Tolkien sinks into the arm of the sofa or snuggles as much on my lap as the computer allows. If I write from the coziness of my bed, he curls against my legs and sinks into the blanket's warmth while I type away. Clearly, he deems me incapable of focused work without his keen supervision.

Of course, he can also be a hindrance to my progress.

Have you ever tried to type when a cat rests on your keyboard? Or continue editing when a feline lounges on your unmarked stack of papers in desperate need of red ink? Or visualize a tricky timeline when the little bugger perches in the middle of all the scene  notecards you've carefully arranged on your dining room table? Or finish research when the furry menace insists on lingering on the open stacks of books?

Tolkien also has a sneaky side to him and a conviction that the desk chair actually belongs to him. The second I stand, he'll leap into my seat. When I try to move him, he becomes an anchor.

How do cats make themselves weigh three times their actual poundage when they do not wish to be moved?

A time or two, the imp has given me a menacing hiss. I'll nudge him over so we can share the seat ... which means I can sit lopsided while he digs his claws into my back. The crosses cat lovers bear for the comfort of their cantankerous babies.

In addition to being my Little Editor, Tolkien is adept at being a conscientious headmaster. When we begin school each morning, he observes and makes sure everyone sits where they're supposed to and has all the supplies they should and pays attention to the teacher. He performs the last task as best as anyone—human or feline—can when it comes to teenagers and their focus on something other than a screen.

People likely laugh and roll their eyes when I talk about my Little Editor and how he keeps me on task. The truth is, he does.

I don't always want to put in the hard work. I would sometimes rather binge-watch a show or play a logic game on my phone than write or revise or edit, especially when I've reached a tricky spot or a place where I have to dig deeper or unearth painful emotions. I believe Tolkien reads my thoughts because those are the times he's by my side, motivating me to plant my butt and move my hands and open my heart and mind to the necessary words.

He was present for pretty much every memory of the emotional months of writing, rewriting—and rewriting some more—*This Good Thing*, my smallest yet most emotion-packed book.

Most of my memories of the drafting of my first novel, *Any Good Thing*, include Tolkien in my lap during my magical middle-of-the-nighttime writing hours. The still quiet of the house was filled with the warmth of his body and the comfort of his breathing while I typed my way—one word at a time, one paragraph at a time, one scene at a time—to the completion of my first full-length book of fiction.

At that point, I had already written a couple of picture books and a narrative nonfiction book. Fiction is somehow more real and true and terrifying, though. Imagined tales are conceived in the depths of the soul, grow in one's heart and mind and are birthed from trembling fingertips; and, more than most mediums, they will be criticized, critiqued, questioned and—by some—discounted.

Will the story resonate with readers? Will they love my characters as I do? Will they criticize the word choices, plot choices, character actions? Will they understand why I wrote a character a certain way? Will they recognize the heart behind the motivations? Will they care at all?

These questions—and more—accompany every book, every story … every word, lovingly crafted and cautiously released.

Companionship, motivation and support enable me to persevere on this author journey. Tolkien Cat knows my needs and provides them. He continues to do so with each new project, every story, every rendering.

With my Little Editor alongside, I'm never alone in my writing, regardless of the critiques, the crickets or the questioning that comes from without and from within.

joyerancatore.com/my-writings/

Vignette Twenty-eight

Butt Scratches & Neediness

WHEN BENTLEY WAS STILL ALIVE, we knew his likes and dislikes. He made them clear.

He loved to lick people. He didn't really like to be petted or doted on. He didn't like chaos. New people and situations stressed him more the older he got. He loved cheese crackers. He tolerated Romy's incessant need to use his butt as a pillow.

Most of all, though, he loved butt scratches, and I was his favorite person to provide them.

Whenever he got the chance, Bentley would back up to me and look over his shoulder, tongue hanging and look impish. I always knew what he was asking for.

Scratch, scratch, scratch.

Scritch-a, scritch-a, scritch, scratch.

He'd lick the air and display a look of perfect bliss for as long as I was willing to scratch his fluffy rump. His contented air-licking and his frequent returns for more provided evidence of his appreciation.

Everyone who spent more than a moment or two in our house knew how much Bentley loved his butt scratches. Every time he enjoyed his special attention, Romy sat nearby, observing. She never approached for her own scritches. She just watched.

A month or so after we said goodbye to Bentley, Romy approached me with a slightly sheepish look. She turned around and presented me with her backside. To make her request clear, she looked back at me. If ever a dog displayed a look of trepidation, in that moment, Romy did.

I proceeded to give her scratches like I used to give Bentley. She attempted the air-licks and made a determined effort to show the joy that used to emanate from her dearly departed buddy.

Attempted being the key word.

After a few seconds, I stopped. For Bentley, that session would have been far too short, and he would have backed into me with enough force to convey his demand for more. Romy, however, turned around to cast genuine gratitude in my direction before happily prancing away to pounce on her chew-chew and carry it to her bed where she spent the next quarter hour happily gnawing on the nylon bone.

Many days, she repeats the process. I know she'll only be content for a second or two of scratching, but she always shows her thanks before trotting off to a more Romy-preferred activity.

I believe that dog considers her requests a service to me to keep our memories of Bentley alive. I was his butt-scratcher. She doesn't want me to feel unneeded.

How many times in life do we seek ways to be needed? Is it human nature? Is it woman nature? Or, is it a desire not everyone shares? I'm not sure.

Many women struggle with a feeling of not being needed once their children are mobile and independent or when they start school or when they move out of the house.

I'm not one of those women.

While I appreciated the feel of a baby in my arms when both of mine were tiny, I reached a point where the constant physical contact and neediness left me looking for respite.

By the time my poor husband would arrive home in the early years of our parenthood and reach to touch or hug me, it was all I could do to keep from punching him away. Clearly, I have a threshold of tolerance for physical touch and being needed.

I also do not fear or dread the empty nest like many people I've heard do. My husband and I have plans, let me tell you!

As much as we love our children, we're of one mind that we've been raising them and training them and pouring into them so they can one day spread their wings and fly into their own lives. We're excited to see how they soar and to watch where they choose to land.

We're also eager to travel—maybe even internationally—or to stay in instead of running here, there and everywhere. A huge dream would be to finally own land where the dogs can run free and we can host large gatherings of family and friends—maybe even large enough to build a retreat center.

I want to learn more languages—Gaelic, Italian, Elvish … maybe Greek or Hebrew if I feel particularly energetic. I always planned to take up a couple of new instruments: the cello and the harp. Life with RA has adjusted some goals. While those desires remain on my list, I may not be physically able to achieve them.

Of course, I also intend to write many more books and stories. I want to invest in the literary community—local, regional, national and international—more than I'm able to now.

As I consider all my plans, I honestly look forward to the time when I'm no longer needed 24/7 and can do what I want, when I want.

Repeatedly in my life, I've held responsibilities—many I never sought out—that, after a season or so, I longed to push away from me. The feeling of being needed constricts me to the point I think of those obligations—and the people within them—as pythons squeezing the breath and life from me.

Every time I've walked away from some role that relied heavily on needing me, I've done so with relief.

Now, I don't think of my children as pythons. I don't want to kick them from the proverbial nest. I simply don't possess a need to be needed. Truthfully, being relied upon by others scares me and always has. The amount of situations I have no clue how to handle and the number of questions I can't answer are staggering. The fact that my kids have survived my mothering should top the list of the Seven Wonders of the Modern World.

Even after they soar, my children will continue to need me. I know that, and I'm fine with that. Honestly, I embrace the new needs that will come as they grow. They will seek advice. They will need a helping hand with decisions, moves, weddings and children. I intend to be there, a willing hand to scratch whatever itch they may discover.

The rest of the time, though, I will be exploring new experiences, opportunities and passions, unneeded … for the most part.

Perhaps we are always needed and like to be needed, even if the one who needs us makes funny faces back at us in the mirror or isn't entirely sure they want the needs they've asked for. Regardless of the need-related situation or the people involved, gratitude will likely be shown from both sides.

Take butt-scratching time—I admit a deep appreciation for the memories Romy and I share in those scattered few seconds. I can't help but wonder … which of us is the needy and which is the need-giver?

Vignette Twenty-nine

Heroes Among Dogs & Men

ANIMALS POSSESS REMARKABLE INSTINCTS, including their abilities to sense the needs of a situation, especially when danger lurks outside human view, and to provide the necessary protection and care. I witnessed that instinct in action during a campout with my daughter.

One month before my daughter's fifth birthday, she and I joined American Heritage Girls, an organization that emphasizes character building, growth in relationship with God, service to community, honor for country and love for family while earning badges that develop life skills and making memories in activities like camping.

Our troop has a special relationship with a wonderful man who has spent much of his life as a Boy Scout Scoutmaster and owns a peaceful property where troops are invited to camp. We have been camping on his property almost every year for thirteen years. Talk about memories!

Especially in the earlier years of our annual stays, the owner and his neighbors had a passel of dogs among them who served as a furry, tail-wagging greeting committee. One neighbor dog stood out from the pack.

He was huge and shaggy with white fur, perhaps a Great Pyrenees. As you can imagine, a dog with a thick coat that color in southeast Louisiana appeared more on the yellow side most of the year and on the brown side during the muddy months.

The heat didn't slow him down, though, and he was usually the first to greet our troop of chattering girls and learning mamas. He'd trot into our camp during tent setup and make the rounds to greet everyone. Before long, the moms would be dripping with sweat; the tents would be up; the girls would be crowded around the dog; and he would hold his head up proudly, a smile on his snout, as he dutifully accepted the hugs and pets of his adoring fans.

We didn't know his name, so the girls dubbed him Snowball, which transmuted to Schneauxball. Years later, we learned his real name—which I cannot remember—but Schneauxball he was to us, and Schneauxball he will always be.

Often, we'd be one of multiple groups enjoying the beauty of the property on our chosen weekend, but Schneauxball always preferred our group of girls to any group of boys—Scouts or Cubs. Most of his time would be spent in the middle of the action at our campsite, and, more often than not, he'd be surrounded by his groupies.

He accompanied us on hikes, oversaw badge work and gratefully accepted rewards at mealtime.

My daughter was a little older, probably fifth or sixth grade, on an especially memorable campout. I had staked my camo pup tent between my friend Casie's tent and our group of noisy, chatty, too-cool-for-sleep girls.

I have no idea what time the girls finally passed out, but not long after peace finally fell in our little wooded grove, something shattered the overdue stillness.

Some sort of creature was tramping through the woods around us. I don't know what it was, but the substantial noise raised images of wolves, bears, Rougarous. Bandits, rogues and outlaws also came to mind.

After a few moments of sheer terror in which I gripped my skinning knife and mentally role-played a scenario of how I was going to take down the intruder before it could reach our girls, a crashing stampede echoed through the underbrush. The commotion was accompanied by rumbling growls and threatening barks.

Schneauxball to the rescue!

The scuffle intensified, and I felt the tension—heavy, thick. My short, shallow breaths may have been because of the action outside my thin fabric walls or the humidity ... or both.

Suddenly, with finality, quiet fell. I heard soft paw-steps and sniffs here and there around each of the tents. And then, I heard a heavy body settle right outside my tent flap.

A few hours later, the *drip-drip-drip* of dew plopped from our tents onto fallen leaves and the sun peeked over the nearby lake. I rubbed the sleep from my eyes and unzipped my tent flap to reveal a scene I'll never forget and will always recall with a smile. Schneauxball still lay right there, head up and ears alert, ready to defend us again should the need arise.

He stayed nearby the following night, but I never heard the mystery invader again. Our furry hero had valiantly defended us and successfully vanquished our invisible, monstrous foe.

Many people are blessed with similar fantastic instincts and proclivities toward heroism. Schneauxball reminds me of the many chivalrous men who remain active participants in my life or who have passed through at some point.

Those who've appeared in small scenes of my life's story have opened doors, nodded and gestured for me to enter the grocery aisle first or reached the top shelf when they witnessed my hopeless attempts at reaching my preferred chai tea.

The knights who've held chapters or longer sections have encouraged who I am as a woman. They've guided, guarded, championed.

Some reminded me I never have to face monsters alone. One day at *The Mississippi Press* in Pascagoula, Miss., a disgruntled citizen stormed into the office, demanding to see me. Something I had written offended him, and he was there to get in my face.

I couldn't tell you why the man was upset or what I had written. I do remember his tomato-red face and the rage and malice in his eyes. I can still feel the racing of my heart and the pooling sweat in every creased spot of my body. When I close my eyes, I picture the reel of rage-induced violent crimes from the news that played through my mind in the few seconds before a hero stepped in.

Not all heroes wear capes or uniforms; some lean on crutches yet stand taller than many able-bodied men.

Our managing editor, Paul South, was the kind of man who took up the pain of people around him, who stood fast to causes he believed in and who would charge into the gaping mouth of danger to protect someone he cared about.

Paul hoisted up the crutches that enabled him to walk faster than most men without cerebral palsy and took his stand on the front lines in my defense. I watched in horror from my desk, directly in the sightline of the irate and irrational intruder, as Paul diffused the situation, talked the guy down and out of the building and called the police to report the threat.

While I was deeply shaken by the incident, I was more stunned and humbled at the immediate defense my boss leapt to provide, with no thought for his safety.

Other protectors have been lifelong influencers for me.

My three older brothers—John, Jim and Justin—have provided their share of teasing but also instilled confidence in the promise that they're only a call away. They've reminded me of my worth and held me when I've cried. Multiple times throughout the years, they've each stood up for me to a person I know it wasn't easy for them to take a stand against. While much of our lives have been lived at a distance, they've always watched over me.

One other knight in my life co-stars in my story. My husband, Tony, has encouraged me to write, even before Day One of this author journey. He has witnessed the reality of how I write because I can't *not* write. He has been a primary voice reminding me of that fact and encouraging me to just write. He has read almost everything I've written, regardless of what else he had going on. He's given me insightful feedback and helped me remain true to who I am and to what stories I want to gift my readers.

He attends book signings and festivals on days off—or days when he has to work later or just finished a stressful shift—and listens to my brainstorming and ideas and frustrations and concerns. He embraces my meandering ponderings about fictional characters who are more real to me than most living, breathing people I encounter and helps me make them come alive for others. He even joins me in pondering what fire faeries might look like and how they would act as we sip bourbon and gaze into the flames contained within our chiminea.

Where many men would discourage or dishearten wives who pursue a passion that will likely never bring in much money, Tony has urged me to persevere on the days when I was ready to throw in the pen. He has reminded me that my words are worthy of readers and valuable enough to be added to the Great Conversation of literature that is as old as written language. He reminds me that the ability to tell stories is a gift from God, and we discuss how I can best use that gift to bring honor and glory to the Creator of creativity.

He also tells others about my books and writings. His pride in me and my work floors me time and again and gives me emotional moments where I am overwhelmed with how much I love that man and how thankful I am for his co-role in our book of life.

Tony gives selflessly of his time to our children, serving as an Assistant Scoutmaster in our son's Boy Scout troop and pitching in to help with our daughter's AHG badgework when needed.

He added to his example of service when he took on the role of reserve sheriff's deputy. He completed the same training and met the same requirements as full-time deputies, while still working his full-time job. He puts his life on the line every time he goes on patrol or keeps the peace at parades or other local events. He is an unpaid volunteer, committed to keeping our family's community safe and shielding innocent citizens from danger.

I am thankful my son has these examples and more to look to in a world that screams from all sides that who he was created to be is a mistake and "toxic." He will grow to be a knight as brave and gallant as those who've shown him how.

Some people in our culture downplay the unique roles of men and women, especially with how they co-exist and complement one another. I embrace our roles and thank God for the beauty of His creation's design and for the instincts He's given us—instincts to sense danger or to trust.

Always, I will smile and express gratitude when a man holds a door for me. I will forever be grateful for how my husband has sweated, sacrificed and bled for us so I could fulfill my role as caregiver, as well as the added role for me to teach our children at home all the way through high school.

When I could have taken on a part-time job to bring in more income a few years ago, Tony encouraged me to pursue this crazy book dream and often gives much of his free time to enable me to produce another book or attend another signing or edit another client's work.

As I thank God for the masterpiece he formed when he created men and women and the roles we each fulfill, I am grateful for chivalry and honor in giant white dogs and giants among men.

Vignette Thirty

Who Says Cats Don't Camp & Families Can't Survive Close Quarters?

IF SOMEONE TOLD YOU THEY wanted to go camping with their dog, you'd nod and not think twice. If someone told you they wanted to camp with their cat, you'd call them crazy. That was my husband's response to me.

Our family loves to camp. Both of our kids are involved in scouting organizations. We've tent camped as a family. We've camped in a camper borrowed from my in-laws, and now we own our home-away-from-home camper.

Once we upgraded to campers, I decided Tolkien should join us. In my mind, I had no doubt he would love the adventure. The dogs would be fine with his presence, and we'd be one big happy family on the road like we are in our home.

I was right, though Tolkien isn't a huge fan of the travel aspect. He doesn't care for his little carrier or the motion of the truck ride or the commotion and waiting while the camper gets parked, leveled and hooked up. He's not a fan of the return transportation, commotion or motion either.

Once our house-on-wheels is fully functional and we settle in, Tolkien relaxes. His favorite lounging spot was in the camper we borrowed from my in-laws. The entire back wall of that trailer was a window above the slide-out which contained our bed.

Tolkien loved to lie there and survey his temporary kingdom. He would bask in the light of each blissful sunrise. He would crouch for more intent observation of the squirrels or geese scampering and waddling around our campsites. He wore the quintessential cats-rule-dogs-drool expression as he gazed at the dogs on their long lead ropes twisted into the ground. He taunted them with the air conditioning he enjoyed while they panted outside in the shade.

Our new-to-us camper isn't without special Tolkien spots. Beneath the kids' bunk bed is a storage area. We can reach it by lifting the bottom bunk or—more conveniently—from a small outside door. That's where we store our camp chairs, two-burner camp stove, kids' outdoor games and hammocks ... and Tolkien's litter box.

Despite his annoyance at and worry over taking a cat camping, Tony created a special cat door for my baby to go to his secluded space.

Tolkien spends most of the day in his hidey hole since we're frequently in and out and causing commotion. When our disruptions calm down, though, he'll lie in the sunshine on top of the velvety blanket at the foot of our bed.

When we leave the solid door open with only the screen door latched, Tolkien sits primly on the doormat, observes the activity around our campsite and sneers at the dogs whenever he can. At night, he explores the camper, annoys the dogs and sniffs around for anything he can get into.

In the camper, he's much more likely to snuggle with me at night than when we're at home. I love his soft warmth and snuffing breaths.

Unlike Charlie, Tolkien doesn't have an audible purr. In fact, unless I lay my head against his stomach, I will never hear him. While

I miss being purred to sleep, I appreciate the special moments when Tolkien allows me to rest against him and listen to his steady rhythm.

Camping—in my opinion—is the best type of family vacation. Except for the travel to and from and the set up and break down episodes, it is most relaxing. Technology is limited. The outdoors are wide open. Cooking is a family endeavor, and s'mores around the campfire elicit conversation and instill memories.

Add animals to the mix, and you get built-in entertainment.

I'll never forget the first camping trip when we all went—my in-laws, their giant Catahoula Leopard/black Labrador Retriever mix, the four of us, our two big dogs—Bentley and Romy—and my Tolkien Cat. Our unusual caravan made quite the sight, I'm sure.

The red diesel pickup with the giant fifth wheel and boat in tow was followed by our gray pickup with Bentley riding shotgun, the bikes and grill in the truck bed and the smaller camper trailing behind. Our van with Romy bouncing about and Tolkien Cat howling his annoyance at his cramped quarters brought up the rear.

I'm sure the image didn't get less odd when we took our menagerie on walks around the campground. Bull—the shy pooper—would sniff out the most private and prickly bush, then he'd back his butt into it and shuffle a little farther before taking a dump.

Bentley and Romy had no such shyness about them. They usually pooped right by the road—bonus points for waiting until a car passed. And then, they stood there, tongues lolling, smiling while we scooped up their presents.

Those are the not-so-glamorous moments of pet parenthood. There are others.

I made a terrible mistake once when moving Romy's tie-down to keep her in the shade. Instead of clipping on her leash before removing the lead, I unhooked her and held only her harness. Rookie mistake!

Romy seized her opportunity to exact revenge on the ducks that had been taunting her all morning.

Ducks really are horrible creatures, quacking at the staked-down dogs and waggling their tails from their positions just out of lead-reach. They aren't as vicious as geese, but they're far more devious, as Romy discovered.

She bolted from my grasp and hit the lake at high speed. The ducks set sail, closer and closer to the middle of the lake. While both her breeds are built to swim well, Romy has never been as strong at or as fond of swimming as Bentley was—he was like an overgrown beaver.

Romy kept up pretty well, though, until the ducks turned the tables. Once they reached the exact middle of the lake and the canine looked like she might catch the foul fowl creatures—what she would have done if she had remains a mystery—they flapped their wings and lifted high into the air in perfect unison.

Back in the middle of the lake, Romy doggy-paddled round and round in tight, confused circles as best she could, while realizing she'd been snookered.

I was less than useful in that situation because I am not a water person. I simply stood there yelling after her like an idiot while my father-in-law acted.

Thankfully, he immediately set out after them in his canoe. I honestly don't think Romy would have kept her head above water much longer had he not reached her when he did.

I held my breath as he tugged her into the wobbly canoe. She nearly capsized them and lost her rescue, but he expertly handled the frantic dog and the tipping canoe. Soon they were heading back to shore. My father-in-law was clearly the hero of the day, while Romy panted, worn-out and perhaps more aware of the dangers ducks pose.

That might have been the same trip she stretched to the very end of her lead and nearly choked herself to scarf down half our chicken—bones and all. She then ended up with most of our sandwich bread because we were worried about the bones. Dang dog!

It's no wonder Tolkien looks down on her and taunts her whenever he gets a chance.

Despite my tattle-tales on Romy, she surprises us with her overall good camping behavior. At home, Bentley was always the good dog; Romy, not so much. For whatever reason, though, camping reversed their roles.

If Bentley couldn't be right beside us—specifically, beside Tony—he would bark incessantly, especially if he could see Tony fishing in the boat. He did not like being separated without a way to reach his buddy. Any time another dog walked by—which happens often, since that is one of the draws to camping for dog owners—he would bark his fool head off. Camping, it seems, stressed him.

Romy, on the other hand (and aside from those two stories of her impishness), becomes a model dog when we're in the fresh air. She soaks everything in: new scenery, new people and dogs, her people nearby, the chance of eating a dropped piece of something tasty or reaching leftover morsels in the trash bag or licking up goose poop, which tends to be plentiful at waterside campsites.

We miss Bentley. He was the first pet Tony and I chose as a married couple. He was our sweet, nervous old man. Loyal and kind, protective and soothing, he was the best dog. He was a comforting guardian in our tent-camping days. We miss him every day and all the more when we roll out for a campout, despite his bad camping manners.

Kaiser is no Bentley, of course. As of this writing, he has only been camping once. Honestly, that experience is not a fair evaluation of the type of camping dog he will be.

After Tony's eight months of P.O.S.T. Academy two weeknights and one or two weekends a month, our family was ready for a vacation and time together.

We chose a resort campground—a first for us. Trees and lots of them are our typical chosen retreat. For another change in plans, we decided to leave Tolkien at home since we hadn't had Kaiser long, and they still played Tom-and-Jerry at full speed around our house.

The campground had a lake with canoes and paddleboards, a lazy river, two pools, miniature golf, basketball and pickleball courts and much more. They also boasted a dog park. The complex sounded like a special treat for the whole family.

We rolled in on Labor Day, eager to enjoy the place mostly to ourselves for the rest of the week as the families of kids in brick-and-mortar schools left.

Unfortunately, the website's reference to all the amenities as year-round was not entirely accurate. We arrived in time for the cafes and swim-up bars and ice cream shop to be closed during the week. Paddles for the canoes and paddleboards lining the beach were kept under lock and key.

Unexpectedly, Tony had to drive home twice during our short getaway. On top of those changes to our plans, a vicious storm whipped through. We contemplated cancelling when we saw the warnings, but we would have lost our money.

Despite the unforeseen challenges, we had enough fair weather to enjoy all the open outdoor activities. We focused on those opportunities and tried to overlook the parking lot nature of the campground itself. Though we are unlikely to stay at a campground like that again, we made memories and found the rainbow through the clouds.

Kaiser, however, failed to see the attraction.

He was away from his comfy dog bed and backyard. Whenever he went outside of the tiny camper that was awfully close to the size of the kennel at the pound, he had to be on the leash or a tie-down.

And the dog park? Forget about it!

The park was clearly constructed for purse dogs, not canines that can run up to 35 miles per hour. Add in the rain that kept him inside most of the second half of the trip, and he may not be too eager to load up for the next camping adventure.

Despite Kaiser's initial reaction, I am eager to head out again with all the animals. Now that he and Tolkien have a better relationship, I think we'll be safe to keep our entire family together. I also believe Kaiser will love real camping—the kind we usually do. We need to look for a campground with a real dog park, though. Belgian Malinois need to stretch their paws and chase a ball, untethered.

Housing three animals, two near-adult kids and two adults in a small camper challenges us. At some point, the teenagers will bicker and complain about the tight quarters of their bunk beds. Tony and I will search for a countdown app to when the kids will move out, and the animals will snap at one another over a stepped-on paw or imagined special treatment.

Challenges aren't always bad, of course. They grow us individually and draw us closer together.

Thankfully, our camper is a sufficient size and proper layout for our family. We are grateful for finding the right one for us. Each kid gets a bunk bed—though our son may have completely outgrown his as he's almost passed his dad in height. Tony and I have a surprisingly comfortable bed. The table breaks down into another bed which is perfect for the pups, and Tolkien Cat gets to sleep wherever he chooses—curled up in his hidey hole on top of cushy hammocks, in the sun's rays casting across the top bunk or snuggled on my butt when I sleep on my stomach.

He's an odd cat, which I suppose we established already with the fact that he enjoys hopping around the camper comparing views from each window and adapting to wherever the road leads us.

Pets are like any other family members—they require time and patience. Time together rarely goes as planned, and a great deal of flexibility, understanding and love are required to manage conflicting personalities and strong emotions. Whether camping or keeping the home fires burning, time spent together produces memories worthy of the effort.

Vignette Thirty-one

Death Is an Invasive Species

ALONG THE GULF COAST AND around the bayous where I live, invasive species wreak havoc on our ecosystems.

Nutria rats—as cute as I think they are—eradicate native marsh plants that keep our shores intact. Wild hogs, with numbers closing in on a million in Louisiana alone, destroy our forests' plant life. Gorgeous water hyacinths with their floating blooms block life-giving sunlight from organisms beneath them.

Those three creatures have something in common: They shouldn't be here; they don't belong.

On the night I stroked two baby birds while they died in my hands, I recognized death as the most horrendous of invasive species. This world was not created with death, and yet death entered. Its repercussions blast concussive shocks over people and nature, disturbing peace and causing chaos.

As I revised and edited this collection, I noticed several of the vignettes hinge on some upheaval or interruption to my carefully planned life. I tend to mark the chapter titles of my life's story by the disruptions along the way.

By the end of each disturbance, though, I uncover some truth or recognize a need in me or around me that I can right or fill. Disruptions become opportunities.

A new opportunity-disguised-as-a-disruption occurred in the midst of initial revisions of this book.

We met my in-laws at the campground where they were celebrating my mother-in-law's birthday. We sat around the remnants of our shrimp po-boy supper and discussed taking a final walk on the beach before birthday cheesecake and the drive home.

Out of the corner of my eye, I noticed something flutter to the ground beneath the hitch of their fifth wheel. At first, I thought it was a bat. I adore bats and rushed toward the unexpected visitor.

As soon as I reached it, though, I realized the tiny creature was not a bat, but a baby bird. A hole inside the tongue of the camper contained the baby's four chirping and rustling siblings.

My son's small fingers and Boy Scout perseverance retrieved the other babies from their well-hidden nest, and my father-in-law scooped up the still-alive jumper from the ground.

The six of us set to work and soon had a paper towel-lined container to house the birds and a cooked and cooled container of scrambled eggs to feed them.

Back at my in-laws' home, a mama bird was scratching her beak and wondering what happened to the babies in the nest she thought she built in the safest possible spot.

Those same babies had been without their mother for at least 24 hours, so we coaxed and pried their little beaks until all five had at least a bite or two of food.

And then, my in-laws popped the lid on the eggs, handed them to us and said, "Good luck! Your turn!"

They'd rescued babies before—similar hatchlings, orphaned ducks and other unfortunate fowl. In fact, they had the same situation with an undiscovered nest in their camper a few years before when we were going camping ... also for my mother-in-law's birthday. They did most of the caring that time. That nest only had one baby, and my kids named him Skittles. I guess they were hungry when we found him.

Fast-forward a few years, we found ourselves in charge of the lives of five downy birdlets. We still had birthday cheesecake, but the final beach walk was completely disrupted ... as were our weekend plans.

Saturday: baby shower and pool party

Sunday: church and Boy Scout meeting

All disrupted, unless ...

OPPORTUNITIES.

My son took charge of the helpless creatures while my daughter and I attended the shower. We zipped home, changed and picked up boy and birds on the way to the pcol party.

Our church family chuckled at the party crashers and helped us listen for chirping. In between conversations with friends, I fed the open mouths while the kids swam and played.

"What kind of birds are they?" Three of the teen girls pulled out their phones to do a search. "Cowbirds?"

Memories made. Care for God's creation observed.

The birds went along for the ride to the gas station and then waited in the car while we fed the pig, cats and chickens at my in-laws' house. Back home, we took turns checking on them between video games, the Kentucky Derby and bingeing *Heartland*.

Sunday morning dawned, and all five babies were still alive. The rush of preparation for church included the teamwork required to make more eggs and scoop up the box and towels and heating pad.

Back in the van, the babies took another ride. When we arrived at church, the kids entered Sunday school while I headed to a quiet room across the hall.

I plugged in the heating pad, opened the eggs, got the tweezer ready to transfer food bits into beaked mouths and pulled back the towel to find ... one deceased baby.

The other four were eager to eat, though, and I was amazed we'd only lost one.

We had a special Sunday school time with all the kids and several of the adults in our church. It was the last time our teacher would lead. He and his family were moving and would be missed.

Our teacher shared wisdom from his years of coaching countless people from businessmen to juvenile delinquents. He gave us a template for how to approach challenges and obstacles in life, and we flipped back and forth in the Bible to find God's guidance for handling disruptions.

Already, I recognized the baby birds as the unexpected opportunities God had in store for our family that week.

The kids and I worked together to care for them. I fed them twice between Sunday school and church. My daughter gave them a mid-service feeding during the hymn right before the sermon. Both kids fed them while I helped serve cupcakes in honor of the family we would all miss.

And then, the last people were ready to leave, so—birds and garbage bags in hand—the three of us headed out. Bags in the can; birds to the van.

Back home, we situated the little ones in my bathroom, and I settled in nearby with my laptop and Tolkien Cat to mini-muse on the opportunities we would have missed without the disruption of a fluttering baby bird.

Lessons await in caring for helpless wildlife. Opportunities to serve neighbors occur when storms knock out power and extinguish lights. Growth and preparation fill times of transition.

Often, God sends fluttering disruptions to show us He has something far better for us away from our comfort zones. When we reach for something we once thought was too high or leap from our nest to soar (even when a disruptive nudge forces us to reach or leap), we may find ourselves face-to-face with the greatest opportunity of our lives.

No matter the outcome, disruptions will teach us, if we're willing to learn. Our episode with the baby birds didn't end the way we'd hoped, but it resulted in a pivotal lesson.

The four feathered babies were doing great—growing, flapping their wings, eating voraciously—until the sixth day we had them. I went in mid-morning to feed them and ... two of them were dead.

Since the other two looked okay, I fed them once more, covered their makeshift nest with a towel and disposed of their siblings.

When I returned to check on them, neither bird looked good. I tried to feed them, give them water. They were rapidly declining.

I realized I could do nothing to stop their inevitable deaths. I felt helpless and guilty and overwhelmed. I had no idea what happened.

The only change was a slight one to their diet on Thursday morning, based on some online information from a vet and/or rehabber. I immediately blamed myself for questioning the diet my in-laws gave us and following advice from the internet.

Another source of guilt was my anger from earlier that morning. I was tired. For nearly a week, I had been the primary caregiver for the demanding creatures. Do you know how often baby birds eat? I was tired and achy and grouchy. I may have uttered phrases like, "I wish we'd never found these stupid things."

A few hours later, they were dying in front of me. I watched as their breaths grew more labored. I stared, unblinking, to see if their tiny chests would rise again.

With tears blurring the scene before me, I watched as the remaining pair painstakingly pulled themselves toward one another. They leaned in, downy heads together, seeking mutual comfort in their distress. I decided all I could do for them was make sure they weren't alone. As their conditions declined, I took them in my palm, one by one. With a single finger, I gently stroked them and whispered, "It's okay. You're not alone."

I continued holding them for a few seconds after they each breathed their last. I felt horrible to have lost them, but I also knew they would have died much sooner had we not given them a chance.

The final weeks of my parents' lives remained fresh in my mind—the caregiving, the decisions, the anxiety. The shock of the sudden loss of my dear friend Casie returned to mind as well. Illness, deterioration, loss—they weren't part of how creation was designed.

Over the still bodies of two tiny birds who never got to spread their wings in flight, I grieved the existence of death. The reminder of its invasive nature, though, made me rise in hope because I know death isn't the end. Eternal life awaits us on the other side, where creation will be restored to its pre-death glory.

I will see all those I've lost again. We will be together for all eternity in heaven where no invasive species can ever creep in or take root. We will enjoy life as our Creator intended, and I expect to experience songbirds perching on my shoulder from time to time. What a joy it will be to watch them soar.

Vignette Thirty-two

On Cats & Aging

I've come to believe that, as we age, we become more cat-like. I'll present my reasoning, so you may evaluate the validity of my hypothesis.

- Cats loathe pushy, rude people.

- Cats are rarely willing to deal with people's drama and rudeness.

- Cats delight in annoying people who are easily annoyed, especially when they tend to be annoying themselves.

- Cats see no reason to do something they don't want to do, and no amount of prodding or cajoling or show of force can make them change their minds.

- Cats remain unapologetic for their finickiness.

- Cats live on their own timetables with their own agendas and see no need to adjust for anyone else's whims.

- Cats simply are who they are; they care very little for what others think of them.

Most of my life had been spent in constant worry over how others perceived me—what people may think I mean by what I say, how I say it or how my face looks before, during and after the saying. The fact that people's conclusions often veer widely from the truth could not dissuade me from my concerns. I didn't consider personal knowledge of the truth to be enough.

When I hit my thirties, I discovered freedom in no longer always caring what other people think to be true. In other words, I began my internal transition to Cat.

While a new decade gave me the genesis of less worry about such things, the subsequent years put me through something like a trial by fire. The result? A confidence that I can withstand the knowledge that other people believe wildly inaccurate things about me and spread those lies.

The lessons didn't stop there.

I grew to a place where I could rest—yes, actually *rest*—in the knowledge that I know the truth and the only people who matter know the truth because—more important than anyone—God knows the truth.

Reaching that peace and maturity took time.

One of the biggest trial-by-fire experiences that pushed me to become comfortable with who I am and what I believe to be right was triggered by COVID.

We were thrust into a fog of uncertainty. To quarantine or not quarantine. To mask or not mask. To vax or not vax.

I remember the day I'd been trying to hold everyone and everything together, but the dike walls burst. Tony caught me and all my free-flowing tears in his arms. I felt torn and jostled from so many sides with some people calling the disease a joke and make-believe; others fearing for their lives and claiming we'd all die; and still others who actually did almost die. I wanted to keep my kids safe physically but also emotionally and mentally and socially. I worried about the at-risk folks in our lives and carefully evaluated every person we chose to live life with.

Tony's job as a restaurant manager did not allow our family a true lockdown. He worked—and, yes, we were thankful for that great blessing—six or seven days a week, often twelve-hour shifts, for longer than was physically sustainable. He persevered, though, and we evaluated whether we should see his parents, our closest friends, anyone.

We debated masks for a long time. I chose to keep the kids and me in them for longer than most of our church family—not for us, but for the at-risk church members around us. We were far more exposed than most people to the world in general because of Tony's job and were also in the group with the most chance of being asymptomatic.

Most of my decisions were made with a carefully balanced combination of science, common sense and gut. I wish I would have leaned on that third aspect every time. When I did, I feel my decisions were right, whether they made sense to anyone—sometimes including me—or not. When I didn't, well, the flaring of pain in my forearms as I rapidly type these words and knowledge that underlying inflammation caused by the "vaccident"—a word I loathe as much as rude people—has added pain to my life's passion remind me of the danger of not listening to my gut.

I rejected several widely accepted aspects of post-COVID life for my family, and I'm thankful I did. I will never regret my decisions—whether I ever gain proof for their wisdom or not. I often acted in ways some found strange or even wrong, but I learned to stick to my guns—do my research, pray, talk with my husband, make the best decision possible for our family and then stand firm in any winds of disapproval.

That learned ability proved valuable because I continue to use it in all aspects of life. Over the years, I've had my words or actions or decisions questioned or even misinterpreted by friends and family. Such attacks would once sink me in a quagmire of depression and despair. Now, however, I remain staid in the decisions my family makes and rest easy in the knowledge of the truth.

While misinterpretations can sometimes still hurt, I recognize them as a part of life—a part that will likely reoccur ... perhaps from a cursory read of this book, likely of this vignette. I choose not to allow them to derail me or cause me to question my choices to an unhealthy extent.

Even without something as unexpected as COVID, challenges fill life. In the social circles I frequent, I'm often faced with people who seem to crave drama and appear to love nothing more than to distort an easily rectified situation into a complex and inescapable web of worry.

A few years ago, I would have jumped in with both feet and a pair of shears to snip at the web's anchors in an attempt to diffuse the situation, smooth rumpled feathers and restore peace in the kingdom.

No longer. Life's too short to stress myself out and pull from time and effort for my family and dear friends to try to fix other people's messes and missteps.

I now intentionally pull away from situations where I see the proverbial web spinning. If I've learned anything over the years, it's that people who love drama will always love drama as much as they love pulling others into it with them, while expecting those poor schmucks to set everything right. I want no part of that crazy, no matter what people think of me.

Now that I'm in my forties, I keep my distance from people or places that don't respect me or my family. Any kickback against my choices means I get to be a duck. Like I tell my kids, whenever others gossip about us or misinterpret our words or generally find ways to be mean or condescending toward us, we simply need to let their words and actions roll off our backs like water from a duck's.

I have progressed greatly in my transition to Cat. See my attributes for yourself and compare to the original list:

- I loathe pushy, rude people.

- I am rarely willing to deal with people's drama and rudeness.

- I—well, maybe don't "delight" in—but I wouldn't lose sleep over annoying people who are easily annoyed, especially when they tend to be annoying themselves.

- I see no reason to do something I don't want to do, and no amount of prodding or cajoling or show of force can make me change my mind—no matter how fierce a red gi would look on me as I step onto a Jiu-jitsu mat.

- I remain unapologetic for my finickiness—unless I have been unreasonable, which I can be.

- I prefer to live on my own timetable with my own agenda—and look forward to the day I can do so—and see no need to adjust for anyone else's whims.

- I simply am who I am; I care much less for what others think of me than I once did, primarily because I'm grounded in and confident in who Christ is and what He's done in and for me and what He's created me to be and do for Him.

Perhaps I have a little way to go to full Cat status. Although … you are reading this book. A few years ago, I would have been too fearful of people's thoughts to write such a book, let alone publish it.

I may be more Cat than I previously thought.

Vignette Thirty-three

Friends of the Best Sort

SOME OF THE MOST PRECIOUS bonding moments with friends have revolved around our pets. This book exists because of the influence of a friend who I will miss until we're reunited in heaven, where lions and lambs will lie down together and we'll never have to say goodbye to friends—furry or otherwise—again.

I will always remember the day I met Casie. She walked into our homeschool co-op, and I was immediately captivated by her striking blue eyes—the bluest I'd ever seen. They sparkled and shone and drew my attention from across the wide, busy entrance of the church building.

A close second in attention-stealing was Casie's smile: full of heart, genuine to its core and generous with all, with a touch of shyness fortified by determination—a visual representation of her character.

Her passing left a giant hole in our community and even more so in the hearts and lives of her beautiful family, including her precious, anxiety-ridden Basset Hound Hank.

Casie adored Bassets with their giant, floppy ears and droopy, mournful, soulful brown eyes. Who doesn't?

Lenny was her Basset baby when we met. I always enjoyed loving on him. He was soulful and Eeyore-ish, as every great hound should be. He loved to be petted, and he adored Casie. He wasn't the only dog who adored her, though.

Bentley may have loved Casie more than he loved me. You see, Bentley was the lickiest Lab that ever was. He loved, loved, loved to lick. Not everyone appreciates slobbery dog affection. Casie was not everyone. She welcomed his sloppy kisses with open arms and puckered lips.

Whenever Casie was set to visit, I would let Bentley know. "Mrs. Casie's coming, Bentley!"

His giant tail would clear the table, and his entire backend would waggle at the announcement. He knew her name and loved to greet her. He would cover her in kisses, and she'd pet him and give him butt scratches and generally spoil him rotten. And, she loved every minute of it.

Lest you think Bentley was a slobbery savage, he could control his tongue. Case in point: my other dear friend, Amy. Amy adores dogs as well. Her generosity abounds with pets and butt scratches, but Amy does not like to be licked ... at all.

After a visit or two with stern talking-tos from her, Bentley learned. From then on, when Amy would visit, he would frantically lick the air all around her as she scratched his butt. They had an understanding, and he loved her nearly as much as Casie ... nearly.

I'll never forget one time Amy and Casie were both at my house. Bentley went back and forth, vigorously licking the air all around Amy and then licking all over Casie as they both showered him with love, pets and butt scratches.

Animals' intuitiveness and the diversity of God's creation amaze me. Each friend I have been gifted with is unique. Each has her talents and quirks and unique personalities. Each has taught me something different and impacted me in ways only she can.

Casie taught me to embrace creativity in all its forms. She reminded me of the beauty in allowing a mess while the kids made memories and art. She taught me that slobber can always be washed off because the light of excitement in a goofy Lab pup's eyes would be worth it.

My Belgian Malinois appreciates the fact that I eagerly accept all of his exuberant kisses. Oh how Casie would have loved him, and Kaiser would have adored her!

When we met, Casie also had Edward. He was a chinchilla, which has to be the softest creature on earth. Edward was the most stately and sophisticated of chinchillas. His wee nose and whiskers twitched rapidly in the most distinguished way possible. For some reason, when I remember Edward, I always imagine him with a bow tie and top hat, sipping a cup of tea. He was definitely a dapper fellow.

We would watch his whisker twitches and chinchilla-y antics and chuckle. Casie's laugh would usually be accompanied by her nose scrunch and an unmistakable twinkle in those stunning cobalt eyes.

Casie exemplified how to be a fearless mama bear and a fierce friend. She fought the battles that mattered most, while more often serving as the chief peacemaker. We shared many joys and sorrows over the years.

During the final few years before we lost her, we didn't get together very often—a truth I will always regret. Casie's family had moved about forty minutes away—a distance that feels like nothing now that she's no longer in driving range. During COVID, we did video chat—interactions we both needed during that stress-filled time.

My sorrow over the moments I missed with her has reduced my use of the phrase "I don't have time" and changed my "We ought to …" to "Let's get together today."

When we did get together, though, no time had passed. We picked right up every time. We caught up on the burdens, the joys, the sorrows—our lives.

My animals were the same way. I'll never forget the time Romy met Casie. Two seconds after laying eyes on her, Romy leapt into my friend's lap and immediately sat down, like a toddler on Santa's knee. Her immediate reaction is another possible proof animals communicate with one another. I think Bentley had told Romy all about his favorite human. Perhaps Romy also knew with one glance—like the rest of us had—that Casie was a person to be adored.

Casie always cheered on my writing. She genuinely loved to hear me ramble about whatever story I was writing. I remember telling her about *This Good Thing* and her saying something like, "Oh my goodness! I don't think I could read that. I'd be bawling all the way through, but I'm gonna buy it anyway. How did you make it through writing that?"

Neither of us had any idea then that she would be saying goodbye to her three children way too soon. She didn't have a final full year, though, like Carolina did in my book. Casie's end raced up and snatched her away.

We shared a love of photography and spent time together behind our cameras. We taught photography classes in our homeschool co-op and took kids of all ages on photo expeditions in nature, at museums and in New Orleans. We took pictures of each other behind our cameras.

She took my author headshots, and that is why I may be 80 years old with fifty-year-old images of me on my book flaps. The thought of replacing her work hurts my heart. We were supposed to take new ones together, had discussed it, decided on "next spring." Next spring doesn't always come.

I miss my friend every day. When I see her beautiful children, I see her. I see her eyes, her smile, her joy and her life. I see her love for animals and commitment to friends. I see her legacy. And, every time, I walk away, allow the tears to fall and whisper, "They're doing good, Casie. You did good. I miss you, my friend. See you again."

My closing statement to her raises a glowing vision of a far greener field and brighter expanse than I've ever seen. Casie and I are laughing over teacups while Bassets, Labs and chinchillas scamper around us.

That's a future I eagerly await.

joyerancatore.com/this-good-thing/

Vignette Thirty-four

Party Hats & Paws

I SUPPOSE SOME PEOPLE WOULD consider birthday parties for pets ridiculous and unnecessary. I, however, find them fun and as much for the humans as the animals. Whether we know their actual birthday or not, celebrating pets provides us an opportunity to give thanks for their presence in our lives.

We were told Romy's exact birthday when we got her—December 14. Bentley came to us with a giant Valentine's Day stuffed bear and the knowledge that he had been born in February, so February 14 made sense for him. I was told a month for Tolkien as well, and I picked a date—March 16.

Kaiser came with an approximate age, which was altered slightly by our vet. Since the updated age landed his birth in January, we initially picked an easy-to-remember date, but instead of celebrating him with black-eyed peas and New Year's poppers, we chose to give him a day to himself—January 2.

When it comes to celebrating the pups, we splurge on peanut butter-flavored dog ice cream. They each get a cup, and the birthday pup gets a candle. Sometimes we don hats, and we always sing.

Romy's food aggression carries over to birthday parties. For one of Bentley's celebrations, Romy swallowed her ice cream whole and butted between Bentley and his bowl to down his as well. Her grimace as she frantically licked the air afterward proved she must have experienced a massive brain freeze.

We ushered her outside to recover while we gave Bentley another cup of ice cream. He hadn't gotten more than one lick from the first.

Since that incident, we set up barricades to keep Romy from repeating such savagery.

Where we get their ice cream, the cups come in packs of four. We felt no remorse in giving the fourth to Bentley a few days later—after putting Romy outside, of course. She knew he'd had a treat, though. When we let her back in, she licked his bowl and the floor around it for anything his thorough tongue may have missed.

In contrast to Romy's attack on the sweet treat, Bentley would take his time, licking slowly, like a kid with an ice cream cone. He never rushed but savored every drop. He would spend a solid minute or two licking the bowl afterward to ensure he didn't miss any of the goodness.

We made Kaiser's first birthday special: a trip to the dog park, a new toy and birthday bandana from the pet store and an entire birthday cake, complete with a #1 candle. Much like human recipients of a first birthday party, Kaiser seemed more confused than anything at the activities.

Cat birthday celebrations, though, require more creativity. I have yet to find any special cat ice cream and don't dare attempt to put a party hat on Tolkien's head. I'm pretty sure I'd step away with some wicked scratches.

We went all out for one of Tolkien's birthdays. We gave him a full day tucked away from the annoyance of Romy. We set him up in our bedroom and went in several times during the day to carry out the next part of his party. Toward the end of the day, we would enter to find him sitting at attention, eyes shining, eager for his next gift.

He had treats, of course, and time with all his toys—something that can only be allowed away from Romy because she can't stand him having fun. She will destroy all his toys to bite down on his joy. She does the same thing to Kaiser—stealing his balls and lying on them if she's feeling more spiteful than playful.

Back to Tolkien's party: we watched a special TV episode about Havana Brown cats. He stared intently at the screen with what appeared to be great pride and appreciation. We also gave him plenty of uninterrupted time to nap.

I'd say he had a cat-approved birthday, and he showed genuine appreciation. When he emerged for supper, he strutted proudly and shot a smug smirk toward Romy who showed jealousy of his day without her by trying to slip into the room with us, pawing at the door and nipping at her feline brother's rump on his way out. I wouldn't be surprised if she uttered a snide remark to him about not getting a party hat or ice cream.

Throughout the year, our animals give us unbridled love and devotion, unquestioning loyalty and a compassionate paw when we're hurting. Celebrating their birthdays allows us a chance to acknowledge what they mean to us and how much their comfort carries us.

Their presence is certainly worthy of a party hat or two and a few silly moments once a year. Besides, who doesn't love a party?

Vignette Thirty-five

Fins & Flushes

FINS ADD DIVERSITY TO OUR pet tales ... and tails. We have had a few tanks filled with a variety of fish over the years.

I think my husband is most fond of the aquatic creatures. We had our biggest tank at the perfect time for Tony. He was working two jobs—teacher by day, server by night.

When he'd come home, he spent extra time in front of the fish after feeding them. The mesmerizing bubbles and colorful, flitting inhabitants helped him de-stress after his long days.

Fish aren't the simplest creatures to keep alive in captivity, though. Most of them don't have long lifespans anyway, and keeping their environments habitable instead of toxic requires a balancing act not meant for the piscine amateur.

It's good our kids aren't overly sensitive about the appropriate disposal of fish bodies. Of course, they don't stand much chance with an extra-sarcastic dad and overly honest and realistic mom. Our influence will either serve them well into their adult lives or be the source of much angst during therapy sessions. Time will tell.

Our daughter had a Betta fish for a while. Actually, she had two. Her first was Prince Ben; the next was Henry. I'm not convinced the second fellow was ever alive. He always listed a bit to the portside.

Henry rarely moved, and when he did it was like watching an inebriated fish try to cross the sea-street. He was a lovely fish, as far as fish go, and we all cared for Henry. He was mourned at his passing.

Truthfully, I may have been surprised at the announcement because I forgot he existed. I'm the kind of person who requires vocally demanding animals. Confession time: I've forgotten I have kids to feed.

When I'm writing or working, everything around me disappears into some mystical void. Nothing exists except the keyboard or pen, the music I'm playing and the task at hand. I believe I have a remarkable superpower and may have revealed how I've published so many books over the years. Thankfully, kids demand food—loudly and often—as do non-fish pets.

Romy has a pronounced, demanding yip that cuts through my most intense focus. Tolkien, also, will not be denied when mealtime closes in. He meows incessantly, gets a frantic case of the zoomies and aggressively claws our couch … directly behind the scratching post he's never even sniffed.

Kaiser adds his distinctive Belgian Malinois vocalization into the regularly scheduled cacophony. When his whinings and howl-yips go unacknowledged by me, he leaps up, paws on my shoulders or head, as I attempt to continue typing. Increasingly aggressive licks inside my ear and snout-jabs to my temple lead me to eventually tear myself from the screen to prep the kibble.

At least the kids are to the ages where I simply have to do my best to keep the freezer and pantry stocked with items they can make.

That reminds me: I forgot to make a grocery order again.

For anyone considering gifting me a pet, please pass the fish aisle. Such a pairing would not end well, especially for them. Instead, you could gift me a grocery delivery—both kids and pets would appreciate the sustenance.

Vignette Thirty-six

Accident-Prone Pets

HAVING PETS IS NOT FOR the faint of heart. You never know what might happen or what issues may arise. Thankfully, animals typically understand the need to accept help when it's given—an attribute I could learn from.

Bentley's fondness for butt scratches may stem back to the time Tony caught his—meaning the dog's, not the man's—butt on fire.

Perhaps the incident wasn't as bad as that statement would lead one to believe. First, you should know, we love fires: in the firepit, in the chiminea, in the fireplace. As soon as our weather allows, we're eager to strike a match and watch the flames dance.

One evening, Tony was lighting a fire in our firepit. He had some gasoline in a small glass jar. In one of the most vivid slow-motion moments of my life, I watched him toss the contents toward the flame. As soon as it licked the first drop, the fire blazed and raced up the flammable stream toward Tony's arm.

His reaction to fling the flammable substance from himself led to the flame arcing onto poor Bentley's backside. Though a flame did flare up on Bentley's furry rump, Tony extinguished it within a second or two and, miraculously, no further damage was done to dog, yard or man.

How? I can only answer with two words: guardian angels. They handle some stuff, let me tell you, and I predict they work the hardest around Southern men and boys with fire, four-wheelers, wide-open dirt roads and the expression, "Hold my beer."

In retrospect, the fire incident also likely explains why Bentley took to lying behind our chairs instead of between them and the fire like he used to do and why he was less than thrilled to discover the black doors in our living room wall opened to an indoor firepit.

Thankfully that accident didn't result in a vet bill. An earlier emergency with him left us with an unexpected wallop to the wallet.

As a puppy, Bentley did what all puppies do: he sniffed and licked and explored and often stuck his snout where it didn't belong. Late one night, he happened upon a frog or hoppy toad or some such creature in our backyard. In true puppy fashion, he pounced after it and—you guessed it—licked it.

His impish curiosity led to a couple of seizures, a midnight drive two towns over to the only open emergency vet and an $800 bill which was demanded in full the following morning.

Romy's gravest injury occurred in her frantic attempt to let a new neighbor dog know whose fence stood between them.

In true Romy fashion, as soon as she whiffed the new dog, she tore across our backyard to the fence, barking all the way.

Our fence isn't what it used to be. Over the years, the wood has cracked in places, and a few open spots have appeared on the bottom. Replacing a fence is expensive, and so we've done our best to patch or cover wherever a new gap appears to buy us time for replacement money to magically appear.

With dogs jumping on the fence and kids playing, temporary barriers to keep our animals in and foreign ones out often get knocked over. That particular day, one of those gaps was revealed, so when the dogs reached the fence, they met midway through the hole for a closer encounter with an unfortunate result.

Romy stuck her paw where it didn't belong and left a trail of blood-drips through my house and under the piano where she scurried to lick her wound.

We don't think the other dog bit her. We're pretty sure she scraped her paw on a nail or sharp piece of the fence. We investigated the scene of the incident but never found a definitive answer.

The wound I thought would heal on its own did not. After unsuccessful attempts to care for the wound ourselves, we made an appointment with our vet and took Romy in for the first of a number of visits.

Whatever she cut herself on went deeper and did more damage than we realized. Dr. Firmin had to graft a portion of skin from elsewhere to cover the affected area, since it was responsible for protecting the base of her nail.

Her fence escapade resulted in a few weeks of frequent vet visits for cleanings, re-wrappings and loads of spoiling from the staff of our vet clinic. It also led to a new style accessory: the cone of shame.

Romy was not a fan. She sported the most pitiful face as she lay on our tile floor, bandaged paw outstretched and chin resting on the clear plastic. Her knobby eyebrows bunched and twitched back and forth as she pondered the tragedy her life had become.

The cone impeded her ability to enjoy her favorite activities: sniffing, licking, eating chicken poop and sticking her head into tight (and likely forbidden) spaces. Tolkien's snickers and looks of condescension did nothing to improve the dog's mood.

Since Romy had always been skittish of having her paws messed with, I worried the location of the injury would result in bites to someone. Thankfully, she did well and became a fan of the vet's office during that time. Despite the bandage changings and cleanings and procedures, she knew she would be doted on, fawned over and given treats—the good kind. She'd also get to see all her newfound friends.

She recognized her paw needed more help than her tongue could provide and we were giving her that aid. In the early days, I would check on her paw often, talking to her about her "poor paw-paw." By the time she was nearly healed, she was presenting her "paw-paw" to me when I'd ask to see it. She'd stick her tongue out and smile her goofy grin whenever I made a big deal of how great her paw-paw looked.

On the way to her appointments, Romy would ride in the van, sitting straight and tall in her seat, like any person. When we entered the waiting room and then the exam room, she would hop up to sit on the benches, again straight as any person.

Romy always has been a diva. Given a captive and responsive audience, she hams it up more than usual.

She would get so worked up and excited whenever we'd enter the office, I swear I could see the exuberance well inside her, bubble and then pop. She'd hunker down with her backend stuck in the air and front half as low as the cone allowed. Her butt would waggle, and her tail would twitch. She'd bounce into a twirling zoomie that usually resulted in her standing on her back legs, twirling more, wrapping herself and/or me in the leash and then running full-speed into a bench or a doorway, thanks to the afore-mentioned cone.

After nearly a month of care and the cone, Romy was healed and free to sniff and lick again. Our biggest concern became keeping her from sticking her paw where she shouldn't again.

I like to think she learned a lesson or two. She definitely recognized she needed help and allowed us to provide it. That's not an easy lesson to learn … for dogs or humans.

So many times in my life, I could have simply asked for help: while silently battling post-partum depression, trying to keep it all together with young children while my husband worked multiple jobs and could rarely be at home with us, feeling overwhelmed and alone in the journey through homeschooling high school to my children's next seasons.

God has put a host of incredible people in my life who are more than willing to lend a helping hand. I'm usually too stubborn to ask for their help. Many times I've also been too stubborn and proud to accept help that's readily offered. How many times have I said, "I'm good!" or "I've got it!" when what I should have said was, "Please and thank you!" or "I'm really struggling."

Perhaps I should be more like Romy—never thought I'd type that sentence.

I need to admit that I can't do everything on my own but also that I don't have to. It's okay to bear the cone without shame, extend my "poor paw-paw" and allow someone to care for me from time to time.

Vignette Thirty-seven

Comfort in Fur

FUNERAL HOMES SHOULD ALLOW ANIMALS. No person comforts a grieving loved one the way a dog or cat can.

When grief's grinder pulverizes our hearts, we don't want platitudes or questions. We need silence, support, empathy. Softness and warmth in which to bury our teary faces or wipe our damp cheeks bring us something extra—lagniappe, as we say in my part of the world.

Animals don't need training to recognize grief or emotional turmoil. They know, and they comfort. No words; no questions—only unconditional loyalty and presence.

I was around the age of ten when I first recognized my symptoms of depression. I didn't know that word at the time, but I knew I was beyond sad. I looked at my wrists and wondered, for the first time, how long it would take for the veins to empty.

Looking back, I don't remember the details that drove my mind to darkness at such a young age. I know much more now about hormones and chemical imbalances and what great therapy journaling and writing are for me. At that point, though, I had God—Who stayed my hand from rashness—and I had Sprit.

Sprit was our tri-color Collie who became my best friend, confidante and constant companion after my first dog, Heather, was killed. Years had passed, and we had moved from Pleasant Hill, S.C., to Mooresville, N.C.

We lived in the split-level manse within sight of the church where my dad preached. My parents were adamant about no animals in the house, so Sprit lived outside. In the oppressive heat of the Southern summers, Sprit and I lingered for hours on the cool concrete at the bottom of the outdoor stairs which led to our basement door.

Whenever I recall those days with Sprit, I feel the icy chill from the concrete that even seeped through jeans to numb my butt and legs. At times, I probably appreciated the numbness the cold caused and wished it could reach my soul.

I can still feel Sprit's long, wiry hair cushioning my damp cheeks. When I close my eyes to picture those days, I inhale a scent memory: cool earth, moss—rich with a hint of spice—sunbaked grass and the dog smell some people don't like but that, to me, means home and safety. I remember burying my hands in his hair to feel the softer fur beneath and the warmth of his velvety skin. Feeling him grounded me, and resting on him dried my tears.

Animals sense emotional distress. We humans have programmed ourselves to mask up, show no weakness, reveal nothing, keep emotions close to the vest. We also choose to ignore, not see, embrace oblivion. Animals aren't fooled. More than that, they don't want to be.

They want to be with their hurting humans. They don't turn around and walk away. They're not content to cling to blissful ignorance so they don't have to get their emotions dirtied by someone else's pain.

Thankfully, my life has been filled with furry comfort.

Right after my college graduation in May 2005, I bought a house in Gautier, Miss., and took my first full-time job as a reporter with

The Mississippi Press. I was completely independent and living the dream. I had my fluffy dog Gembeaux and my sweet Charlie cat.

Charlie enjoyed lying around and snoozing. He also loved to snuggle, while rumbling his jet-engine purrs.

He got his name from the tiny black smudge over his mouth. Thankfully, whoever named him chose to reference Charlie Chaplin and not the other fellow with the distinctly short black mustache.

I lived with Charlie and Gembeaux for a year before Tony and I married. During that time, I transitioned to the real adult world. I basked in my independence and rebelled against certain aspects of my past as I tried to decide right and wrong and worldview without wearing other people's lenses.

That was a year of good, bad and ugly. It was the year of Hurricane Katrina and the shellshock that followed as I drove up and down the Coast reporting on the devastation with armed soldiers alongside the bumper-to-bumper trafficked roads. It was a year of learning and growth and depression.

I cried a great deal during that time period, which makes sense. That was one of the most emotional years of my life. Being on my own was both the best and scariest of transitions. Right as I felt my feet were more firmly planted beneath me, Katrina rocked the foundation. I questioned myself, my home, my profession … everything.

Tony and I got engaged and decided to get married much sooner than we'd originally planned. We didn't want to wait until he finished grad school. He transferred from a school in Kentucky to one in North Carolina mid-way through that year, and we made plans for me to join him in July. Just over a year after starting at *The Mississippi Press*, I said goodbye to our news office and my colleagues.

Hindsight provides great clarity. Looking in the rearview mirror to that time of my life, I see a girl who felt like she was losing her independence, her freedom and herself.

As much as I love Tony and as thankful as I am that we got married and that we have a solid marriage now—gratitude that took time, prayer and years of communication and counseling and love and mostly God—I recognize now that I met marriage with icy cold feet. I can confirm, that is not the ideal way to begin life as a wife.

I hadn't yet learned the secret to contentment in identity or how being independent and being married could coexist. Above all, I knew the words of Ephesians 5 about husbands and wives and love and respect and submission and what they seemed to mean, but what I'd observed to that point didn't match.

While I knew I didn't want what I'd witnessed, I was unclear on the words' meanings or how to pull them into real life. I believe I subconsciously viewed marriage as something ominously final. Perhaps I'll add that to the table of contents in our future book on marriage.

During the down times of that first year of marriage, though, I had my Charlie. Wherever I was, he curled up in my lap and purred. He knew I loved having him with me, and he contentedly rested his paws on my shoulder as I carried him on my hip while I busied around the house or cooked dinner. He continued his routine of purring me to sleep every night.

A few months later, he stayed close during the eight months I silently suffered from post-partum depression following the birth of my first child. I didn't understand my situation during that time. All I knew was I didn't recognize myself. Nothing in my life had gone according to my plans. That was before I understood how imagined futures and real life don't always match.

Married life was harder than I had pictured; it wasn't "happily ever after, the end." Marriage—like any committed relationship—requires hard work. We faced typical and atypical life challenges, as all couples do. Our lives didn't mimic the ideal family examples of  TV. For one thing, money is a necessity in the real world. We sank more in debt each day, and my anxiety grew.

My carefully researched and thought-through birth plan flew out the window with the entrance of the one obstetrician from my practice I didn't want; the one who showed no emotion or care when she announced I'd be going in for surgery instead of welcoming my baby the way I'd envisioned.

And then, there was motherhood. Nothing prepares for how hard that role can be. Sudden responsibility for a tiny human when I was still unsure how to care for myself left me flailing in ice cold rapids on a swift trajectory toward rocks, a waterfall or both.

During that time and in that place, I didn't have a support system. Part of the cause for that reality had to do with the lack of expected support people for a multitude of reasons beyond my control. Another aspect had everything to do with my stubborn resistance to ask for help or open myself up in vulnerability to others.

I remember the day it dawned on me that I would never be able to call in sick again or have another day off. I'd been awake most of the previous night. I sat in the rocking chair in my daughter's room while she lay in her crib, crying still. I'd tried everything and decided she would likely cry forever.

That was also the moment I understood why recordings of wailing infants are utilized in wartime torture situations.

The feeling of exhaustion that pressed down on me was unlike any I'd felt before. I didn't think I could make it to the end of that day, and part of me didn't want to. But I did.

My child did stop crying. We have made it through many more years and challenges of parenthood. Charlie was right there with me for many of them, curled in my lap and purring.

When I finally admitted to myself that I had been depressed for the first eight months of my daughter's life, I felt freed. Also, I looked around and realized many other moms were going through the same struggles.

I wasn't alone. Those three words healed me more deeply than I expected they could.

Charlie had always known my inner turmoil. When I was lowest, he'd seek me out. If my lap were occupied by the baby, he'd curl up beside us—always there; always purring, steady and sure.

A fresher grief of my heart was the day I found out one of my best friends in the world was dying. She hadn't wanted to tell anyone she had cancer until she had a plan in place to fight for her life.

Thankfully, I got to see her the night after I received the call, got to hold her hand, kiss her head, stroke her hair. I had planned to return the following day, but I arrived home later than intended from visiting my mother, recently widowed and alone in a personal care home.

When I texted another friend that I was about to visit Casie, she called to tell me the family had gathered to be with her as she said goodbye to this earth.

That evening, my family went to small group. I couldn't go. I let myself grieve and allowed the tears to flow. Romy, our Chesapeake Bay Retriever mix, padded over to me and rested her snout on my lap. Her soulful eyes conveyed to me that she was there, that she grieved with me, that she wouldn't go anywhere; and then she lay down at my feet and comforted me with her presence.

I cried. I prayed. I wrote a letter to Casie with all the words I'd never get a chance to say this side of heaven. I wrote poems, and I played the piano—songs about heaven, about light, about love and friendship; a soundtrack to play her home.

The whole time, Romy was there, close by and comforting.

If anyone says animals don't understand emotions, I would counter that they understand them better than we do. We should learn from our pets.

We do and say all the wrong things, especially in times of grief. When I saw one of my friend's teenage daughters at her mom's funeral, I blurted, "How are you doing?" and gave myself a swift internal kick and lecture.

She's doing absolutely horrible right now, Joy; she's trying to process losing her mother. She's not okay and she won't be okay and that's okay for her to not be okay. None of us are okay because losing Casie is as far from okay as you can get.

If I were more like Romy, Charlie and Sprit, I would have simply hugged her and stood with her while my eyes said all she needed to hear.

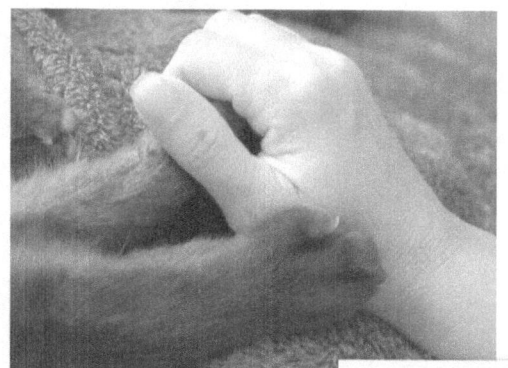

If we were more like our pets, imagine how much more silent funerals would be and how much more time we would spend with one another. Imagine how much more comfort and light we would receive during our darker days.

We would be supported through both the hurt and the healing, and we'd never feel alone.

Until we learn to be more like dogs and cats, I'm thankful for comfort in fur.

Vignette Thirty-eight

One of the Kids

SOME ANIMALS ACT LIKE PEOPLE. I think Romy firmly believes she's one of the kids, and many of my memories of their younger years have her smack dab in the middle of their activities.

Whenever our kids have friends over, Romy inserts herself. Nerf wars or ball in the backyard? There she is—chasing darts and stealing balls. Video games in the living room? She's at the boys' feet, head perked up, watching the screen with a grin on her snout, ready to pounce whenever a snack gets set down without a guard.

When our daughter has her friends over and they escape, giggling, into her room, Romy paws at the door and whines. I swear she thinks she's one of the girls and wants to bask in the smells of lotions and candles while hair is fixed and gossip flows. She allows her nails to be painted and prances to show off bows and tutus. Once my daughter and her two friends were ready for their junior prom, on went the leash and outside went Romy for pictures with her girls.

One Christmas, the kids' big gift was a new-to-us wooden playset with swings and a slide and a three-story tower. It was a hit with the kids, as expected, but we had no idea how much Romy would love it.

She'd leap into the tower, scale the ladders to the top and sit for hours, overseeing her kingdom, barking at neighbor dogs and stray cats.

That was around the time some of our closest friends were foster parents. I remember many times when my two kids, their two kids and however many fosters they had at the moment climbed all over that play structure, swung on those swings and zipped down that slide—all with Romy in the middle of them, tongue lolling and smile flashing.

I'm not sure who was most upset when we finally disassembled that structure. My money is on either me or the dog.

While items like love-worn playsets are special reminders of great moments, our hearts are the real memory holders. With the aid of photos and family storytime, we can summon special moments whenever we're feeling nostalgic.

As I've gotten older—and most of my keepsakes have been broken or chewed by kids or animals—I have learned that "things" aren't as important as heart-held memories, including the adventures of Romy and the other kids in their magic tower.

Vignette Thirty-nine

Quarantine Companions & Reemergence

PART OF ME HATES TO give it ink. Part of me wishes I could never speak of it again. Part of me wonders if it was a horrible nightmare.

All of me knows 2020 and COVID will always be as much a part of our stories as 9/11, Katrina and all the other life-changing, peace-shattering events that mark our lives.

I think it's worth acknowledging how COVID specifically impacted moms. Across the board, the moms I've observed are not the same women they were pre-2020. Many of us are just now—four plus years later—reemerging. I don't know that any of us have recovered. We're timidly rising from emotional ashes, most of us in some sort of altered form.

While I had always homeschooled my children, I know many women who thrashed around in the deep end of the sudden necessary endeavor with no one to toss them a life preserver.

For my family, the lockdown felt more like a lockout. We saw very little of my husband and held our breath in anticipation of getting sick at any moment as he continued managing at the restaurant.

He was working twelve-hour days, at least six days a week with the rest of the skeleton crew that had been retained. He was front and center, handing meals to every person who drove through the blazing heat in the restaurant's South Louisiana parking lot.

We can debate the effectiveness of masks in another space. The facts were that it was a while before the powers that be declared they should be worn. After that, workers like Tony sweated even more and dealt with respiratory issues because of wearing face coverings for hours on end in oppressive heat conditions.

For us, we were never locked away from the disease and so we strove to protect friends and family from ourselves. Do we mask; do we not? Do we let the kids play with their friends? Do we visit our parents or not?

Tensions ran high over the seriousness of the situation, the validity of masks and so much more. We knew people on each extreme side of every debate, and we tried to use wisdom and discernment to live life in care and moderation ... while continuing to live.

Finally all the worry and anxiety over what people would think about our various choices overcame me. We knew people in the at-risk category, and they didn't seem to share our concerns. I led the kids in steps to protect whoever we happened to be around. That constant worry finally erupted as I collapsed on the end of our bed, close to hyperventilating, until Tony took me in his arms and shifted my burdens from me to him.

The way I felt is how I believe many of my fellow moms felt during that time. As women, we tend to be the ones most tuned in to the needs, especially emotional ones, of those around us. We then proceed to take on the responsibility of caring about each one and attempting to fix them.

I do worry that tendency has always been harmful to many women. I've heard of far too many young mothers who die suddenly and leave behind three, four or more little ones. Sometimes they have a disease; other times, the family discovers no cause for their loss.

How much damage do we mothers do to ourselves by trying to care for everyone around us and forgetting to care for our own physical, emotional, mental and spiritual needs? How much is our burden increased by society's expectations for us to do all the things, and social media's filtered lens of how our lives should look?

The truth is mothers, especially of young children, need extra help from time to time—a break, a shoulder, a respite … someone to say, "You're not alone." Unfortunately, the places that should be reaching out are often the same places that demand their service since they "just stay home" or because culture's expectations dictate they mark off some sanctified checklist.

Women are gifted in caring for others, but we can't utilize that power to our own detriment. Without ourselves at full strength, we definitely won't be able to help.

What a weight of needs there were in the aftermath of the pandemic!

Our world was overloaded with emotions. Uncertainty morphed into fear. After a few months, that emotion turned rabid. In the United States, our country's fear became super-charged by hate. Prejudice. Riots. Threats. Deaths.

The news overflowed with trauma. I watched our world, wondering if it would implode or explode. As I did, I clung to my pets. They calmed me, lay nearby, never fretted. They were stability in one of the most unstable times I've experienced.

I am naturally an empath. And no, I don't mean it in some sort of fantasy world, magic sort of way; although, all fiction is based in fact, and I suspect most humans are oblivious to the invisible world that exists all around us and to the incredible powers our emotions and minds contain.

Watching what looked an awful lot like our world ripping itself to shreds, seeing friends—especially mom friends who were lonely, struggling, disconnected and reaching—and then hearing the reports of the deaths … each tragedy sliced at my soul.

The deaths from COVID were horrendous—the ones who died alone, the family members deprived of final goodbyes. But then, there were the other deaths. The ones who could no longer take the pain, the isolation, the fear, the burden. Their losses hacked chunks from my heart.

After a while, I felt like a hollow shell. I stopped watching the news; I steered clear of social media. I built a solid steel wall around my heart and refused to let the hard things in. For any that did break through, I shut my eyes and what was left of my heart. I became void of emotions because the accompanying pain was too much.

While some people began to write during that time period or became more creatively productive, I shriveled ... like grapes hanging beneath our oppressive high summer sun. I curled in on myself. If no one else noticed, I felt the barbs of my emotional disconnect from society. And yet, the alternative was pain-filled as well. Which would be worse?

I had welcomed 2020 with the brightest optimism I'd ever felt. I laughed about having 2020 Vision for my author future, and my smile beamed.

In February, I published *This Good Thing* with high hopes. By then I knew two more books were coming to complete a four-book collection. I had planned author events hours away. And then, the world shifted.

Events got canceled. I lost the desire to market a book that told the story of the last year of life of a young wife and mother. Weren't we already living too much real pain, grief, loss?

It took me a while and a beautiful, heartfelt review to finally embrace my desire for my littlest book to meet its readers.

"This book isn't long, but it will change your life, if you let it."

That one came from a reader—Terri—who's been with me and encouraged me from the beginning. Hers was the review I so deeply needed to read. I needed the reminder that my words—my passion, my *empathy*—were needed. They had a place. They could make a difference for someone.

With that truth in mind, healing began. I uncurled from my shriveled state and felt again. With feeling came pain, but through pain emerged growth and strength.

In many ways, the pain only began for me toward the end of the restrictions. A series of events fell, like life-crushing dominoes, upon me in the fall of 2021.

The first was my body's adverse reaction to the vaccine I never wanted to get—and wouldn't have, had I waited one more week when the powers dropped their mandates.

It was in the early days of physical pain as I attempted to wrap my mind around how, before age 40, I would never be able to do many activities again, Hurricane Ida blasted nearby.

Though we were to the east of the storm's strike, we felt her wrath and picked up the pieces of debris around our house and on our van. We remained mostly disconnected from the world for a couple of weeks while crews worked to restore power and internet lines. I was also at the height of my inflammatory pain during that time period without air conditioning.

After the first of 2022, I pushed forward—finally in hope—with my physical recovery and found a doctor who supported my desire to naturally combat what manufactured drugs had caused. I launched a commitment to overhauling my diet, finding ways to exercise again and losing the weight I'd put on during my COVID depression. I found myself unable to do some of my favorite workouts but rejoiced when I did thirty-second rounds of pushups. I had believed that was an exercise I'd never do again.

I reduced sugar and increased fresh foods. I reduced the amount of wine I consumed and discovered a love of avocado and salmon and tuna. I learned what worked and what didn't for my body. And, I determined I would listen to my body and my intuition from then on. When I believed the no-carb, no-gluten aspect of my diet was detrimental to my health, I listened and chose moderation instead.

As 2022 progressed, I shed weight and gained strength. Constant pain was replaced by more minor flare-ups with triggers I could recognize—extreme temperatures, specific foods, improper posture and sitting too long, standing too long or overexerting myself.

And then, the season of grief hit. The first to go was our sweet Bentley, after a month or two of constant caregiving.

Next was the early morning phone call that set into motion a few months of total upheaval.

Jim, my middle brother, apologized for waking me so early. Our father had a massive heart attack. They took our mother—whose body and mind were ravaged by Parkinson's—with him in the ambulance to the hospital, but she needed someone to be with her. Jim was on his way, but it would take eight hours. I was the closest.

At that point, I was within about eight pounds of the weight-loss goal I'd placed for myself earlier in the year and knew I should achieve it by Christmas. As it turns out, caregiving can be a crash weight-loss program. I wouldn't recommend it, though. Preparing healthy foods while caring for a person with round-the-clock needs proved nearly impossible. I typically skipped meals, rather than trying to juggle tasks.

The pain returned full force. I wasn't able to exercise, but I was getting a workout, lifting and lowering my mother from wheelchair to chair to bed to other places. Through the course of physical anguish, I dealt with emotional turmoil as well—a lifetime of hurt and scars I'd never dealt with or even named.

At one point, I took advantage of the two hours of a sitter and enjoyed my first shower of the week. I used the running water to mask the sound of my heart releasing through tears and sobs the many internal challenges I'd never acknowledged.

Somewhere in that course of events, we lost my favorite chicken, Cinnamon. While a chicken may not be anywhere near the same level as a beloved dog or as a parent, her death was yet another sting during a time of raw, open-wound grieving.

In addition to caretaking, grocery stocking, meal preparing and dashing to drug stores and doctors' offices, I had to convince my father to relinquish a couple of freedoms he didn't want to release—his car and their house.

He was not pleased with me when I took his reluctant permissions and rushed to institute them so both of my parents could receive the care they desperately needed in a safe environment. From there I continued caregiving from a distance and with frequent long drives— another trigger for my inflammation.

Before my father had bounced back to full strength, my mother fell and broke her hip. He refused to leave her side at the hospital where she underwent surgery, which resulted in a rapid decline that brought my family together from around the world for the first of two funerals.

I received that call and found myself responsible for informing my four siblings of our father's death. Our father had made it past his eighty-eighth birthday, celebrating with a cake and his wife and some of his children in the personal care home.

Our mother missed her eightieth by a few weeks. I was thirty minutes away when I got that second call of closure. I can testify a phone ring takes a wholly different tone at those times—I believe I knew both times what message waited after "Hello?"

In between those two black dress occasions came an unexpected goodbye that—more than all the rest—sent me into a tailspin.

Casie—the woman all her friends agree was the best companion—was diagnosed with cancer. Before she could travel to Texas to map out an aggressive plan to fight and before she could share the news with more than a few people, she ended up in the hospital.

Thankfully, I got the news. I missed getting to see her awake, but I did see her one more time while she was alive.

I held her hand, spoke to her, kissed and hugged her. The next night, I felt the slice and rip of the knife in my heart as I heard the family had gathered to say goodbye. I was too late to see her again, and so I sat with my grief and memories as the weight of another impending call tugged and squeezed and battered further at my ragged heart.

"Casie's not hurting anymore."

But we all were.

The months passed—forward motion no grief can stop. 2023 brought glimpses of light, but the pain lingered.

April brought my fortieth birthday. I've never liked birthdays, especially as candles have increased on my cakes. That birthday, though, felt least joyous of all.

Casie and I shared a birthday month, within the same week. We hadn't made the time to celebrate together the year before. We texted that we should, but we didn't. And now, we can't.

That day was tough, but my husband recognized, when I told him I definitely didn't want a party and really didn't want to go anywhere, that I meant it on a deeper level than usual.

My family gave me space and allowed me to sit in my favorite place—the back porch—with Romy and the chickens and just be still. I randomly and spontaneously cried a few times.

Grief is like that. It whips without warning—like a summer squall on the beach—but it passes quickly when left to its own devices. That birthday of grief was therapeutic, as was visiting Casie's grave on her birthday five days later. How much I wished we'd celebrated together on all the birthdays we had on this earth.

For me, 2023 was my year of restoration of peace and of truly feeling—without drowning in the emotions. Light that had disappeared for many seasons filtered through the haze—stream by tiny stream—until, finally, I felt its warmth again.

Even through heavy grief, we can experience a renewal, a reemergence. As I watch old friends peek back into the online world and speak quietly of former interrupted writing projects and new happenings once more, I smile.

When my birthday rolled around in 2025, I didn't view it with dread. Perhaps I've even come to a place where I'll accept a small amount of celebration in the years to come.

All things do become new one day. We find our way to recovery after the storms of life. Grief cannot chain us forever.

One day, Casie and I will sit together again, our hands around warm tea mugs and our feet resting near snoozing dogs. We'll celebrate all the birthdays then ... together.

joyerancatore.com/this-good-thing/

Vignette Forty

Lessons in Begging

SOME OF THE MOST HUMOROUS personality traits of animals center around their unique begging techniques. No two creatures are alike in their approach to obtain some morsel of tastiness.

My in-laws' dog Bull had the most confident demeanor when he begged. Actually, I can't accurately call it begging. He sat at attention with total confidence that whatever we were eating was as much his as ours. He would accept his reward without surprise or timidity.

Bentley, however, did his best to look like he wasn't begging. His expression was sheepish with a hint of worry and a dash of hope. If anyone dared to pet him while he was begging-not-begging, he would pull away, and his expression would shift to total annoyance. If looks could talk, his would have said, "How dare you pet me when you're hogging the chow?"

Romy and my in-laws' dog Clyde have a similar look when begging. Romy would not appreciate that statement since she hates Clyde with a passion and considers him the worst blight to ever enter her life—even worse than the little weird brown furry puppy (Tolkien Cat for the rest of us) and the pup with giant ears. Truth is truth, though. Both dogs look completely confused and baffled as to why people are eating and not including them.

They attempt to make sense of the conundrum by tilting their heads this way, then that, arching their eyebrows and occasionally leaning closer to the good-smelling nuggets and the humans holding them.

Both have to be sternly warned or any kind (*cough* gullible *cough*) human runs the risk of losing a finger.

With Kaiser we've not experienced full-on begging because—so far—all four humans in our household have followed the absolutely-no-table-food-to-Kaiser rule ... for the most part, anyway. He will sniff and raise his snout toward us, though, in a purely curious manner.

What Kaiser does love to do is watch every step of the cooking process. His attention is laser-focused as he observes each task, from ingredient gathering to mixing to oven timer chirp. He'll pop up and run to see what we remove from the magic hot box.

One day, my daughter put an apron on him, and he wore it with great pride all afternoon. I call him my Little Chef and swear I'm going to learn to cook for the pups so he can finally eat something he helps me make.

Lest you think cats are above begging, they are not. Of course, Tolkien would heartily disagree that he would stoop to such a peasant level.

Now that I think deeper about it, he doesn't really beg either.

Once, I was working in bed—a socially acceptable work spot for writers, by the way—with my computer on my lap desk. I'd had a long morning and had just made myself a turkey and avocado sandwich. I set my computer aside to make room for my plate.

Fulfilling his role as my Editor-meow-Chief, Tolkien had been lying alongside my legs. After I'd taken a bite or two, he raised his head, and his chocolate-chip nose set to work.

Sniff! Sniff!
Sniff! Sniff!

Four sniffs in, he had discerned that I had turkey. Tolkien has a particular affinity for turkey.

His eyes widened. He hopped up, pulled an impressive U-turn on the narrow strip of bed beside my leg and proceeded to plant paw after paw on top of the desk in my lap.

I tried to take a bite; he struck in to bite from the other side.

"No, sir!"

I raised the sandwich. He followed. Higher—he followed. Higher still ... the cat sat on his furry haunches and then stretched himself upward, a paw raised to take what, clearly and rightfully, belonged to him. He literally reached a point where he was perfectly balanced yet extended to his full height on his back paws, one front paw clawing at what he felt belonged in his nearly toothless mouth. Never have I eaten so quickly while also staving off a crazed cat with the smell of turkey in his nostrils.

Well, I may have eaten faster once: the terrifying time I attempted to eat a sandwich on a park bench at the New Orleans Zoo.

Every free-range chicken in the vicinity circled me—tighter, closer—eyes crazed and clucks manic. Before I knew it, I had a chicken perched behind each shoulder, another beside me on the bench and closing in on my lap. Two more hopped around my feet, alternating fluttering up toward my food.

If Stephen King hasn't written a horror tale about pecking chickens, he should. They're far more terrifying than clowns.

Back to Tolkien and turkey sandwiches: he has a firm grasp on what he believes is his due and is stealthy about his attempts to claim them. When he hops onto the dinner table, he'll give an innocent-looking initial sniff toward my plate and turn away with an air of indifference. Then, with bird-of-prey speed, he drops his head toward my meal. I barely react quickly enough to push him away before I lose a pork chop.

Each animal has its own approach to begging; which one works best or is the most endearing, I'm not sure. I can't help but wonder, though, if I resemble a begging creature when I'm at an event selling my books.

I hope I don't appear as confused as Romy and Clyde, as conflicted as Bentley or as crazed as Tolkien. Perhaps I should channel the confidence of Bull before my next event. Although, I'm not sure I can pull it off. He was quite the regal and commanding canine.

Perhaps I could weave together the confidence of Bull with a shot of Kaiser's innocent curiosity and Bentley's eager hope.

"You're a reader? I'm a writer!"

"You like books? I've got books!"

"You want to read goofy animal tales? I've got goofy animal tales!"

I could be a reader's best friend.

That's a good author!

Vignette Forty-one

Schooling Kids & Pets

FIFTEEN YEARS OF HOMESCHOOLING (seventeen total after we celebrate the second graduation) have been an adventure that came with many perks and humorous anecdotes ... some of our family's best memories.

Our kids have experienced community service in ways they wouldn't have if we had sent them to school. We would have missed peaceful family vacations after Labor Day, and they wouldn't have been able to follow their interests on weekdays during the school year. We wouldn't have had the freedoms to tailor courses to their needs and interests or explore rabbit trails of learning or pet animals whenever we want.

Homeschooling with pets makes the experiences extra memorable. Charlie was always close by during school time, and I have several pictures of him lying, passed out, on the kids' schoolwork or being snuggled while one kid or the other learned to read.

The dogs loved to lie in the mix of everything. Bentley's favorite class was history. I know that because that's when his snores rumbled loudest. Romy took her best naps during health and chemistry classes.

Toward the end of his life, Bentley's flatulence became much more ... pronounced. We spent most of our school days guarding our noses from his noxious fumes. Classes were frequently interrupted with nose-squinching exclamations of "Ugh! Bentley!"

On the rare occasions our outbursts woke him, he would furrow his eyebrows and give us his best sheepish and embarrassed expression. Poor guy; he couldn't control it.

Tolkien might think he's our headmaster. He has certainly mastered a stern look as he perches at attention on my desk to oversee school time. He glares disapprovingly at the messy dining room table that doubles as our school space and side-eyes me now and then for what he seems to consider my subpar attempts at teaching.

Often, he'll nap in one of the dining room chairs during school hours. He often chooses my son's chair, which means he—the boy, not the cat—sits on the edge and frequently pets the brown feline as he diligently completes his Advanced Math. The boy willingly sits catawampus, while the cat lies sphinx-like, regal and outstretched across the chair's length.

Kaiser rarely sits still. He assists with PE by requesting the back door to be opened at least fifteen times per class.

I won't speak for my kids on the topic, but I'm thankful they've grown up studying and learning with furry companions within reach. I'd like to think the ability to pet an animal at any point during the day made for a more peaceful and less anxious school experience.

Any distractions the animals have caused during the school day—Tolkien's insistence on napping atop books, the parakeets' occasional squawk sessions, Bentley's gaseous eruptions—provide welcome breaks. They afford us a moment to pause—sometimes in an overwhelming moment—for a laugh or simply an extra breath. A thirty-second break to snuggle with a furry friend allows a mental recharge and an emotional refuel.

Perhaps our society could address two problems with one solution if we empty our overcrowded animal shelters and offer young people paws of comfort for their long, anxiety-causing school days.

Imagine the tales students could tell of their furry classmates and the gratitude of the animals for such unique and attention-filled homes.

Vignette Forty-two

Natural Disasters & Close Companions

WE HAVE ACCEPTED HURRICANES AND tornadoes as regular parts of our lives in southeast Louisiana.

In 2021, Hurricane Ida rocked our neck of the woods. Neighbors to the southwest of us received a far worse impact than we did, but the storm did enough damage to earn a place in our historical roll call of storms.

We were without power for a week and internet for two. Our roof took damage. One side of the fence was uprooted by a giant tree from our neighbor's yard. Thankfully, it only minimally damaged our chicken coop on the way up.

A giant pine tree in our other neighbor's yard snapped high in the air and crashed on top of our van, impaling the hood and coming within inches of our front door.

When the tree hit, all of us—two adults, two teens, two dogs and one cat were in our walk-in closet. Well, technically, Tolkien was outside the door in our bedroom. We had been under a tornado warning for a while. At that point, the warning had been extended at least once.

The kids were scared. The animals were scared. I had visions of every horrifying news story I'd ever seen replaying in my head. And then the tree hit.

The crash sounded like an explosion. Its impact shook our entire house. I was certain we were going to emerge to half our house missing—a gaping yawn to the bawling sky.

Thankfully, the tree avoided serious damage to our house, and our van was mostly repaired. (I'm still convinced the frame is warped, but what do I know?)

The kids still remember the fear of huddling in that closet. I sometimes wonder if the animals do, too, and if we can convince Tolkien to join us inside the closet next time. I'm thankful we were spared further damage or serious loss, and my heart breaks for all who lost loved ones or beloved pets.

Part of the reason we purchased a camper was so we can escape a storm and take our pets with us. Perhaps before the next big one hits our area, we can unravel a way to attach a chicken coop to the back of our camper so we can evacuate them as well.

If Hurricane Katrina—which hit 16 years to the day before Hurricane Ida—taught us anything, it's that pets should never be left behind when a massive force of nature is barreling toward inhabited areas.

I was encouraged to see Floridians making evacuation plans on social media for pets—small and large—as well as for themselves in the days leading up to Hurricane Milton.

A few days before that storm's landfall, I saw a long post with fantastic tips for preparing before a storm. The poster listed everything from preparing a house, including flipping off breakers, to having pet items like leashes and food and medicine within reach.

We often refer to our pets as part of the family. In times of impending disaster, I fear some people forget those words. One of my challenges to myself before the next hurricane season is to review checklists and make any preparations I haven't thought of before, including for our furry friends.

The danger of a natural disaster no one can prepare for, like what Hurricane Helene did to the mountains in 2024, does exist. Those precious people could never have imagined the catastrophe coming. Too many of them were unable to save themselves, let alone their animals.

In the days that followed the flash floods and tragedy, I grieved for the massive loss in an area I have a special bond to. I was heartened by a different type of flood—the flood of neighbors who raced to help humans and animals alike ... to rescue the lost, to recover the fallen.

While none of us will forget that cataclysm and its destruction, I pray we also remember the beautiful images of people and children pulled from the mud by heroes and the horses and animals miraculously spared and reunited with their humans.

Vignette Forty-three

Inspiration & Horses' Hooves

WHAT IS IT ABOUT HORSES that stirs my soul? Is it the majestic arch of their necks as they run? Is it the wild spirit that crackles in their eyes—no matter how calm and tame they may be? Is it their ever-present sweet scent or the warmth in their huffed breaths?

Perhaps it's the fact that my heartbeat matches their hoofbeats when I watch them run or that I've been captivated by them as far back as my memory goes.

As a child, I spent many late nights wide awake, envisioning myself atop a horse. Most of my post-bedtime activities included imagining and acting out stories that came to mind. Whatever I envisioned was always clearer than a movie. If a story were sad, I would cry real tears; if it were hilarious, I'd muffle my laughter in a pillow.

When I imagined riding horses, I could feel the power beneath me and the wind in my hair as the whipping mane stung my face.

In my heart, I'll always be the same horse-crazy girl I've been since I was tiny. Which is why, for my thirty-eighth birthday, I leapt at a chance to visit an equine rescue ranch only a couple minutes from my house.

Like many families, we got new bikes during COVID. On one of our rides together, Tony and the kids led me to a hidden gem they had discovered on a previous ride: Wind Dancer Ranch Equine Rescue Service. When we got home, I searched for them online and found a nice website. They offered visits with the horses, and I told my family that's what I wanted to do for my birthday. I submitted the form and received an automated reply with confirmation of our visit.

What I didn't know was the website was old, and the current manager didn't have access to that form or email address. When we arrived, no one was there to greet us.

I can't remember exactly how, but someone let us in the gate. We met a woman who boards her horses there. She called Aubrey, the manager, who wouldn't return until later that day, and we cleared up the website confusion. Our new friend, Paula—who turned out to be a talented artist and children's book illustrator—gave us an impromptu tour.

We spent more than an hour walking the ranch, petting horses and donkeys the whole time. We heard a few of their rescue stories and fell in love with the place and the animals.

For some time, all my daughter had wanted to do was volunteer at a stable and help horses. The closest opportunity we had found would require a huge chunk of driving time, and I didn't have that to give. My daughter and I wondered if she may be able to volunteer at Wind Dancer.

Fast-forward to 2023, my daughter started volunteer work there. Before long, she was bathing and grooming horses, leading them around as easy as if they were five-pound puppies instead of nearly half-ton animals and helping on shoeing days with horses and donkeys. A little over a year later, a need arose for a morning feed person, and she was the first choice.

A primary aspect of involvement in American Heritage Girls is volunteering in the community. My daughter's opportunities serving at Wind Dancer led to her first job but also to the setting for her

Stars & Stripes Award Project—the highest honor in AHG, earned after a massive amount of work and commitment to raise funds for and staff the building of a massive run-in shed in one of the pastures.

Watching my daughter experience opportunities I only dreamed of and seeing her blossom into a responsible young woman as she rose to each task and challenge thrilled my horse-lover soul and reignited my horse-craziness in a new way.

Through discussions with Aubrey, I learned about the livestock slaughter pipeline that stretches across the United States and dumps into Mexico and Canada. Cows, donkeys and horses (among other animals) are expensive. Too often, when life happens (as it inevitably does), the big animals are the first to go. Off to auction go the animals—sometimes from caring homes who genuinely think they're making the best choice for their animals.

Unfortunately, wherever money changes hands, greed resides. Some of the unsavory factions of the livestock world are individuals whose goal is to buy low and sell high. They have no regard for who they sell to as long as they make a buck, and a great way to increase profit is to spend as little as possible while the animals are in their possession.

Many of those animals are shipped to one of our neighboring nations where they are sold to slaughterhouses, most of which don't abide by any humane treatment guidelines. The journey there is typically in horrendous conditions in trailers packed with animals of all ages—ill, aged, pregnant, newborn.

Often before the animals get to the point of transportation, they're corralled in what most folks call "kill pens." Those are the settings for many photos of horses and donkeys available for adoption that we see on social media. Many times their food and water is limited, if available at all.

Their "bail," as the demanded price is called, ranges from a few hundred to more than a thousand dollars. Often, a deadline accompanies the price. If the animal's bail doesn't get paid in three days, you miss out. In other words, they'll be on their way to slaughter.

While some animals are older or have physical issues, many I've seen are two to eight years old—far too young and healthy for the fates awaiting them.

The people behind the photos can be cruel, devious and dangerous; and rest assured, whatever "rescue" they're providing is for their wallets. A number of the horses and donkeys at the ranch near us were rescued from such monsters.

As a life-long horse lover, I've read countless books about horses—from encyclopedias to care and training manuals to fiction. I've written academic papers and news articles about horses, read horse magazines and spent untold hours researching many equine topics.

Until becoming close with someone in the rescue industry, I had never heard of the slaughter pipeline. I had no idea the depths of inhumanity and cruelty that exist in our nation.

A combination of that education, the opportunity to be close with the majestic animals several times a week, a vivid image of a man I saw once in Wendy's and a love for and appreciation of Native American culture resulted in a story seed planted in my mind. The research, though heartbreaking, has led to a sprouting contemporary western book that has been magical to write.

Through fiction, writers can deliver truth to people they may never get elsewhere. That's one of the many benefits I love about literature.

Another golden nugget of the writing life is the fact that ideas await wherever we open our hearts and can lead us to unexpected places.

Each book I've written originated as a seed of inspiration that I nurtured to full bloom. Some rose from reality; others from imagination. For each, I had to be willing to accept where they might lead.

My entire fantasy world, glimpsed through "Ealiverel Awakened" in *The Crux Anthology* and my collection of "Tales of the Faerie Shepherds" on my website, emerged with the imagined appearance of a wee faerie on my shoulder while writing on a sunny autumn afternoon.

Carolina's Legacy Collection was birthed from a tragedy reported in a local newspaper. As I wrote *Any Good Thing*, the characters inspired the other three books.

Necessity fueled the writing of my co-authored nonfiction book for writers, *Finders Keepers: A Practical Approach to Find and Keep Your*

Writing Critique Partner, and the plans for an entire Author Resource Series. We wanted to write books about topics we had to learn the hard way.

I never expected this book to happen. While grieving for the sudden loss of my friend Casie, I realized how important animals have been throughout my life. I also recognized how much stories of animals have influenced me as a person and as a writer.

Honestly, I wanted to stop many times while writing this book and some of my others because the task of taking inspiration and following it through whatever emotions it elicits can be draining.

Every story—real or imagined—reveals something to me about myself. Such disclosures can leave my heart and soul raw, but embracing and evaluating that pain usually results in powerful growth and deeper empathy.

Open hearts to the beauty and ugliness of the world around us allow our souls to be stirred. Such an awakening often begins with something as simple, yet majestic, as pounding hooves.

joyerancatore.com/my-writings/

Vignette Forty-four

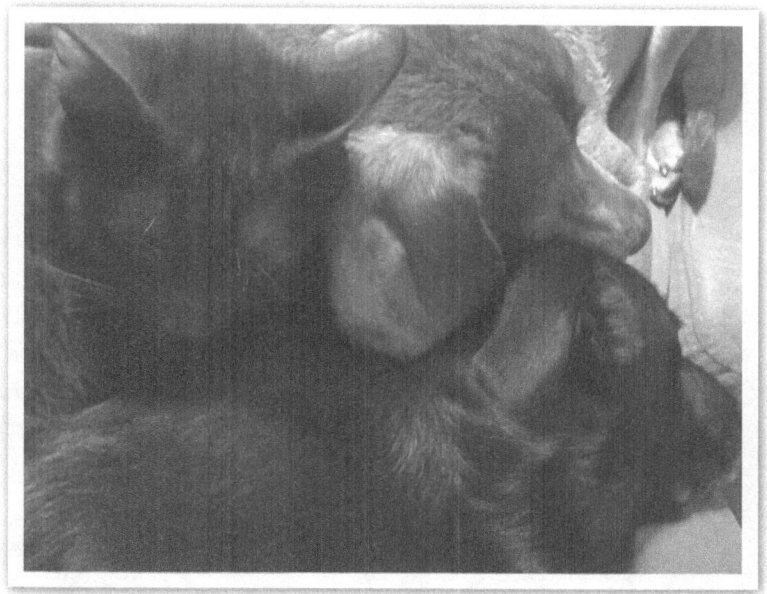

Loving Like Cats & Dogs

FEW RELATIONSHIPS ON EARTH ARE as amusing to observe as those between dogs and cats. Now, I'm not talking about the type where the dog is actively seeking to destroy the cat. I'm referring to the household scenario where a canine and a feline discover how to coexist.

Charlie was well-established when we welcomed Bentley. I'm sure some chasing ensued, but my memory sees them coming to an agreement fairly quickly.

Dogs take their job as guardians seriously. As documented earlier, Bentley aided in finding Charlie when he ran off. In some cases, guarding—in regard to felines—means protecting others ... or others' property ... from said cats.

Romy takes her role as Tolkien's disciplinarian seriously. When we yell at him for scratching the sofa, she leaps into action and proceeds to paw at him, chase him and/or nip his rump.

For his part, Tolkien takes full advantage of his agility and wide range of the house—counters and high windowsills included—to dominate and lord over Romy. He loves to crouch out of sight on the other side of a wall and twitch his tail in anticipation of Romy rounding a corner … right into his waiting claws.

Lest anyone believe Tolkien's haughty glances in Romy's direction, I witnessed his love for her one of the many times I accidentally rolled over her tail with my desk chair.

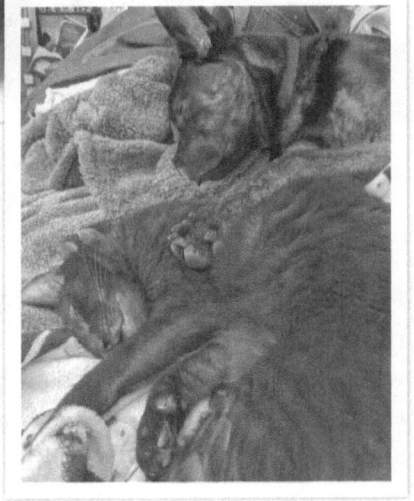

Tolkien had been napping on the dining table chair closest to my desk when Romy uttered a pitiful yelp. As I inspected the dog, I noticed a little brown face peering around the back of the chair, extra-long whiskers bent and disheveled. He was eyeing the brown dog with the second-most concerned face I've ever seen on him.

The most concerned I've seen him is when it's nearing mealtime, and no one's moving toward his food.

Back to his perturbation over Romy's well-being: Tolkien pressed his chocolate chip nose closer toward the dog, who eased her snout nearer until noses touched. Apparently satisfied that I hadn't horribly maimed his worthy adversary, Tolkien disappeared behind the chair, turned, stretched and lay back down to resume his slumber.

Tolkien delights in perching on the table and leaning over to swat Romy's butt as she passes. He did that once, maybe twice, to Bentley. He definitely didn't do it more. As chill and calm as Bentley was with Tolkien, he would not stand for any tomfoolery. His tail and posterior were entirely off limits to the cat and his batting claws. Bentley made that position clear with his *snarl-growl-snap*.

When we opened our home to Kaiser, he and Tolkien got off to a rocky start. Kaiser's favorite thing in the world—next to water and running and food and balls and comfy beds and kisses and snuggles on the sofa—is to chase other creatures: dogs, chickens, humans or cats. If it runs, he will chase it with glee ... whether the other creature is in on the game or not.

As you can imagine, Kaiser's first few weeks in our house were ... chaotic. Tolkien's instinct was to run from the wild pup, which triggered the dog's chase reflex. Round and round our small house they raced.

We never know how such situations may play out. What would happen if Kaiser caught the brown cat? How many household items would be broken in their wake? Was that our new household existence—lifting drinks as the cat rips across the table while the dog with giant paws leaps up in hopes of stopping him?

I was fairly certain Kaiser meant no malice. Tongue lolling, tail wagging and goofy grin intact, Kaiser definitely considered their interaction a fun game. Tolkien, however, looked terrified.

After a couple weeks of keen observation of the new canine, Tolkien decided the pup posed no threat and could, instead, be used

as part of his grand master plan.

Anyone who's ever been around cats knows each of them has some diabolical plot for world domination. Tolkien clearly deemed Kaiser's size and skill set and access to outside as beneficial to his scheme.

While the chasing continued on occasion, the activity morphed into a sparring match between Taekwondo classmates. Tolkien would leap onto some mid-level perch—like the coffee table or piano bench—and sit back on his haunches before raising both forepaws to *slap-slap-slap* Kaiser on his snout.

Kaiser would return the strikes with gentle swipes of his bear-sized paw. The chase would continue until the pup cornered the feline who's less than a quarter his size and covered Tolkien's neck with his open mouth.

Neck fur mussed and damp, Tolkien would slip away with a precise pivot and leap across the house again ahead of his companion, bound to higher ground (like a bookshelf) and crouch, tail twitching, while awaiting the next approach. I sincerely believe Tolkien views their interactions as training to whip his new soldier into shape.

Regardless of Tolkien's feelings of superiority over his canine siblings, he has curled up with all three of them on enough occasions over the years for me to know they care for each other in their own special ways.

Observing the peaceful interactions of two species who, instinctually, should be enemies reminds me how interacting with people different than me can be an enriching and beneficial opportunity. We can learn from one another, challenge each other and develop a bond—perhaps even a lasting relationship.

What great things could happen if we all make efforts toward loving our fellow humans like cats and dogs do to one another?

Vignette Forty-five

Photo taken by Joy E. Rancatore at the Southeast Louisiana Veterans Cemetery.

Unexpected Funerals & Connection Strings

THE INVISIBLE STRINGS OF LIFE'S connections linked me to a woodpecker and a Vietnam hero and taught me the value of every life around me—even the ones I never meet face-to-face.

Nothing in life prepared me for the evening I pulled in our driveway and emerged from my van to be greeted by a stiff and silent red-headed woodpecker.

He lay perfectly straight alongside the basketball goal base. He was on his back, and so he faced up toward me. If he weren't so obviously dead, he would have looked peaceful. He maintained a stately demeanor with his brightly painted head.

I recalled all the times I'd glimpsed a flash of red overhead or heard a *tap-tap-tap*. I chuckled at the times I'd heard his attempts at pecking something metal. Do woodpeckers have headache medicine?

My daughter joined me in remembering and wondering. Our son saw us standing still, looking down at something, and met us at the edge of the driveway.

We speculated on what happened. Was it a cat? He was still intact. Did he hit the van? I examined the side and the windows.

When we bent toward the bird, we found blood stains at the top of his beak. Had he tried to drill a hole in the metal basketball goal again?

We will never know what happened, but we decided the winged creature deserved a proper burial. Our neighbors likely thought we'd gone mad as my son brought out a shovel, and my daughter dug a hole in our front yard. Into a zipped baggie went the bird and into the gaping earth we placed him.

Every creature's life deserves to be celebrated. That woodpecker brought joy to us with his bright feathers and cheerful sounds, so at his death, we remembered his contributions to our lives. Words were spoken. Dirt was returned, and leaves were scattered.

May he rest in peace.

One of the most moving funerals I've ever attended was for a Vietnam hero. He was to be buried in the Southeast Louisiana Veterans Cemetery. The call spread for people to attend since he had no family nearby.

We live close, so I took the kids who were younger then. I explained the man's story to them. They understood he was someone who sacrificed for them long ago and who deserved a morning of our time.

The Patriot Guard Riders rumbled past on their bikes, flags fluttering—Old Glory, POW/MIA—sounds and sights fear-inducing for those who deserve it, comforting and protective for those who need it.

"Taps" was played. A hero was laid to rest. Tears were shed for a man from a whole other generation who I likely never would have met.

We learned about him and his service. At age nineteen, SGT Billy Edward McClure joined the Army during the Vietnam War. He was stationed in Vietnam for one year between 1970 and 1971 and celebrated his twentieth birthday there. He served our country for more than eight years before being honorably discharged. He passed away in December 2016, a few days before his sixty-fifth birthday, and was laid to rest in March 2017.

Attending SGT McClure's funeral was a privilege. I think it was important for my children—then ages nine and seven—to witness veterans, active military and civilians congregate to show respect for someone they never knew.

Each life has an impact—whether it's a woodpecker whose busy pecking brightens people's days or a man who served his country with honor during a tumultuous time.

Connections are interesting. We rarely think about the lives we touch as we go throughout our day. Perhaps a smile during a stressful grocery store moment helps someone keep going through their day or an opened door for a frazzled mother with a stroller calms her heart for a moment.

Many lives have touched ours without us even recognizing them—military, first responders, the person whose speed limit adherence kept us from racing ahead into a wreck. Some have greatly affected us; others' influence was smaller.

Regardless of the impact's magnitude or our awareness of it, others' lives improve our own, encourage us or inspire us.

One member of the Patriot Guard at SGT McClure's funeral evoked a poem from my creative heart. Although I'm no skilled poet, I'll share it here.

Photo taken by Joy E. Rancatore at the Southeast Louisiana Veterans Cemetery.

The Patriot

Gentle breezes rustle flags at half-mast.

Beneath them he stands

Erect upon his walking aid,

The Flag set carefully atop.

He smilingly requests a photo.

Life and positivity flow from him.

He snaps the photo and continues on;

I turn away to honor one now gone.

One by one, men advance to say so long

To the brother they may have never met.

A stiff salute, a bowed head;

Tears caress worn, hardened cheeks.

He shuffle-steps at attention,

Flag held firmly at his side.

He goes to pay respect—a brother-in-arms—

And never leave a man behind.

At the front he slides away his assist.

Slowly, painfully he kneels, head bent.

He pays respect to the urn and the hero within,

Unconcerned with the exertion it cost.

He rises shakily and haltingly,

The Stars & Stripes his one support,

And unfurls to resolute attention,

An earlier era's strength stalwart.

His salute snaps up, out and down,

Emotions following each movement.

He turns around with a soldier's precision

And reaches a shaking hand for his wheeled friend.

A Patriot to the end, his service true;

This man shuffles past with honor shining through.

He'll say goodbye to every brother he can

And join them one day for their eternal leave.

That veteran captured my attention and heart. Although I didn't say anything to him, his expressions and actions spoke to me. He reminded me of the greater band of brothers that includes all who have served our nation and the bond they share as our beloved guardians.

Opportunities like the one we had with SGT McClure allow us to say thank you and to recognize the hidden influences in our lives.

His funeral also inspired a scene for "Life Lessons in Courage & Woodworking" in *Every Good Thing* where a young character says, "Everybody should have somebody to remember them. I can be a memory keeper for heroes who don't have family to share their stories."

Strings connect people throughout time and space in ways that are often impossible to see, and yet we feel them. Those of us still living get to keep others' strings alive through memories—whether we knew a person deeply or only learned of them after they were gone. That soldier wasn't alone at his burial, plus we got to learn his name and story.

SGT Billy Edward McClure, we'll be your memory keepers.

joyerancatore.com/every-good-thing/

Vignette Forty-six

Clarity Amidst Chaos & Giant Ears

WITH THE DAWNING OF EACH new year, I reflect on the setting one and then focus on all the desires, goals and plans ahead. As I do, a few words rise until one flutters above the rest and assigns itself to the new year.

That word becomes a touchstone of sorts for decisions and goal-making. It can even become a mantra and often pops to mind as some event or opportunity falls into place or as an epiphany rises or a challenge or trial attempts to block my path.

One of those last scenarios most reminds me of my 2024 Word of the Year: Clarity.

Many times, challenges or trials that arise are of my own making. I tend to take on more responsibilities than I should or say yes when I shouldn't. I've also been known to follow rabbit trails on occasion.

Just when I thought I'd gotten a handle on when to say no and how to minimize my commitments, my kids hit high school. As a homeschooler, that stage means far more school preparation and planning and teaching. In addition to the deeper course load, their responsibilities and yeses grew exponentially. They added activities to our schedule: several dances a year, Jiu-jitsu (which can consume up to four nights a week), jobs and co-op.

With getting a driver's license being a far more complicated and expensive feat than it was when I was a teen, I served as chauffeur for all those events until after my oldest's senior year.

At the same time we added most of those activities to their previous commitments of Boy Scouts and American Heritage Girls, Tony applied to become a reserve sheriff's deputy and began his basic law enforcement training.

After his initial eight months of training, on top of his full-time paying job, he was called upon for patrol 24 hours a month, plus parades and special events. The next stage of Road Certification took even more of his time, often resulting in him going straight from management at a restaurant to pursuit of bad guys with three to four hours before his next work shift.

We had always split driving duties for the kids' activities. Tony's new schedule shifted a more even balance to a 90/10 share ... on his less busy weeks.

Our schedule complications overlapped my writing a couple more books and chasing two ill-timed dreams: buying a bookstore (for the second time—clearly that's not in the cards) and owning a larger house with more land—a case of bad timing.

The bookstore had been our family's dream a few years earlier. Tony and I each silently desired to be bookstore owners. We thought our town was going to be without one, so we revealed our secrets and laughed at how we shared the same dream. At that point, our family of four envisioned and planned together.

We had a name, an overall concept of what the shop would contain and how daily life would look as we would continue homeschooling while opening the business. Each of the kids discussed what their shop responsibilities could be.

I had started work on an official business plan, and we had a day blocked off to meet with our bank about business loans. Then we learned our town would continue to have a bookstore.

We met the new owner and fell in love with her, her kind heart and her beautiful smile. Mrs. Mary Lou became a special person in our lives for a number of reasons.

She instantly became one of my biggest fans and told every person who entered Mary Lou's Book Sack about my books. She loved my kids like her own grandchildren, and we looked forward to decorating the store for each holiday.

Mrs. Mary Lou was also the one who opened our eyes and hearts to learn more about the Lutheran Church Missouri Synod—the church home I didn't realize I'd been seeking all my life.

A few years later, she was ready to sell, and I wanted to buy. I drew a rough sketch of how I would rearrange the shop. Tony and I discussed the pros and cons. I sent messages to a few business owner friends and spoke with the storefront's owners about rent.

I slowly recognized that second pursuit of bookstore ownership was different. Before, we had a united family dream; then, I dreamed alone. I committed a week-and-a-half to bookstore dreaming, planning, researching and five-step grieving at the loss—again—of an unrealized dream.

And then there was the house search I started—I suppose—out of discontent but also out of a realization that the kids' years at home were growing short, and junior and senior years should contain parties and get-togethers.

Also, we were becoming Lutheran and desired more fellowship with family and friends—old, new, church and not. While we can pack some people into our 1100-square-foot house and our fantastic covered patio, it gets cramped.

When I saw the wooden ranch-style house with the massive covered outdoor space and pool on three acres with a pond, I fell in love. I saw our family there. I envisioned all our friends and family hanging out and Romy running around in the middle of all of us.

After a few days of exhilaration and hopefulness and starry eyes, we hit the reality that those soft spots we'd walked on in the house meant far bigger issues than we could or should tackle.

The tease of more space kickstarted me into a frenzy of updating my resumé and building an online portfolio and giving myself a crash course in a brave new world of job hunting—of which I'm not a fan. In order to purchase anything near what we wanted, we could no longer be a one-income family.

The search also required us to finally compose the long list of projects our house needed, especially if it were going to bring in the most money at closing. Tony started working, but his time was limited with his job and law enforcement.

And then my vivid imagination kicked in again. I envisioned what showing a house would look like: having to leave it—our office and schoolroom—for hours at a time, worrying that Romy would jump on someone or Tolkien would get out or someone would leave the door to my son's room open and the dog and/or the cat would attack his parakeets, leaving nothing but feathers behind. I may have had a few minor panic attacks as potential horrific scenarios played out in my mind.

Through those time-consuming rabbit trails, I was working on this book and my horse novel. I also edited a couple books for a special client and completed my kids' junior and freshman school years.

As I was completing an edit and researching jobs and planning revisions—all tasks pieced together in the pocket moments between kids' appointments—clarity parted the sea of chaos in my mind.

The house that had pulled at our heartstrings was off the table. Nothing else as great had surfaced. Even if one did, we couldn't get our house in shape any time soon. If I could find a great job and prove myself hirable in this weird digital age, the chances of finding the flexible hours I'd need to handle everyone else's schedules were slim to none.

I needed to pump the brakes on applications, focus on completing at least one of my books and hosting my annual Summer Reading Challenge, planning and organizing book events for the summer and fall and keeping up with the kids' schedules. Nothing could happen for me job-wise until after P.O.S.T. and our family trip to follow.

Clarity.

And then we adopted a dog who happens to be one of the most energetic breeds on the planet and needs daily walks, runs and/or visits to the dog park. Kaiser has added quite a bit of responsibility to my list … and I love him for it.

He has pushed me outside my comfort zone. I even occasionally take both dogs to the park by myself. He's added depth to this book as my interactions with him have taught me more about myself and my deepest desires. His affection and demands for attention warm my heart, and his vocal nature and expressive faces have added much laughter to our home.

Adding a job would limit Kaiser's dog park time and keep me from memory moments like senior Homecoming dress shopping with my daughter that became a most-of-the-day experience or cooking dinner and watching *The Flash* with my son.

Puppy moments pass in a few months. Round-the-clock time with my kids at home will be gone in a few brief years. Clarity precedes contentment and reminds me how powerful words—and a dog's giant ears—can be.

joyerancatore.com/summer-reading/

Vignette Forty-seven

But What a Way to Go

NOT ALL MY PETS HAVE been cats and dogs. I once had a wee hamster who was so cute I cleverly named him QT.

QT had quite the personality and kept me entertained. He and I were both nocturnal. Well, he actually was nocturnal; I liked to stay up late making up stories.

I've always relished the quiet of night and the blanketing comfort of its darkness. The powerful aloneness of that time of day heals me from the noise and social activity of the daytime and refuels my creative and social tanks for the following day's responsibilities and expectations. As an adult, I still like to make up stories under nighttime's quiet cover. Most of *Any Good Thing* was written, revised and edited between the hours of 10:00 p.m. and 2:00 a.m.

Nighttime was QT's favorite time to run on his wheel. In case you didn't know, hamster wheels are noisy. So are the balls that allow them to securely run around a house.

I've always wondered what hamsters think when they're in those balls. What does the giant, pink-tinted world look like to such a tiny creature? Are they scared? Confused? Do they get hamster whiplash when they run into walls and furniture?

QT's little claws scratched and pricked when he rested in my hand or crawled on my shoulder. His teensy nose and whiskers twitched constantly, and he always looked like he was one breakaway run from mischief.

One day, we had to go out of town. We left plenty of food and water for him in his cage. I petted his tiny, silky head and said, "See you soon. We'll be back in a few days."

His nose twitched in response. Mischief twinkled in his beady black eyes.

When we returned, QT was not in his cage. I found the corner where he had gnawed his way to freedom, but QT was nowhere in sight. Finally, my parents found him.

Next to his cage was a box full of pecans. QT's final resting place was in that box where he ate more than his fill and died with a smile on his whiskery face.

I cried and cursed the impractical and unsafe plastic cage we had for him, but I eventually admitted, "If he had to die, what a way to go!"

joyerancatore.com/any-good-thing/

Vignette Forty-eight

Fabricated Rescue Missions

I HAVE A CONFESSION. WHEN I drive, my mind wanders ... quite imaginatively, I might add. One day I'll carry through my idea to design and produce bumper stickers with the message: "Warning: author at the wheel; prone to imaginative wanderings."

As I zip along the interstate, I fantasize about spying a wobbly kitten tottering dangerously close to the perilous road, stopping a few yards away and racing to his rescue ... just in time.

Of course, that little baby would be eternally grateful and completely committed to me—his hero without fur. I envision the emotional scene as I scour the roadsides for an endangered creature. I've been tempted to pull over and examine discarded trash bags or boxes.

That's when my overactive imagination spins a story about a serial killer who dumps pieces of his victims in unassuming trash receptacles alongside interstates and captures his next victims as they snoop through their predecessor's remains.

After a few horrific scenes, I force my twisted mind back to kittens and cuddles.

I have shared this fantasy with my husband—the kitten one, not the dismembered body one. His reaction is usually somewhere along the lines of, "Don't you dare show up with a roadside kitten."

While drafting this book, I nearly tested his commitment to adamant opposition to more cats in our house. While Tony was out of town for one of our son's Boy Scout camps, I was doomscrolling on social media. An image stopped me, mid-scroll—the face of a bright white, tiny kitten with sutures where eyes should have been.

Snow was four months old, blind and in need of a home. I clicked on his picture, read the details and skimmed the comments. I was about to send a message to make him mine—I even decided I'd deal with Tony later, after he got home—when I found a comment that someone had already adopted the kitten. I texted Tony that someone beat me to adopting a blind kitten, and I could feel his eyes roll.

While I'm very happy sweet Snow got a loving home—and Tony is relieved it wasn't ours—I admit to being a little jealous. In the fifteen seconds it took me to see the picture, read the info and scroll to the update, I had already pictured Snow in my lap or on my shoulder while I work and in a little baby sling wherever I go—book signings, kid taxiing, grocery shopping.

My imagination may be helpful for writing, but I fear it will get me in trouble one day—if in no other way, most likely with my husband. Although, he knows the risks with me. I once told him a story from my childhood that probably explains my odd animal choices.

Whenever I was allowed to choose a new stuffed animal, I would scour the shelves for one with some imperfection—a flopped over ear, a dangling tail, a loose eye. My reasoning was, "No other kids will want them."

In case you wondered, "The Island of Misfit Toys" remains my favorite part of *Rudolph, the Red-Nosed Reindeer.*

Now, please don't accept this tale as an invitation to hunt down my house and drop a box of kittens on my doorstep. I would want to keep them, but my husband would say no. I would cry. He would say no.

The kittens would mew. It would be an emotions upheaval.

At the end of the day, pets are expensive: food, vet bills, toys. Book sales don't even cover my author business expenses—sad, but true.

I will focus on helping however I can: supporting local animal assistance organizations, sharing babies in need of homes, urging people to spay and neuter and writing about issues like the livestock slaughter pipeline and threats to wild horses and their land.

Who knows? Maybe I can rescue a blind baby if I hit bestseller status. You can help—simply tell all your animal-loving friends about my books!

#OveractiveImagination
#AuthorSeeksBlindKittenForBookTourCompanion
Oh, and
#AdoptDontShop!

Vignette Forty-nine

A Mini-Musing on Grief

ONE OF THE BLESSINGS ABOUT animals is we can be our truest selves when we're with them. We're free to be the people we hide behind the masks and shields of daily survival. We can bare our secrets and the dark spots on our souls. The trauma and the pain we hold inside can be rubbed into their fur as the motion of petting them soothes our inner turmoil and bonds us with them.

When we grieve with a pet, we can do so unfettered. We can unpack grief's many layers in ways we can't always do with fellow humans. Our relationships and emotions are often complicated and usually more complex than we can express. When we grieve the loss of someone, we don't always do so in expected or accepted ways.

Sometimes trauma lingers in the past that makes our loss a wholly other type of grief. That's not something most people around us can understand, and often it's not something we feel comfortable explaining.

Perhaps our animal doesn't understand our conflicted emotions, but they accept them and us. They don't judge us or the person who's gone. They don't question our relief. They don't wonder if the person really did or caused what we say. They accept us and our pain and our blended emotions of grief, anger, sadness, joy, worry, relief, guilt.

They'll also be there when we accept the truth of a past we've tried too long and too successfully to hide from the world. When we finally put a name to what happened to us—trauma, abuse, manipulation—and the weight of its meaning and the reality of its effects on our entire lives sink in, our pets will comfort us.

As we grieve the truths of our pasts, our animals will remain close, soaking in our tears and sprouting warming tendrils of comfort and peace.

Unlike people, animals accept and embrace who we are—the good, the bad, the broken. Unlike us, they see us as we truly are. They did so on day one, and they'll do the same on day 4,015. They have no agenda, no ulterior motive, no preconceived notions, no prejudice, no misbeliefs.

Our pets gift us pure love. Thankfully, on darkened days of grappling with the past and unveiling deep-rooted pain and experiencing the complexity of grief, love's healing light radiates all we need.

Vignette Fifty

How to Train a Malinois

THE REALITY OF ADOPTING HIGH-ENERGY breeds, like the Belgian Malinois, is they require frequent training and extra attention.

I often see dogs like him in our local shelters. I suspect one of the primary reasons they are often discarded is people get this beautiful, popular dog and then realize they have no idea how to handle or care for them.

Despite the challenge of freeing time to train Kaiser and engage with him in high-speed activities, we knew we had to. Adopting a dog is a lifetime commitment. We want him to be part of our family forever and in many situations that require a well-behaved, responsive dog.

We camp with our pets, and we like to eat at restaurants that welcome animals. Plus, any dog bred for military and law

enforcement use must be carefully trained to avoid life-changing tragedies down the road. We also wanted Kaiser to be happy, and not much makes him happier than running full throttle after a ball.

Training and committing to Kaiser remind me of setting a firm foundation for my author business and greatest writing-related dream.

Any business is tough. Very few are out-of-the-gate successes. The biggest "overnight" success companies or authors reach that status after years or decades of hard work, careful planning and foundation shoring.

Like training a dog, these endeavors require intentionality and care in both the details and broad picture planning.

Thanks to my experience in public relations and web development, I know the value in a well-built website and brand cohesion across all facets of my public image. I focused on those needs first—from the overall platforms to the minutiae of identical names and profile pictures across social media platforms and identifying favicons on websites.

Many times over the years I've wanted to leap ahead and do something bigger—run ads, purchase some big publishing something-or-other that the "big guys" always use. What I had to remind myself, though, was I wasn't ready for that leap.

Small Steps Every Day: those words marked a cup that became my favorite for its saying, although I often forget them in the slog of my daily grind.

Many times since launching this author journey, I have felt my wheels spinning. Some days, my steps are too tiny to count, or they propel me backward instead of inching me forward.

Other times, outside forces have pushed me back. Around the time I was battling self-doubt about releasing this book, I learned that at least one of my books—*Any Good Thing*—had been stolen by a website that shares their pirated goods with readers. Their reasoning is that publishing companies and authors make enough money and books should be free to everyone.

To add insult to the injury of their crime, one of the biggest developers of AI used the works on that website to train their technology. I was stolen from ... twice.

I already felt uncertain about the value my words may add to the world. Having those words taken from me without any hope of retribution left me wondering what the point even was. Why bother?

The truth of the publishing world is that, yes, some big publishing companies and their senior level staff make significant amounts of money. The majority of authors—traditionally published with those big companies and self-published like me without any monetary advances and every author in between—makes pennies on most book sales.

I want readers to know where their $20 to $35 goes when they choose to buy a book—or at least what part of it gets to the author. Writers spend years writing, revising and editing each book, and then they spend tons of time and money promoting them (even the writers published with bigger companies whose executives have massive salaries).

My reality is that I make $5.62 to $9.79 profit on my Carolina's Legacy Collection paperback books, but that's only when I sell them in person. Typically, that means I'm at an event, many of which charge a fee to participate. Even the free ones require some out-of-pocket expenses—donated books, gas and mileage, food or lodging. The profits I mentioned don't account for those expenses.

Those same books sold through an online retailer or in a bookstore bring me returns as low as $2 each. Most bookstores that carry my books do so on consignment, so my profit margin with them falls between the two scenarios I've shared. The downside to those situations is I spend a great deal of time and gas visiting the stores with whom I have relationships. I also have to be proactive in receiving payments from sales.

I have had negative experiences where some stores have tucked my books away on shelves out of sightline, done nothing on their end to sell them, damaged the books (which I have to pay for upfront) or even kept all the profits from sales I know happened.

Because I am a business, I have overhead expenses. I currently have four websites, plus additional hosting sites, as well as two email addresses that have to be paid for in order to legally send out newsletters. I'm a member of a few professional writing organizations. Of course, the government also requires money so I can be a business. My baseline budget for a year—with no money to put toward advertising—is about $1500.

On top of that, I have to pay for all the editing, designing and printing costs associated with producing a book and buy my books upfront for any sales I do in person or for any stores that take my work on consignment. In 2024, I spent $1151.23 on copies of my books to resell and sold less than 70 books total (online, in stores and in person). Four of those sales, I shared royalties on, and one doesn't give me a penny since the purpose of that anthology was for charity.

Times are tough for everyone, and I completely understand not being able to buy new books. Thankfully, readers have great options for that, as well. Authors sometimes release an e-book for free or a reduced price on reputable sites—ask your favorite authors for links to those or watch their social media and newsletters for alerts.

Most libraries encourage their patrons to request great books. If your library doesn't carry a book you want to read, ask! If they do carry books by your favorite author, check them out and encourage all your reader friends to do the same. Better yet, read the book together and host a book club discussion. Many authors—like me—offer free book club kits and even virtual (or local in-person) visits for clubs.

Supporting authors can also include sharing book news on social media—another free option. All of these simple, mostly free activities combine to aid authors in ways readers may never imagine.

On my own, my endeavors often feel fruitless. I sometimes embrace the lie that I will never move forward. On more than one occasion, I have contemplated quitting. Each time, though, something has happened.

A kind email appeared. A library checkout of an e-book dropped a whopping $0.32 in my bank account. An invitation flew my way. Five generous readers applied to beta read this book on the first day I released a request form.

Those small, powerful gestures reminded me my words are needed. They also reminded me that, like our commitment to the animals we've brought into our home, I made a commitment to share stories throughout my life. As part of that responsibility, I committed to my weekly newsletter and prayed that every week it would touch someone or bring something useful to them. I would post on social media—something funny, helpful, true.

And then, I suddenly had more than 400 followers on one social media platform after being stuck under 200 for what felt like ages, 1500 on another. Overnight (in its seventh consecutive year), my LAM Summer Reading Challenge group exploded to 53 active members, up from two or three in prior years.

More people in my region recognized me as an expert resource for writing-related topics. Suddenly, my library couldn't keep my books on their shelves. "All copies in use" is one of the most beautiful phrases an author can discover next to their book listing.

I will continue to make small steps each day, surrounded by the friends—human and animal—God has gifted me, while dreaming of the end goal: for my stories to reach more readers and finally earn money so I can write more of them. I don't desire riches or fame. My greatest dream revolves around two goals: the opportunity to use my platform to give publicity and/or money to incredible organizations that care for animals and veterans and the freedom to pen stories of soul-deep importance from my heart for readers who need them.

As a lonely child, I needed stories—true and imaginatively true. As a new mother wearing a mask to hide her pain, I needed their reminders of life's big picture. As a more confident and content woman with a cat in her lap, I still need their encouragement, escape and education. I know I'm not the only reader who needs books.

God gave us creativity and imagination. He also gifted us the written word and made it clear in His great Book how much importance He places on penned and spoken messages. I resolve to use His gifts for our good and His glory as long as He allows me to do so with whatever time I can carve out around paying work, family responsibilities and life in general.

To celebrate my resolution to my literary commitment, I will end this book and release the manuscript for publication. I send it into the world with the prayer that it will touch at least one person's heart and that the small $1 per book sale will miraculously multiply to do great things for some incredible animal and veteran organizations that are dear to my heart.

Next, I will take a brief break before opening a new manuscript to spend time with Kaiser and some training treats. I envision him sitting by my side until I command, "Release."

bit.ly/JoyERancatoreNewsletter

Thank You

THANK YOU FOR READING THIS COLLECTION.

While these stories are personal and significant to me, I hope they have been meaningful for you as well. Thank you for helping me contribute to some of my favorite rescue and veteran organizations. At least $1 for each purchase of this book (in every format) goes to groups I've personally vetted. If you enjoyed this book, please share it with your friends and write a brief review to help other readers discover it. Help me reach my goal to donate a helpful quarterly check to fantastic organizations.

Let's #ShareTheRead!

joyerancatore.com/animal-vignettes/

Acknowledgments

To God: We wouldn't be here without Him, and we wouldn't be as comforted without His gift of animals.

> *We give thee but thine own, whate'er the gift may be;*
> *all that we have is thine alone, a trust, O Lord, from thee.*

"We Give Thee But Thine Own" by William W. How

To The Animals I've Loved Throughout My Life: Many of the reasons I'm thankful for you comprise the pages of this book. Thank you for the comfort, compassion and camaraderie you've selflessly given.

To My Husband: Tony, you gave me the encouragement, advice and love that made these stories a book. Thank you for always being my Alpha Reader and my biggest fan. Thank you, too, for the willingness to take a convoluted crash course in photography to capture a couple hundred images at sunrise and sunset for the resulting single shot that, thanks to some extra magic, the world will now see.

To My Kids: These past few years have been some of the most chaotic ones, and I fear I've failed in my role as your mother. Thank you for loving me anyway, cheering me on and making these past few years also some of the most memorable and special. I am proud of and thankful for the Christ-like young adults you are becoming.

To My Critique Partner: Mea, thank you for always making time for me and my stories and for speaking the truth in love and making me a better writer. Love you, QWERTY!

To My Beta Readers: This book rests between two covers greatly because of the encouragement, feedback and support of each of you, my incredible beta readers. Thank you, Emily, Faith, Justin, Martha, Rachael, Terri and Yvette.

To My Cover Designer & Formatter: Rachael, you care deeply about my words and my readers and your design shows it. You amaze me more every time we work together, and "I thank my God upon every remembrance of you ...." (Philippians 1:3)

To My Named Friends: Thank you to each friend, family member and business named in these stories for your kind permissions to share our mutual experiences. Each of you are special to me, and I am thankful to have you in my life.

To My Church Family at Redeemer Lutheran Church (LCMS) in Mandeville: Thank you for your prayers and encouragement. They are critical for Christian creatives, and I don't take your support for granted.

To Those Who Work in Animal Rescue: Thank you for your emotional sacrifices and for the love you bring to animals who, many times, have seen too little of it.

Colophon

The main text and primary headings are Baskervville font (10.7 pt and 18 pt) from Google Fonts.

Baskervville is a revival of Jacob's revival of Baskerville's typeface. It was distributed by the Berger-Levrault Foundry from 1815. The font Jacob produced was sold as a "Caractères dans le genre Baskerwille" i.e. "Baskerwille alike fonts" — with a w instead of a v. The particularity of Jacob's Baskerwille is that the roman is very close to Baskerville's typefaces while the italic is closer to Didot's typefaces. The ANRT workshop that took place for five days aimed to digitize Jacob's font in order to show his work which moves from transitional to modern styles. The typeface was then developed and engineered by Rosalie Wagner.

Baskervville was designed by the ANRT students from 2017 (Alexis Faudot, Rémi Forte, Morgane Pierson, Rafael Ribas, Tanguy Vanlaeys and Rosalie Wagner), under the direction of Charles Mazé and Thomas Huot-Marchand.

In 2025, a bold weight designed by Thomas Huot-Marchand was added. Rosalie Wagner fixed some kerning and glyphset issues and improved the font's outlines for a better rendering on screen.

Information from: https://fonts.google.com/specimen/Baskervville/about

The subheadings are Square Peg font (30 pt) from Google Fonts.

This happy font is great for scrapping and casual situations. Square Peg has a shaky, rough, and almost mono-weight with slightly heavier horizontal strokes. Its handwritten style lends itself to situations that require playful and casual themes.

Information: https://fonts.google.com/specimen/Square+Peg/about

Meet the Author

Legacy and identity, founded on hope-filled faith, infuse the tales of

the soul written from the heart of Joy E. Rancatore. An award-winning, multi-genre Indie Author, Joy believes extraordinary things await her characters and their tales. She lives in Southeast Louisiana with her loving husband and their two children, where she is guarded and snuggled by a furry entourage of animals.

Subscribe to Joy's author newsletter for two free short stories and weekly updates from Romy, Tolkien and Kaiser ... in their own words.

Photo: Casie Jones Photography

bit.ly/JoyERancatoreNewsletter

FREE Book Club Kit

When you share *Animal Vignettes: True Stories of Friendship* with your pack of book-loving friends, you can receive a digital Book Club Kit, complete with exclusive treats:

- • Printable Bookmarks
- • A Discussion & Club Activity Guide
- • A Pawty Planner &
- • MORE.

You'll also receive weekly:
- • Book News &
- •Notes From My Furry Friends.

As if that's not enough, simply reply to one of my emails if you'd like me to visit your club virtually or in person.

https://bit.ly/AV-Book-Club-Kit

Love to Listen?

Hear *Animal Vignettes: True Stories of Friendship* narrated by the author. Listen as each tale comes alive through the voice of the woman who lived them and who loves the featured animals.

joyerancatore.com/animal-vignettes/

MORE STORIES BY THE AUTHOR

FICTION

CAROLINA'S LEGACY COLLECTION:
"Our Good Thing: A Short Story"
Any Good Thing: A Novel
This Good Thing: A Novella
Every Good Thing: A Short Story Compilation
One Good Thing: An Epistolary

The Crux Anthology, "Ealiverel Awakened"
Edited & Compiled by Rachael Ritchey

NONFICTION

Animal Vignettes: True Stories of Friendship

*Finders Keepers: A Practical Approach to
Find and Keep Your Writing Critique Partner*
Joy E. Rancatore and Meagan Smith

joyerancatore.com/my-writings/

Logos & Mythos Press LLC
Slidell, LA, USA

www.ingramcontent.com/pod-product-compliance
Lightning Source LLC
Chambersburg PA
CBHW021218130626
46554CB00004B/1267